Rethinking Global Governance

This book argues that long-ignored, non-western political systems from the distant and more recent past can provide critical insights into improving global governance.

These societies show how successful collection action can occur by dividing sovereignty, consensus building, power from below, and other mechanisms. For a better tomorrow, we need to free ourselves of the colonial constraints on our political imagination. A pandemic, war in Europe, and another year of climatic anomalies are among the many indications of the limits of global governance today. To meet these challenges, we must look far beyond the status quo to the thousands of successful mechanisms for collective action that have been cast aside *a priori* because they do not fit into Western traditions of how people should be organized. Coming from long past or still enduring societies often dismissed as "savages" and "primitives" until well into the twentieth century, the political systems in this book were often seen as too acephalous, compartmentalized, heterarchical, or anarchic to be of use. Yet as globalization makes international relations more chaotic, long-ignored governance alternatives may be better suited to today's changing realities. Understanding how the Zulu, Trypillian, Alur, and other collectives worked might be humanity's best hope for survival.

This book will be of interest both to those seeking to apply archaeological and ethnographic data to issues of broad contemporary concern and to academics, politicians, policy makers, students, and the general public seeking possible alternatives to conventional thinking in global governance.

Justin Jennings is Senior Curator of the Archaeology of the Americas at the Royal Ontario Museum and Associate Professor of Anthropology at the University of Toronto. His research interests include early cities, states, and cultural horizons in the Andes and in other regions of his world.

Rethinking Global Governance
Learning from Long Ignored Societies

Justin Jennings

LONDON AND NEW YORK

First published 2023
by Routledge
4 Park Square, Milton Park, Abingdon, Oxon OX14 4RN

and by Routledge
605 Third Avenue, New York, NY 10158

Routledge is an imprint of the Taylor & Francis Group, an informa business

©2023 **Justin Jennings**

The right of **Justin Jennings** to be identified as authors of this work has been asserted in accordance with sections 77 and 78 of the Copyright, Designs and Patents Act 1988.

All rights reserved. No part of this book may be reprinted or reproduced or utilised in any form or by any electronic, mechanical, or other means, now known or hereafter invented, including photocopying and recording, or in any information storage or retrieval system, without permission in writing from the publishers.

Trademark notice: Product or corporate names may be trademarks or registered trademarks, and are used only for identification and explanation without intent to infringe.

British Library Cataloguing-in-Publication Data
A catalogue record for this book is available from the British Library

ISBN: 978-1-032-44671-4 (hbk)
ISBN: 978-1-032-44673-8 (pbk)
ISBN: 978-1-003-37332-2 (ebk)

DOI: 10.4324/9781003373322

Typeset in Times New Roman
by Apex CoVantage, LLC

For my children and their children

Contents

List of Figures	viii
Acknowledgments and Credits List	x
1 Toward a More Perfect Union	1
2 The Western Roots of Global Governance	18
3 Dividing Sovereignty	38
4 Building Up and Standing Down	57
5 (Re)Building Consensus	75
6 Powering From Below	94
7 Ordering Anarchy	114
8 Finding Better Futures	133
Index	147

Figures

1.1	du Simitiere's initial sketch of the Great Seal of the United States	2
1.2	Hopkinson's first sketch (left) and final sketch (right) for the Second Committee's Great Seal of the United States	8
1.3	Thomson's design of the Great Seal of the United States that was accepted by Congress in 1782	12
2.1	Wenceslaus Hollar's celebration of the Peace of Westphalia that underlines the connections made to divine intervention and Greek and Roman traditions	19
2.2	Prinald's world map published in 1766	19
2.3	A United States Office of War Poster from 1943 that celebrated the United Nations	24
3.1	Tee Yee Neen Ho Ga Row (left) and Sa Ga Yeath Qua Pieth Tow (right) were two of the Mohawk delegates to the Queen of England who were dubbed "The Four Indian Kings" by the London Press	40
3.2	An Indus Valley Civilization seal depicting a two-horned bull with an inscription. Some seal motifs may have been linked to clans	44
3.3	Henri-Paul Motte's late-nineteenth-century imagining of Vercingetorix preparing to surrender to Julius Caesar	48
4.1	A 1892 drawing from the London Illustrated News of the Buganda capital in a kingdom neighboring the Alur. The Buganda shared the Alur's emphasis on connections between a ceremonial capital and outlying regions	61
4.2	A roll-out drawing of a Colonial-era cup depicting (center, upper register) the encounter between the Inca emperor on the left and one of the Colla kings on the right	64
4.3	Philip Baldaeus' drawing of the reception of Dutch General Gerard Hulft by King Rajasinghe II of Kandy in 1656	65
5.1	A tablet from southern Mesopotamia, circa 3000 BC, that records a possible ration distribution of barley and emmer wheat from a temple precinct	79

Figures ix

5.2	A detail from *Althing in session* by William Gersham Collingwood that was painted around 1897 after his visit to Iceland as part of his fascination with the Viking sagas	80
5.3	Men considering stakes in the ground for pigs before a moka event in the Hagen area of New Guinea. Note the neck ornament, *omak*, that some wear to mark their generosity at past mokas	84
6.1	The Royal Residence of the Zulu King Cetshwayo, circa 1875	96
6.2	A seated Cortés meets a contingent from Tlaxcallan in the Lienzo of Tlaxcala.	99
6.3	An artist's impression of what Maidanetske would have looked like, circa 3700 BC, after buildings took over the main plaza	102
7.1	Shoteah Pomo dancers in 1923 preparing for the Expulsion of Sahte ceremony. The ceremony's goal is to drive malignant spirits (the Sahte) away from the community	117
7.2	Jenne-jeno was abandoned around 1400 AD when its last inhabitants moved to nearby Djenné. This street scene from the later settlement was photographed in 1906	121
7.3	The gateway (foreground) to the Akha village of Phate in 1971. The gateway helps to keep evil spirits at bay	123

Acknowledgments and Credits List

I write this book during a period of considerable pessimism in world affairs. There is widespread concern about current systems of global governance, but few options are being offered that go beyond tinkering with the status quo. My reaction as an archaeologist to these concerns has been to dive into the past—from thousands of years ago to the 1970s—to see what might be learned from societies that approach common collective action problems in ways different from my own.

This book has often been a solitary pursuit, written in early mornings or in chunks of time during the day when other pressing tasks were avoided. I thank the Royal Ontario Museum for its support throughout this project, as well as the libraries at the Royal Ontario Museum and University of Toronto. A book like this cannot be written without sitting at the feet of millions of people, both those who lived in the past societies described in this book—in some cases, these societies very much endure amidst the pressures of globalization—and those outsiders who, like myself, struggled to understand them. There is still so much to learn from what we have already done.

As in my previous projects, profound thanks are due to my family. My wife, Adrienne, has been my rock once again, and my children, Isla, Poppy, James, and Finn, continue to be my inspiration. Though still young, I dedicate this book to them, and to the children that they may have, in the hopes that the next generations will inhabit a renewed world inspired from the teachings of people who have lived in every corner of the world.

In 1940, Walter Benjamin famously wrote of an Angel of History who saw the past as an unrelenting cycle of destruction and despair. I see a more optimistic vista unfurling below Benjamin's Angel as he flies backward into the future. There are also considerable cooperative successes in our past that can help build a better world for tomorrow.

Images from the following sources were used in the book. I especially thank Pamela J. Stewart, Andrew J. Strathern, and William Sage for their kind permission to reprint their photos in this book.

Figure 1.1—Courtesy of The Thomas Jefferson Papers at the United States Library of Congress

Figure 1.2—Both images of seal sketches are courtesy of the United States Archives (Papers of the Continental Congress, 1774–1789)

Acknowledgments and Credits List xi

Figure 1.3—Courtesy of the United States Archives (Papers of the Continental Congress, 1774–1789)

Figure 2.1—Courtesy of the Te Papa Museum. The Peace of Westphalia, 1648, Antwerp, by Wenceslaus Hollar, Cornelis I Schut. Gift of Bishop Monrad, 1869. Te Papa (1869–0001–204)

Figure 2.2—Courtesy of the University of Texas at Arlington Library

Figure 2.3—United States Office of War Information Poster, courtesy of Hennepin County Library

Figure 3.1—Images of both paintings are courtesy of Library and Archives of Canada (1977–35–4), bought with a special subvention of the Government of Canada in 1977

Figure 3.2—Courtesy of the Cleveland Museum of Art, Purchase from the J. H. Wade Fund, 1973.160

Figure 3.3—Courtesy of the Musée Crozatier de Puy-en-Velay, Vercingétorix se redant á devant César, Henri-Paul Motte, 1886, 2014.4.5.45

Figure 4.1—Unsigned drawing from 1892, Illustrated London News, Unsigned drawing, Vol. 101, Issue 2790, p. 9

Figure 4.2—Adapted by the author from Plate 28 in Teresa Gisbert (1980) *Iconografía y mitos indígenas en el arte* (La Paz: Gisbert & Cia)

Figure 4.3—Philip Baldaeus (1744 [1672]) *A True and Exact Description of the Most Celebrated East-India Coasts of Malabar and Coromandel; as also of the Isle of Ceylon.* (London: A. & J. Churchill), Vol. 3, p. 745

Figure 5.1—Courtesy of the Metropolitan Museum of Art, Purchase, Raymond and Beverly Sackler Gift, 1988, 1988.433.2

Figure 5.2—William Gersham Collingwood, Althing in Session, British Museum, OA.10759, by permission of the Board of Trustees of the British Museum

Figure 5.3—The Pamela J. Stewart and Andrew J. Strathern Archive. Pittsburgh: University of Pittsburgh Digital Research Library, www.Stewart Strathern.pitt.edu, by permission of the Pamela J. Stewart and Andrew Strathern Archive

Figure 6.1—Walton, James. [s.a]. Drawing depicting the King's Kraal. The Zulu War. *In James Walton Collection*, MS 247-a-3-1-4-5.jpg (1.876 Mb), accessed on September 23, 2022

Figure 6.2—Courtesy of the University of Texas at Austin Library

Figure 6.3—Painting by Kenny Arne Lang Antonsen for book with Jimmy John Antonsen titled *Old Europe—First Civilization (7000–3000 BC)* (2019, Copenhagen: Saxo Publishing)

Figure 7.1—Plate 12, C. Hart Merriam (1955) Studies of California Indians (Berkeley: University of California Press)

Figure 7.2—Postcard 414 by François-Edmond Fortier

Figure 7.3—William Sage, Arizona State University Library. Rare Books and Manuscripts: MSS-281 8.2.60. Courtesy of William W. Sage Collection on Laos, University of Wisconsin Digital Collections

1 Toward a More Perfect Union

On July 4, 1776, the Second Continental Congress ratified a Declaration of Independence. The document was both a list of grievances against King George III and a treatise on the American colonies' right to revolt because of these grievances. With its 56 signatures, the colonies were now rechristened, in their words, as the "thirteen united States of America."[1] To celebrate, Congress struck a committee to create the new nation's Great Seal. The committee members—Benjamin Franklin, John Adams, and Thomas Jefferson—elicited the help of local artist Pierre Eugene du Simitiere who sketched out some of their ideas (Figure 1.1).[2]

du Simitiere's first sketch was packed with symbolism. The seal would be dominated by a great shield flanked by Lady Liberty and an American soldier. The artist also drew the Eye of Providence hovering above and depicted below an unfurled scroll with the words "*E Pluribus Unum*" (Out of Many, One). Smaller shields within the great shield featured the initials of each of the new states. These smaller shields surrounded symbols of the countries—England, Scotland, Ireland, France, and Germany—from which most of the colonists had originated.

Over the next month, du Simitiere, Adams, Franklin, and Jefferson toyed with the seal design before presenting their idea to Congress. Lady Justice replaced the soldier, and the shields of each state were now prominently displayed in a ring around the seal. Congressional delegates, however, hesitated to bring the design to a vote, ultimately tabling work on the seal for more than three years. The war with Britain was already heating up, and they were reluctant to endorse a seal that evoked particular relationships between the states as they tried to both form a working government and field a beleaguered army.[3]

I begin this book with the Second Continental Congress because its members were facing a seemingly insurmountable collective action problem. Much of the British Parliament was dead set against divided sovereignty in the years preceding the Revolutionary War, with commentators like Sir William Blackstone thundering that parliament's power was "so transcendent and absolute, that it cannot be confined."[4] Sovereignty, as traditionally conceived, is a claim to possess the highest source of legitimate power over people and their associated territory.[5] *Imperium in imperio* (empire within empire) was a Latin phrase bandied about during the period to underline the lunacy of the American desire for greater control over its own affairs. As traditionally conceived, "a polity cannot be a little bit sovereign."[6]

DOI: 10.4324/9781003373322-1

Figure 1.1 du Simitiere's initial sketch of the Great Seal of the United States

In declaring independence from Great Britain, the American Congress was not just trying to build a national government from the ground up. They were also trying to build a different kind of government that could somehow act as one entity while at the same time preserving the independent decision-making of each state in the union. They thought that empires within an empire were not only possible, but also desirable, and the delegates countered their doubters with their own Latin phrase that they highlighted on the early sketches of the Great Seal, *E Pluribus Unum*. "Out of many, one" had a nice ring to it, but how would it actually work?

To solve their collective action problem, late-eighteenth-century American intellectuals sought a "judicious modification and mixture" of past experiments in divided government.[7] The first sketch of the seal had highlighted the European origins of the United States and the governance models that the nation's founders drew upon to form first the Articles of Confederation and then the Constitution would come from the writings of that continent.[8] They looked to the Bible, for example, as well as to English common law, the Ancient Greeks, and contemporary Enlightenment thinkers. What they chose not to draw on were non-Western governance traditions.

Today, we face another seemingly insurmountable collective action problem. This time, it is not about getting 13 former colonies on the same page, but some eight billion people in 194 countries. Global governance, the combination of formal and informal institutions that mediate the world's affairs, remains anchored in the almost 80-year-old United Nations. Although still effective in many areas, the governance system that has developed around the United Nations has struggled with pandemics, climate change, immigration, unfettered capitalism, and other issues that defy political boundaries.[9] A new answer to the world's "*E Pluribus Unum*" is required, and we would be well served to look for ideas among those traditions that Benjamin Franklin and his contemporaries largely ignored.

This book is an argument for how a wider exploration of the past can improve contemporary global governance. For millennia, humans have found ways to work together to fulfill common objectives. Collective action problems, of course, have changed over space and time—how many of us have had to team up to kill a woolly mammoth?—yet the basic contours of many of these problems remain the same. Global warming, for example, is another iteration of the "tragedy of the commons," wherein the self-interest of individual users runs counter to the common good, and echoes of today's debates on immigration can be found in the negotiations of where and how people should live in the world's first cities.[10] Although the specifics were often vastly different, the past, both quite recent and from thousands of years ago, provides us with a wealth of possible ways to work together that we ignore at our peril.

The intellectual origins of the United Nations and many other intergovernmental and non-governmental organizations can be found in the same sources that inspired the members of the Second Continental Congress. The solutions offered to collective action problems from within the Western canon are powerful ones that should not be ignored. Yet the world has seen—and continues to see—many other ways of getting disparate people to effectively work together. This book presents approaches to governance that fall outside of the Western canon, while demonstrating how a "judicious modification and mixture" of these alternative experiments in collective action could help make the world a better place.

The Problems of Collective Action

Put simply, collective action is the tasks done by a group to achieve a shared goal.[11] The ability to cooperate is particularly acute in humans. We are the only species that routinely chooses to cooperate in large groups of non-related kin, sometimes enthusiastically volunteering to join activities that go against our self-interest.[12] We *want* to work together. The evolutionary underpinnings of this desire have vexed evolutionary biologists since Darwin because, over time, more altruistic individuals who routinely put others in front of themselves should theoretically lose out to those who are more selfish.[13]

Darwin's solution to the problem of human cooperation was group selection, the idea that a collective could raise its reproductive success over its rivals by working together more effectively.[14] The debate on why humans cooperate has nonetheless endured because scholars—along with everyone else—recognize that working together is often quite hard, especially over long periods of time, within

4   *Toward a More Perfect Union*

larger collectives, and among those who do not know each other well. The many challenges of broader collective action projects often make them fail, and we return to living within the lower-level organizations to which we are accustomed.[15]

Of the many barriers that plague collective action, there are six that are perhaps worth highlighting in this book. Collective action's free-rider problem is when those who benefit from resources and services fail to pay their share.[16] Sometimes these free-riders are cheats—a kid sneaking into a movie theater—while in other cases, it's a suburban driver using streets paid for by city taxes. Given a choice, a person often chooses to pay as little as possible, creating a disincentive for others to pay their fair share for more publicly available resources and services.[17]

A related barrier to collective action is the expectation for equity.[18] People think that they should be appropriately rewarded for their efforts. When both the task and reward are clear to the parties involved, then equity might be easily resolved: two people divide in half the fruit they picked together from a tree. The problem, of course, is that equity is rarely straightforward.[19] Even in the case of our fruit pickers, what if one worked harder or had a larger appetite? The challenges to determining equity only increase as groups get larger and rewards become opaquer or delayed.[20]

People tend to object to being told what to do by outsiders. Hierarchical decision-making is often deemed acceptable within one's group but tolerated under narrower circumstances when the orders come from those perceived to be outsiders in the area under consideration.[21] This is another barrier to collective action because tight circles of autonomy tend to be drawn around segments of society, such as ones sanctifying household decisions or aspects of the market economy. These can become no-go zones for government innovation, requiring far more buy-in for changes to the status quo.[22]

Breakdowns in collective actions also often stem from a lack of trust, our fourth collective action barrier.[23] Years of working together with family and groups of friends build within-group trust. You are therefore willing to take on a task with your cousins knowing that they will show up to perform the required tasks and that your individual efforts will be properly rewarded.[24] Family, however, can only solve some problems. Larger, more complicated, tasks require that strangers work together, but strangers are inherently less trustworthy because there is no track record of previously successful collective actions.[25]

Another barrier to collective action is permanence.[26] As a collective grow larger, its members end up working more often with more strangers and taking more orders from them. People can acquiesce to this situation if the objectives are clear and mutually desirable, especially when the collaboration is short-lived. Few would balk at working under an expert's tutelage for an afternoon. More sustained collaboration, however, tends to require far more negotiations, and heightened concern about trustworthiness, free-riders, and other issues can quickly derail efforts.[27]

Finally, collective action becomes more difficult when property and resource rights are unclear.[28] Is a tool privately owned? Does ownership of that tool alone entail a portion of the reward? Who has water rights? These and other related questions must be resolved for fruitful collaborations to continue. Answers can be particularly hard to come by in the case of commons that are shared among many groups.[29] When a salt source needs to be visited by thousands and debris must be cleared from low earth orbit, enduring institutions need to be developed to coordinate activities between independent, and at times antagonistic, groups.

These and other barriers to collective actions are considerable obstacles that have prevented every other animal from cooperating widely. Humans have nonetheless found a way to thrive because of an ability to work in larger and larger groups. Vast irrigation systems, pyramids, and writing systems are all testaments to sustained success in collective action; their eventual ruin is also a testament to how these relationships inevitably break down.[30] When things fall apart, some societies atomize, even creating structures dead set against forming relationships beyond the minimum required for survival.[31] In most cases, however, other kinds of groups emerge with the hope of better solving the collective action problems that families continue to face.

The Declaration of Independence announced the break-down of a collective. The delegates of the Second Continental Congress had gathered in Philadelphia because they were not happy with their position within the British Commonwealth. Their primary complaint was "taxation without representation."[32] Previous attempts to obtain direct participation in Parliament had failed, and Benjamin Franklin's Albany Plan of 1745 to create a unified American government fizzled out because of both the colonies and Britain's concern over divided sovereignty. The Stamp Act and other British revenue-generating efforts after the French and Indian War, however, brought renewed interest in an American confederation that would be a collective group independent from the commonwealth. Books and pamphlets urged action on either side of the Atlantic, violence erupted, and suddenly the "thirteen united States of America" were declaring independence.

The Articles of Confederation and Perpetual Union created a "league of friendship" between the states that was designed to allow the fledgling United States government to continue the war. The 1777 document approached the collective action problem at the level of the state—the pact was between states rather than between the people of the United States—and sought to do two things: provide for common state interests and protect state sovereignty.[33] Many collective action obstacles lurked unresolved within the document, and it soon became clear that the federal government as designed was ineffective. After independence was won in 1783, the state's league of friendship seemed destined to fragment. The nation's founders looked for alternative models of governance.

The Paths Not Taken

While working as a diplomat in Europe after war's end, John Adams wrote *A Defence of the Constitutions of Government of the United States of America*, a three-volume work that sought to legitimize the various constitutions being created by each state in the tumult following independence. The work was a historical justification for the American political experiment, covering the European

6 *Toward a More Perfect Union*

federations of his time like those in the Netherlands and northern Italy, along with earlier republican systems all the way back to ancient Greek and Rome. The first volume of *Defence* was published in January 1787 and made its way to Philadelphia a few months later as the Constitutional Convention deliberated its plans for the revising of the Articles of Confederation.

Adams wrote *Defence* at a feverish pace—his wife said that he was "much Swallowed up" by the project.[34] He cast his net widely, trying to convince both a European and American audience of the righteousness of the Constitutional Convention's intellectual project. Among the groups that he wished to consider were the Seneca and other nations of eastern North America with which he was familiar. In the preface to the first volume of his *Defence*, Adams wrote:

> To collect together the legislation of the Indians would take up much room, but would be well worth the pains. The sovereignty is in the Nations, it is true, but the three powers are strong in every tribe.[35]

John Adams knew that insights could be gleaned from Native Americans. Yet he would never actually take the pains of describing the Indian legislation that he so admired.

A Defence of the Constitutions of Government of the United States of America sprawls across almost 1,500 pages. More than 40 governments are discussed by Adams, almost all of them belonging to Europe. Native Americans' political structures were discussed in passing only a few more times in Adam's *Defence*. He generalized and mischaracterized the political structures of these societies when he wrote of them, and ultimately rejected them as inferior to those of Europe. Despite his assertion of the comparative value of Native American political organization in the preface, Adams rested his defense of the governance models being proposed for the United States of America on Western traditions.

Similar arguments could be made for the other arguments circulating at the time. Despite his frequent interactions with Indians, for example, James Madison's *Federalist Papers* cite many of the same Western governments that Adams had cited as inspirations for the United States government.[36] Benjamin Franklin, a great admirer of many aspects of Native life, made few explicit references to their systems of government when both privately and publicly supporting his vision for the future of the United States.[37] Although the Founding Fathers alluded to the Native American confederacies when addressing Native leaders—Franklin wrote that the "Great Council fire of our Nation . . . will again be rekindled" when speaking of the Constitutional Convention[38]—they returned time and time again to European models as sources for ideas on how to create a well-functioning federalist government.[39]

A counterargument has been made for a far more significant degree of Native American influence on the evolution of the government of the United States of America than is argued here.[40] These authors suggest that Native Americans significantly influenced colonial thinkers through their advice and example. They point to various meetings between the groups, including one that took place when the Constitutional Congress first convened, and highlight scattered references to Natives in delegate's writings or parallels in symbols and phrasing. This counterargument has considerable support, even resulting in a 1988 Congressional resolution that the formation of the United States was "influenced by the political system developed by the Iroquois Confederacy as were many of the democratic principles which were incorporated into the Constitution itself."[41]

The evidence of Native Americans offering advice is indeed compelling. Their leaders were often gifted orators and their words to colonial delegates are sometimes recorded as part of treaty conferences and other interactions. Time and time again, Native leaders noted the flaws in colonial governance and attempted to turn the settler's attention to aspects of their way of life that might prove useful.[42] Perhaps the most quoted of these speeches is the speech by Canasatego, an Onondaga leader who spoke to colonial commissioners from Pennsylvania in 1744:

> We heartily recommend Union and a good Agreement between you our Brethren. Never disagree, but preserve a strict Friendship for one another, and thereby you, as well as we, will become the stronger.
>
> Our wise Forefathers established Union and Amity between the Five Nations; this has given us great Weight and Authority with our neighbouring Nations.
>
> We are a powerful Confederacy; and, by your observing the same Methods our wise Forefathers have taken, you will acquire fresh Strength and Power.[43]

The commissioners thanked Canasatego for his thoughts, signed the treaty, and then did nothing to strengthen "Union and Amity" with the 12 other colonies.

The Jesuits and other early-seventeenth-century Europeans in the eastern woodlands had found themselves drawn into debates with Native leaders about the merits of core aspects of their culture from Christianity to a class-based society. These exchanges pushed settlers to interrogate their own culture and led to the creation of a popular early-eighteenth-century book genre based on fictional encounters between Europeans and others.[44] The Native ways of life of North America were thus ripe for exploration and emulation, and Native Americans leaders had long encouraged the colonists to better organize their affairs by learning from them. Through much of the first two centuries of British and French colonization, there *was* an engagement—albeit one rife with misunderstandings and abuse—with Native American ideas.[45]

Yet the voluminous late-eighteenth-century writings associated with the development of the United States Constitution barely mention Native confederations. Despite Canasatego's exhortations, a serious attempt to learn about the confederacy put together by his forefathers was not undertaken. The reasons why are many. Ideas of cultural evolution were beginning to congeal in Europe that put "savages" on the lowest rung of a ladder of progress that led to "civilization."[46] The allegiance of most nations, including the Onondaga, to the British during the War of Independence was also a factor in alienating the two groups,

8 Toward a More Perfect Union

Figure 1.2 Hopkinson's first sketch (left) and final sketch (right) for the Second Committee's Great Seal of the United States

as was the colonists' desire to place their constitution within the currents of European thought.[47]

The shift away from an intellectual engagement with Native Americans is hinted at in the second draft of the Great Seal. In 1780, Francis Hopkinson—the designer of the United States flag—drew up a new design that had a Lady of Peace on one side of a shield and a Native warrior on the other side. The shield's 13 diagonal red and white stripes hinted at the push toward greater federalism and would be retained in future drafts. The committee sent Hopkinson back to the drawing board, however, to replace the Native warrior with a Roman soldier.[48] There would be only one kind of American on the Great Seal of the nation (Figure 1.2).

The exclusion of Indians from the Great Seal was emblematic of a further negative shift in attitude as settlers pushed westward in the wake of the Revolutionary war. Violence escalated, and calls mounted for the eradication and forcible removable of Native Americans in the early nineteenth century who were now seen as standing in the way of prosperity. Gone was a time when Natives could be seen as equals. The more progressive voices of the time argued for education and assimilation: Indians, in their view, could be integrated into society if their backward ways were corrected.[49] Lewis Henry Morgan and other mid-eighteenth-century scholars would argue that we could still learn much from the Seneca, Onondaga, and other nations, but the Natives now served as a window to the past rather than an inspiration for a brighter future.[50]

What Could Have Been

No one knows what the United States Constitution would have looked like if the Founding Fathers had seriously considered Canasatego's Confederacy as a governance model. The Iroquois are a linguistic and cultural group that, at the time of European contact, resided in the eastern Great Lakes region of what are now Ontario, Quebec, Pennsylvania, and New York. Families lived in villages composed of longhouses that were typically occupied by a group of related women, their spouses, and children.[51] Men were often on the move, participating in diplomacy, trade, and warfare.[52]

The first longhouses in the region appear circa AD 1000, growing in average size through the fifteenth century until each held as many as 100 residents.[53] Matrilineages formed the backbone of these longhouses. While the related women were typically from the same clan, their spouses were outsiders, creating social bonds between males that crosscut regions.[54] Villages remained small—often just one or two longhouses—until about the fifteenth century when rising warfare triggered the creation of larger, often palisaded villages.[55] Negotiating relationships within and between neighboring communities spurred the creation of nations whose members, in turn, formed multinational confederacies for mutual aid and support.[56]

Coalition-building created two competing confederacies among the Iroquois. A northern confederacy was in what is now southern Ontario, but the America Colonies dealt largely with the southern Iroquois who had formed the Haudenosaunee Confederacy ("People of the Longhouse"). The Haudenosaunee Confederacy was composed of five nations: the Seneca, Cayuga, Onondaga, Oneida, and Mohawk. A sixth nation, the Tuscarora, would join the five nations in the eighteenth century. Some 30,000 people strong,[57] this confederacy was the one that Canasatego suggested that the colonies should emulate in order to achieve their own political aims.

The Haudenosaunee Confederacy was maintained by the Great Law of Peace, a living document passed on orally and celebrated on wampum belts. The Great Law is the story of Deganawida who united the warring five nations through his teachings. Deganawida's teachings were not written down until the late eighteenth century, so the nature of how the Great Law of Peace was delivered made its details difficult to assess for outsiders during the Colonial era—one had to sit with a nation for hours to begin to understand how peace was to be maintained. Even the act of being there was in-and-of-itself a fundamental part of the Great Law: Deganawida preached the virtue of listening to others.[58]

The members of the Constitutional Convention are unlikely to have heard the Great Law of Peace recited, but they would have known the broad contours of Haudenosaunee political organization through their diplomatic interactions. Each of the five nations maintained a council of *sachems*, male leaders who were nominated by the clan mothers. These same women could remove them from office. The sachems led the conversations of their assembled communities, but decisions were often by consensus—all had to agree on a course of action.[59] When the need arose, a meeting was called of the sachems of the five nations. Decisions among this group were once again made by consensus. In most cases, the assembled sachems rendered a decision, but in matters of great importance, a sachem was tasked to bring the matter back to his people for consultation. The issues deliberated by the assembled sachems were on external matters that impacted the five

10 *Toward a More Perfect Union*

nations. Internal decisions, including the right to go to war, were made at the level of the nation.[60]

The Great Law of Peace, as enacted by the eighteenth-century Haudenosaunee Confederacy, offered governance alternatives to the American colonies that were well-worth considering. The Great Law of Peace, for example, provided a blueprint for a far more inclusive democracy. Despite the soaring "We the People" opening of the Constitution, the states chose who could vote, and by the beginning of the nineteenth century, the vote was largely restricted to white men in the United States.[61] The Great Law of Peace, in contrast, enshrined the rights of all to speak, including outsiders who agreed to respect the law.[62] One's vote, moreover, was not placed at a ballot box but heard in a longhouse after hours of deliberation. Someone spoke, there was a long pause to reflect, and then another replied. These discussions could go on for hours until a consensus was reached.[63] Deganawida's teachings on listening and open-mindedness were imbedded within the procedures of these deliberations, as was his urging to avoid unwarrantable dissent. Playing politics nonetheless occurred—the subtle variation in oration of the Great Law, in part, were used to favor one nation's interests over another[64]—but council meetings had a completely different tenor than the often-pugilistic debates that were occurring in the early days of Congress.

Congress' adversarial approach to debate was the same as that seen in British Parliament, and it had a similar makeup of landed gentry. Although the composition of the Senate and House of Representatives has changed over the last 200 years, its adversarial winner-take-all attitude has only hardened. Transposing aspects of Haudenosaunee governance, then or now, would require translation. Iroquois politics, among many differences, was premised on a system of descent and residence far different from the one that were common in eighteenth-century colonial America. Yet surely a deeper engagement with the Haudenosaunee decision-making would have proved valuable.

In the Preface to his write-up of the debates of the Constitutional Congress, James Madison remarked:

> [T]he radical infirmity of the 'ar[ticle]s of Confederation' was the dependence of Cong[res]s on the voluntary and simultaneous compliance with its Requisitions, by so many independent Communities, each consulting more or less its particular interests & convenience and distrusting the compliance of others.[65]

Madison recognized that he and his fellow delegates were facing a collective action problem that had been left unresolved by the Articles of Confederation. Their first attempt had failed in less than a decade, and the Founding Fathers *knew* that the Iroquois had developed a confederacy that had proved far more enduring. They could have learned a lot from their neighbors.

There was much more to the Iroquois secret sauce of confederation beyond their system of decision-making. A community-shared responsibility for an individual's wrongdoing was integral to maintaining peace, as was their law demanding that hospitality be given to those who sought refuge. The symbols of the Haudenosaunee Confederacy—a tree with roots across the Six Nations, as well as a great longhouse where all the council fires were tended—emphasized unity over the parts that made the whole. As many before have argued, there was, and remains, much to admire in the Haudenosaunee Great Law of Peace.[66]

The delegates in the Constitutional Congress, however, chose to look elsewhere to model their nation's inchoate government. Inspired by European examples, they built a federalist system that provided only an uneasy solution to their collective action problem. Amendments followed, as well as a civil war, as groups continued to protest that their government was not working for them. Widening the scope of intellectual inquiry in the eighteenth century could have produced a different constitution of the United States of America and given rise to a more cohesive, inclusive, and understanding country.

Toward a Better Future

The final version of the Great Seal of the United States was unveiled in 1782 when American victory in the Revolutionary War was all but ensured. The seal now depicted a bald eagle clutching arrows and an olive branch in its talons. An "*E Pluribus Unum*" scroll was grasped in its peak. The 13 colonies were still there: 13 olive leaves, 13 arrows, 13 stars above, and the 13 stripes on the heraldic shield (Figure 1.3). Yet the eagle held the states firmly in its grasp. The Great Seal was a harbinger of the projection of federal power over the states that would be laid out seven years later in the Constitution.

The Constitution provided one solution to the former colonies' collective action problem, a solution that ultimately led to a far stronger federal government and a more robust national identity than was originally intended by those who first assembled in 1776. The Haudenosaunee Great Law of Peace and other non-Western confederation had been left unexplored by the delegates, and one can only wonder at what could have been if colonists had listened to Canasatego's advice. Perhaps the Civil War could have been averted, suffrage movement made superfluous, and the American imperial impulse redirected. The history of the United States, of course, may have remained the same, but options left unconsidered are options that cannot be taken.

There is rarely a single solution to a collective action problem. As societies grow larger with more moving parts, the range of possible solutions widens. History, culture, climate, and happenstance ensure that means used to solve common goals vary widely. Over millennia, we have come up with thousands of different ways to work together. None of these solutions were perfect; few were easy. The solutions nonetheless show different ways to resolve many common collective action concerns, such as those of free-riders, trust, and equity. Agriculture, urbanism, and other fundamental transitions in human history have been made possible by our ability to cooperate to solve new challenges. Over time, the collectives have gotten larger, and we are now faced with the dilemma of coordinating global action.

12 *Toward a More Perfect Union*

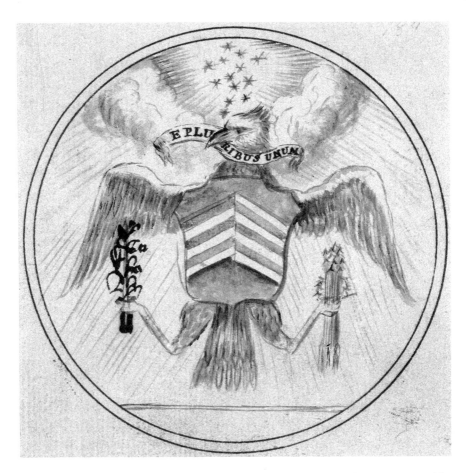

Figure 1.3 Thomson's design of the Great Seal of the United States that was accepted by Congress in 1782

The Founding Father's indifference to the Haudenosaunee Confederacy is emblematic of a broader late-eighteenth-century's turn away from the non-Western world. The intellectual curiosity of the Enlightenment was replaced by the manifest destiny of European expansion.[67] Other ways of being were seen as inferior, resulting in a far narrower suite of political possibilities. When people began to think more seriously about global governance, there was therefore not even a nod to non-western systems. They instead returned to the same mix of federalist and confederate solutions that the Founding Fathers had explored a century earlier.[68]

By the end of the nineteenth century, there was no debate: *E Pluribus Unum* would be best achieved at the global level by an intergovernmental institution composed of representatives of sovereign states.[69] The League of Nations, and

Toward a More Perfect Union 13

then the United Nations, emerged out of these convictions. Both were beneficial, with the UN responsible for the betterment of billons of lives. Where the UN faltered, other organizations have stepped in, trying to find solutions to collective action demands that have only grown in scale and intricacy in the decades following the Second World War. These efforts, by and large, have sought to maintain at least a semblance of a world in which independent states are the primary actors.

Many of today's problems can no longer be solved strictly at the level of the one's town, state, or nation. Yet globalization is eroding the current geopolitical order with dynamic flows of ideas, people, and objects. Many scholars thus recognize that the welter of global governance mechanisms that have grown up around sovereign states and the United Nations are ill equipped to deal with the most pressing collective action problems of our increasingly hyperconnected world.[70] We need to find new ways to improve global governance, but once again many scholars are returning to the same Western sources for inspiration.[71] A vast array of other political systems remain unexamined for their potential insights.

The "uncivilized" governments that were dismissed, marginalized, and dismantled by colonial administrators were often built to thrive on unstable political ground. Constantly adjusting relationships between constituents to address the problem at hand, these governance mechanisms are flexible yet durable, inclusive yet open-ended. The mechanisms used to organize large-scale activities in mid-first millennium Mexico or nineteenth-century highland Burma may feel untenable to readers who are used to a certain way of doing things. The status quo of organizing global affairs, however, is not working. The alternative governance systems discussed in this book can inspire new ways of navigating through today's globalization processes that seem hellbent on disruption.

Although yesterday's solutions cannot solve today's problems, they can help us think creatively about how to best deal with free riders, inequity, common property, and the other common problems of collective action that threaten, once again, to overwhelm attempts to solve the critical problems faced by our community. In *Rethinking Global Governance*, Thomas Weiss and Rorden Wilkinson argue:

> [M]uch of our current understanding of global governance is shaped by what we know, and a great deal of our reluctance to wrest it from the common associations that have hampered its analytical utility result from a lack of knowledge and appreciation of other views.[72]

Today, we cannot afford to turn to only to the West in our search for useful solutions to such pressing global issues as managing pandemics, curbing wealth inequities, and mitigating climate change. Our past contains a rich diversity of proven solutions to the common obstacles of collective action that have long been marginalized by the West. Amidst an existential crisis, can we afford to ignore so many of our earlier successes?

14 *Toward a More Perfect Union*

Notes

1 See Thomas Jefferson (1776) *Declaration of Independence*. The text begins with "The unanimous declaration of the thirteen United States of America."

2 For history of the Great Seal, see Richard S. Patterson and Richardson Dougall (1976) *The Eagle and the Shield: A History of the Great Seal of the United States* (Washington, DC: Department of State).

3 See Gordon S. Wood (1998) *The Creation of the American Republic: 1776–1787* (Chapel Hill: University of North Carolina Press); and Forrest McDonald (1985) *Novus Ordo Seclorus: The Intellectual Origins of the Constitution* (Lawrence: University of Kansas).

4 William Blackstone (1765–1769) *Commentaries on the Laws of England*, vol. 1, pp. 156–157 (London: Clarendon Press).

5 See Peter H. Russell (2021) *Sovereignty: The Biography of a Claim* (Toronto: University of Toronto Press), p. 10.

6 See David A. Lake (2003) The New Sovereignty in International Relations. *International Studies Review* 5(3): 303–323, p. 306.

7 Alexander Hamilton. The Federalist #51 in Jacob Cooke, ed. (1961) *The Federalist*, p. 353 (Middleton: Wesleyan University Press).

8 See Jack N. Rakove (1997) *Original Meanings: Politics and Ideas in the Making of the Constitution* (New York: Vintage Books); and Alison L. LaCroix (2010) *The Ideological Origins of American Federalism* (Cambridge: Harvard University Press).

9 See Thomas G. Weiss (2011) *Thinking About Global Governance: Why People and Ideas Matter* (Routledge: New York); and Thomas G. Weiss and Rorden Wilkinson (2019) *Rethinking Global Governance* (Polity Press: Cambridge).

10 See Garrett Hardin (1968) The Tragedy of the Commons. *Science* 162(3859): 1243–1248. For the long-term relevance of collective action problems, see Richard E. Blanton, with Lane F. Fargher (2016) *How Humans Cooperate: Confronting the Challenges of Collective Action* (Boulder: University Press of Colorado).

11 See Russell Hardin (2013) *Collective Action* (Abingdon: Routledge).

12 See Sarah F. Bronson and Frans B. M. de Waal (2014) Evolution of Responses to (Un) Fairness. *Science* 346(6207): 12511776.1–12511776.7 and Yvonne Rekers, Daniel B.M. Haun, and Michael Tomasello (2011) Children, but Not Chimpanzees, Prefer to Collaborate. *Current Biology* 21: 1756–1758.

13 See Richard Dawkins (1976) *The Selfish Gene* (Oxford: Oxford University Press).

14 See Charles Darwin (1871) *The Descent of Man* (London: D. Appleton).

15 See Joseph Henrich (2018) *The Secret of Our Success: How Culture Is Driving Human Evolution, Domesticating Our Species, and Making Us Smarter* (Princeton: Princeton University Press).

16 For a now classic discussion of the free rider problem, see Mancur Olson (1971) *The Logic of Collective Action: Public Goods and the Theory of Groups* (Cambridge, Harvard University Press).

17 See Thomas Laudal (2020) *A New Approach to the Economics of Public Goods* (Milton: Routledge).

18 See James H. Fowler, Oleg Smirnov, Tim Johnson, Richard McElreath, and Christopher T. Dawes (2007) Egalitarian Motives in Humans. *Nature* 446(7137): 794–796.

19 Psychologists have probed this nuance in equity expectations. For example, see Felix Kölle and Simone Quercia (2021) The Influence of Empirical and Normative Expectations on Cooperation. *Journal of Economic Behavior & Organization* 190: 691–703.

20 See Peter Corning (2011) *The Fair Society: The Science of Human Nature and the Pursuit of Social Justice* (Chicago: University of Chicago Press).

21 For example, see Joey T. Cheng (2020) Dominance, Prestige, and the Role of Leveling in Human Social Hierarchy and Equality. *Current Opinion in Psychology* 33(2020): 238–244. Dominance, in particular, is resisted, while hierarchies based on prestige are not.

Toward a More Perfect Union 15

22 See Brent Simpson, Robb Willer, and Cecilia L. Ridgeway. Status Hierarchies and the Organization of Collective Action. *Sociological Theory* 30(3): 149–166.
23 See Joyce Berg, John Dickhaut, and Kevin McCabe (1995) Trust, Reciprocity, and Social History. *Games and Economic Behavior* 10(1): 122–142.
24 More generally, there are problems with collection actions across diverse communities because of trust issues. See James P. Habyarimana (2009) *Coethnicity: Diversity and the Dilemmas of Collective Action* (New York: Russell Sage Foundation); and Laura Coello and Baukje Prins (2010) *Significant Difference?: A Comparative Analysis of Multicultural Policies in the United Kingdom and the Netherlands* (Amsterdam: Aksant).
25 See Francis Fukuyama (1996) *Trust: The Social Virtues and Creation of Prosperity* (New York: Free Press).
26 See John M. Anderies and Marco A. Janssen (2013) *Sustaining the Commons* (Tempe: Center for the Study of Institutional Diversity, Arizona State University).
27 See James A. Kitts (2008) Dynamics and Stability of Collective Action Norms. *Journal of Mathematical Sociology* 32(2): 142–163.
28 See Sara Singleton and Michael Taylor (1992) Common Property, Collective Action and Community. *Journal of Theoretical Politics* 4(3): 309–324.
29 See Elinor Ostrom (2003) How Types of Goods and Property Rights Jointly Effect Collective Action. *Journal of Theoretical Politics* 15(3): 239–270.
30 See Blanton (2016).
31 See Robert Bettinger (2015) *Orderly Anarchy: Sociopolitical Evolution in Aboriginal California* (Berkeley: University of California Press).
32 The concern was not only about a lack of representation but also the financial decisions that the British Empire was making. See Justin du Rivage (2017) *Revolution Against Empire: Taxes, Politics, and the Origins of American Independence* (New Haven: Yale University Press).
33 See Keith L. Dougherty (2001) *Collective Action Under the Articles of the Confederation* (New York: Cambridge University Press).
34 See letter from Abigail Adams to John Quincy Adams, November 22, 1786. In C. James Taylor, Margaret A. Hogan, Celeste Walker, Anne Decker Cecere, Gregg L. Lint, Hobson Woodward, and Mary T. Claffey, eds. (2005) *The Adams Papers, Adams Family Correspondence*, vol. 7, January 1786—February 1787, pp. 394–396 (Cambridge: Harvard University Press).
35 John Adams (1787–1788) *A Defence of the Constitutions of Government of the United States of America*, vol. 1, p. xxii (London: Dilly and Stockdale).
36 See James Madison (1788) *The Federalist* 18, 19 and 20 (Washington, DC: The Colonial Press, 1901).
37 See Timothy J. Shannon (2012) Benjamin Franklin and Native Americans. In *A Companion to Benjamin Franklin*, edited by David Waldstreicher, pp. 164–82 (Oxford: Wiley-Blackwell).
38 See Benjamin Franklin to Cornstalk, Cherokee Chief, 30 June 1787, *Franklin Papers*, Library of Congress.
39 See Samuel B. Payne, Jr. (1996) The Iroquois League, the Articles of Confederation, and the Constitution. *The William and Mary Quarterly* 53(3): 605–620 and Jürgen Overhoff (2011) Benjamin Franklin, Student of the Holy Roman Empire: His Summer Journey to Germany in 1766 and His Interest in the Empire's Federal Constitution. *Germanic Studies Review* 34(2): 277–286; and James D. R. Philips (2021) *Two Revolutions and the Constitution: How the English and American Revolutions Produced the American Constitution* (Lanham: Hamilton Books).
40 See Donald A. Grinde, Jr. and Bruce E. Johnson (1991) *Exemplars of Liberty: Native American and the Evolution of Democracy* (Los Angeles: American Indian Studies Center, University of California); Elizabeth Tooker (1988) The United States Constitution and the Iroquois League. *Ethnohistory* 37: 279–291; and Jose Barreiro, ed. (1992) *Indian Roots of American Democracy* (Ithaca: Awkewkon Press).

16 *Toward a More Perfect Union*

41 See the Congressional Resolution passed by Senate at: Select Committee on Indian Affairs (1988). H. Con. Res. 331, https://www.senate.gov/reference/resources/pdf/hconres331.pdf, accessed on July 11, 2022.

42 Many of these attempts are discussed in Grinde and Johnson (1991).

43 Canasatego's speech is recorded on p. 785 of the *Minutes of the Provincial Council of Pennsylvania,* vol. IV published in 1851 (Philadelphia: Theo Fenn).

44 See Chapter 2 of David Graeber and David Wengrow (2021) *The Dawn of Everything: A New History of Humanity* (New York: Signal). For examples from the genre of European dialogues, see Volume 2 of Baron de Lahontan (1703) *Nouveaux voyages de Mr. le Baron de Lahontan dans l'Amérique Septentrionale* (The Hague: Chez les Freres l'Honore); and Françoise de Graffigny (1747) *Lettres d'une Péruvienne* (Paris: A Piene).

45 For early relationships between Europeans and Native Americans, see Colin G. Calloway (2013) *New Worlds for All: Indians, Europeans, and the Remaking of Early America* (Baltimore: John Hopkins University).

46 See Chapter 5 in Bruce Trigger (2006) *A History of Archaeological Thought* (New York: Cambridge University Press).

47 For the Iroquois, see David L. Preston (2009) *The Texture of Contact: European and Indian Settler Communities on the Frontiers of Iroquoia, 1667–1783* (Lincoln: University of Nebraska Press); and Gail D. MacLeitch (2012) *Imperial Entanglements: Iroquois Change and Persistence on the Frontiers of Empire* (Philadelphia: University of Pennsylvania Press).

48 See Patterson and Dougall (1976).

49 See Claudio Sant (2021) *Unworthy Republic: The Dispossession of Native Americans and the Road to Indian Territory* (New York: W. W. Norton) and David Wallace Adams (2020) *Education for Extinction: American Indians and the Boarding School Experience, 1875–1928* (Lawrence: University of Kansas Press).

50 See Lewis Henry Morgan (1851) *League of the Ho-dé-no-sau-nee, or Iroquois* (Rochester: Sage & Brother).

51 See Elisabeth Tooker (1978) The League of the Iroquois: Its History, Politics, and Ritual. In *Northeast*, edited by Bruce Trigger, pp. 418–441. *Handbook of North American Indians,* vol. 15 (Washington, DC: Smithsonian Institution); Bruce Trigger (1978) The *Children of Aataensic: A History of the Huron People to 1660*, vol. 2 (Montreal: McGill-Queen's University Press); William Engelbrecht (2003) *Iroquoia: The Development of a Native World* (Syracuse: Syracuse University Press); and Jon W. Parameter (2010) *The Edge of the Woods: Iroquoia, 1534–1701* (Lansing: Michigan State University Press). Note that the term "Iroquois" is used here to speak more generally of the various nations that speak a group of related languages and share a general set of traditions and lifeways, and "Haudenosaunee" when speaking of the southern six nation confederacy. Today, the nations that formed the Haudenosaunee confederacy generally use "Haudenosaunee" to describe themselves, rather than "Iroquois" that is derived from a term used by the Huron (another Iroquois-speaking group to the north) to refer to Haudenosaunee nations.

52 See Engelbrecht 2003 and Anthony Wonderley (2005) Effigy Pipes, Diplomacy, and Myth: Exploring Interaction Between St. Lawrence Iroquoians and Eastern Iroquois in New York State. *American Antiquity* 70: 211–240.

53 See Mima Kapches (1990) The Spatial Dynamics of Ontario Iroquoian Longhouses. *American Antiquity* 55(1): 49–67; and John Creese (2016) Growing Pains: Explaining Long-Term Trends in Iroquoian Village Scale, Density, and Layout. In *Process and Meaning in Spatial Archaeology: Investigations Into Pre-Columbian Iroquoian Space and Place*, edited by Eric E. Jones and John L. Creese, pp. 45–77 (Boulder: University Press of Colorado).

54 See Susan Jamieson (1981) Economics and Ontario Iroquoian Social Organization. *Canadian Journal of Archaeology* 5: 19–30; and Elisabeth Tooker (1970) Northern Iroquoian Sociopolitical Organization. *American Anthropologist* 72(1): 90–97.

Toward a More Perfect Union 17

55 See Jennifer Birch (2010) Coalescence and Conflict in Iroquoian Ontario. *Archaeological Reviews From Cambridge* 25(1): 29–48.
56 See Anthony Woderley and Martha L. Sempowski (2019) *Origins of the Iroquois League* (Syracuse: Syracuse University Press).
57 See Gary Warrick (2008) *A Population History of the Huron-Petun, 500–1650 AD* (Cambridge: Cambridge University Press).
58 See Bruce E. Johannsen and Barbara Alica Mann, eds. (2000) *Encyclopedia of the Haudenosaunee* (New York: Greenwood Press).
59 See Tooker (1970); Elizabeth Tooker (1980) Women in Iroquois Society. In *Extending the Rafters: Interdisciplinary Approaches to Iroquoian Studies*, edited by Michael K. Foster, Jack Campisi, and Marianne Mithun, pp. 109–123 (Albany: State University of New York); and Bruce Trigger (1978) Iroquoian Matriliny. *Pennsylvania Archaeologist* 48: 55–65.
60 See Johannsen and Mann (2000).
61 See Richard R. Beeman (2011) *The Varieties of Political Experience in Eighteenth-Century America* (Philadelphia: University of Pennsylvania Press); and Michael A. Smith, Kevin Anderson, and Chapman Rackaway (2014) *State Voting Laws in America: Historical Status and Their Modern Implication* (New York: Palgrave Pivot).
62 See John Arthur Gibson (1899) *The Deganawifdah Legend: A Tradition of the Founding of the League of the Five Iroquois Tribes*," as told to J. N. B. Heweitt (Washington, DC: Bureau of American Ethnology Archives, No. 1517C).
63 See William N. Fenton (1998) *The Great Law and the Longhouse: A Political History of the Iroquois Confederacy* (Tulsa: University of Oklahoma Press).
64 See Christopher Vecsey (1986) The Story and Structure of the Iroquois Confederacy. *Journal of the American Academy of Religion* 54(1): 79–106.
65 See p. 692 of James Madison (1842) *Notes of Debates in the Federal Convention of 1787*, vol. II (Mobil: Allston Mygatt).
66 See Grinde and Johnson 1991, Tooker 1988, Jose Barreiro (1992); Donald S. Lutz (1998) The Iroquois Confederation Constitution: An Analysis. *Publius: The Journal of Federalism* 28(2): 99–127; and David Bedford and Thom Workman (1997) The Great Law of Peace: Alternatives to Inter-nation(al) Practices and the Iroquoian Confederacy. *Alternatives* 22(1): 87–111.
67 See Enrique Dussel (1993) Eurocentrism and Modernity (Introduction to the Frankfurt Lectures). *Boundary 2* 20(3): 65–76.
68 See Chapter 2 for a discussion of deliberations on global governance.
69 See Chapter 2 for a discussion of the Western influences on global governance.
70 For example, see Thomas Hale and David Held (2017) *Beyond Gridlock* (Cambridge: Polity); Amita Acharya (2018) *Constructing Global Order* (New York: Cambridge); and Thomas G. Weiss (2016) *What's Wrong with the United Nations and How to Fix It* (Cambridge: Polity).
71 On the international level, see for example Augusto López-Claros, Arthur L. Dahl, and Maja Groff (2020) *Global Governance and the Emergence of Global Institutions for the 21st Century* (New York: Cambridge University Press). For a discussion at a more local level, see Jedidiah Prudy (2022) *Two Cheers for Politics: Why Democracy Is Flawed, Frightening—and Our Best Hope* (New York: Basic Books). Both emphasize a return to the Western governance roots.
72 See Thomas G. Weiss and Rorden Wilkinson (2019) *Rethinking Global Governance* (Cambridge: Polity Press).

2 The Western Roots of Global Governance

The idea of the United Nations can be traced back to a particularly bloody chapter in European conflict that left more than eight million people dead.[1] Everyone seemed to be at war in the mid-seventeenth century AD. The Holy Roman Empire was imploding, the Dutch were fighting for independence from Spain, and England was being torn apart by a civil war. Rapes, torture, and massacres were endemic, and few people lived without fear. The Protestant Reformation had begun 100 years earlier, and two of the primary causes of the mid-seventeenth-century conflicts were the disputed role of the Papacy and a lack of religious freedom. Bilateral agreements between nations were insufficient to stem the bloodshed. Europe needed to change the basic rules of engagement.[2]

To end the wars throughout much of Europe, diplomats came together in Westphalia in 1648. Fundamental ideas of philosophy, law, religion, and international relations were discussed before a widely celebrated peace was brokered that both limited the power of the Pope and gave each state an inalienable right to choose its religion (Figure 2.1).[3] The inchoate idea of state-based sovereignty would become more fully developed over the next century, buttressed by works like Hobbes' *Leviathan* that collapsed together an absolute ruler, the ruler's subjects, and the government into a single bounded entity.[4] This scholarship coincided with the decline in much of Europe of feudalism with its local ties to lords in their manor. Rulers grew in power and trumpeted the idea of a state- or imperial-wide commonwealth that benefited all citizens.[5]

By the mid-eighteenth century, sovereignty was seen as unlimited, undivided, and unaccountable, flowing down from the top in a pyramid-shaped hierarchical society. Rousseau and a few other writers offered up other kinds of ideal government organizations for the state,[6] but no one questioned the idea that polities were sovereign, independent nation with supreme authority over its citizens. The idea of state sovereignty would thus be seen as the bedrock of international relations when Europe began dividing up the world. The reality, of course, was far messier on the ground—there were shifting answers to fundamental questions about colonial empires like what was the relationship of the East India Company to Great Britain and in what sense might Indians be thought of as British?[7]—but the great games of geopolitics were now conceptualized in terms of the relationships between leaders who led differently colored, hard-edged states (Figure 2.2).

DOI: 10.4324/9781003373322-2

The Western Roots of Global Governance 19

Figure 2.1 Wenceslaus Hollar's celebration of the Peace of Westphalia that underlines the connections made to divine intervention and Greek and Roman traditions

Figure 2.2 Prinald's world map published in 1766

20   *The Western Roots of Global Governance*

As the colonial powers grew stronger, the possibilities of cataclysmic violence loomed larger. Enlightenment thinkers therefore began proposing models for global governance that might avoid most warfare. These modelers also thought in terms of state actors, both in how they might be best internally organized and most effectively work together.[8] Kant's *Perpetual Peace: A Philosophical Sketch*, written in 1795, is an influential example on this subject that argued for representative governments and a federation of free states.[9] Others, of course, had different ideas about the optimal state government structure and the organization of international relations.[10] Ideas beyond a world order structured by states, however, were never seriously questioned.

With a nation's absolute sovereignty taken as given, the collective action problems of global geo-politics were seen as problems of state relationships. The barriers that impede collective action, such as free-riders, permanence, and a lack of trust, were thus seen as *inter-national* problems making it possible for people to imagine, once again, that problems could be resolved by getting a few dozens of the right people into a room together. As violence continued to consume Europe throughout the nineteenth century and spread into its colonies, there were heightened calls for a new intervention that could forge a more enduring, Westphalian-like peace.[11] The horrors of the War to End All Wars finally brought some of these ideas into reality when the League of Nations formed in 1920, an organization born from high hopes that would soon be replaced by the United Nations after a Second World War proved more terrible than the first.

Following other researchers, this chapter argues that global governance today remains largely a product of the Western imagination.[12] Basic notions of how the world order should work remain anchored in Enlightenment ideas and European examples, both in terms of how international organizations currently operate and in the possibilities that scholars offer for their reform. We *see* the problems of global governance in a certain way, and this shapes how we think these problems might be best addressed. One of these notions is that sovereign nation-states could and should control world politics. Both the League of Nations and United Nations were founded on this principle, and, often, ideas for fixing the world's problems maintain this status quo. This chapter uses the idea of sovereign nation-states to illustrate the broader grounding of global governance in Western thought.

The United Nations' conceptualizations of how global interactions should work were ill-fitted to the reality on the ground when the organization first formed, and the increasing pace of globalization since the Second World War has now only multiplied entanglements between more and more actors.[13] Global relationships are now deeply embedded in the fundamental day-to-day functioning of families, interest groups, companies, and states. In many cases, these relationships cut across national borders, weakening the state's ability to set political, economic, and social policies. More organizations enter the fray to facilitate collective action, but they almost invariably follow the same Enlightenment-inspired playbook as their competitors with the solutions that they offer—even the self-proclaimed disrupters end up behaving like everyone else. Gridlock ensues.[14]

Many working in global governance have long recognized that the status quo is not working.[15] In 2003, Koffi Annan gave his famous "Fork in the Road" speech as the United Nations Secretary General.[16] In the context of the first salvos of the War on Terror, Annan suggested that radical changes might be needed to the United Nations to improve global security. Twenty years later, the need for sweeping changes in this and many other areas of global governance grows ever more acute. We nonetheless continue to trudge down the same rutted paths that are proving increasingly ineffective. The force of tradition makes certain paths seem like the only ones that are feasible—they have been seen as the only viable options for a long time—and much has been invested in pursuing these routes. This book argues that other paths are worth considering.

A League of Nations

When the First World War ended in 1918, nine million soldiers and five million civilians were dead. Over 20 million more would die in a flu epidemic that circled the globe in four deadly waves from 1918 to 1920. Families were shattered, economies were in ruin, and simmering political tensions threatened to engulf the world in another war. The societal costs of modern warfare were becoming astronomical, but counties kept on getting drawn into fighting in the early twentieth century. Leaders once again sought a way to find lasting peace and, once again, they looked to European examples and ideas for solutions when they gathered at Versailles to discuss a possible confederacy of nations in the spring of 1919.

One way of understanding the influences behind the League of Nations is through the eyes of its two greatest champions: Woodrow Wilson and Jan Smuts. Wilson was the President of the United States, a country that had avoided some of the horrors of the First World War because of its later entry into combat. Wilson remained an optimist and he led a group of thinkers who felt that the world was destined to grow into a global community as international interdependencies deepened. Wilson thought that an American-like federalist system, paired with free trade and the extension of international law, would both hasten this transition to a global community and minimize bloodshed.[17] He wanted the league to be a space of open debate. All states would be invited; reason would reign supreme.

Wilson's vision was a strand of liberal internationalism that drew from John Stuart Mills, Herber Spencer, and other nineteenth-century European philosophers who argued about how democracy could be best nurtured.[18] Wilson was an academic before he was President, long wrestling with how the United States and other governments could best serve their people.[19] He rejected approaches like those offered by Madison and Kant that argued that government should be built to resist the base ambitions of its leaders and mob impulses.[20] Wilson instead argued:

> Government is not a machine, but a living thing. It falls, not under the theory of the universe, but under the theory of organic life. It is accountable to Darwin, not to Newton.[21]

22 *The Western Roots of Global Governance*

Government should thus be built up organically in dialogue with the people, applying the state's "full spiritual vigor" to restore to American families "its purity, its self-respect, and its pristine strength and freedom."[22] Good government could be achieved by talking things out.

Applying this principle to global governance, Wilson thought that free trade, open diplomacy, disarmament, and self-determination of nation states would put countries on a more equitable footing. This footing was necessary for fostering real dialogue, with the idea that the league's structure would then grow organically over the course of its deliberations. Since a state's interests would be so closely tied to global affairs, Wilson felt that force or sanctions would not be needed to keep countries from destructive acts against their neighbors, since interests would so frequently align. There would therefore be little need for censures and an independent army to enforce league decisions.

When the League of Nations was being discussed, Jan Smuts was the Prime Minister of the Union of South Africa, a self-governing dominion of the British Empire. As a combat veteran of both the Boer and First World Wars, Smuts also wanted to create a global governing body. Like Wilson, Smuts was a racist—as were many at the Paris Peace Conference when the league was debated.[23] Smuts believed in the inherent superiority of Western ideas and explicitly sought to advance a "Christian doctrine of human brotherhood" through an organization that would ensure freedom and equality for all nations.[24] While Wilson thought that these ideas would come to the fore over the course of the League's deliberations, Smuts believed that such ideas should be built into the structure of the organization.

Smuts saw the League of Nation as an opportunity to put into practice his abiding interest in how parts integrated into wholes. He argued that an entity—be it an insect or a civic government—was "a system of co-ordinated structures and functions"[25] which was formed over time by the "ordering, organizing, regulative activity in the universe" that created "synthetic unity."[26] More complex entities were seen as more "holistic" containing features that were more than the sum of their parts. As an entity became more "holistic," it passed through "different grades of Evolution" until it achieved, if properly fostered, "the last and highest reach of its evolution."[27] Smuts, like Wilson, therefore thought that the League of Nations must develop organically, but he believed that regulatory guardrails were needed to ensure that the League prospered. For Smuts, a functioning league was one with teeth not only to deter states from going to war but also to ameliorate sickness, poverty, famine, and other life conditions that were often the root causes of conflict. Smuts' hope was to do so without significantly impinging on state sovereignty by adopting a federalist system that allowed both the parts (the states) and the whole (global governance) to evolve properly.

Smuts read more widely than Wilson, incorporating psychology, philosophy, biology, physics, and other disciplines into his speeches and writing to inform his political thought.[28] Drawing inspiration from Darwin, Plato, Freud, Einstein, and many others, Smuts saw progressive change leading toward ever larger, better functioning wholes. The West, for Smuts, was at a "higher grade of Evolution"

The Western Roots of Global Governance 23

than others, so it should best serve as a model for structuring the League. Western federalist systems were thus seen as worthy of emulation, and so those tasked with forming the League of Nations would explore many of the same federations that America's Founding Fathers had pondered almost a century and a half earlier.[29]

When the principles of the League of Nations were drawn up in 1919, most pertained to territorial integrity, warfare, and conflict arbitration. Social and economic issues were given less emphasis, although already existing organizations like the International Red Cross were also placed under the League's purview. The focus on armed conflict was thus narrower than Wilson or Smuts had envisioned. Smuts also lost out in terms of enforcement—there would be no League of Nations Army—but he managed to put the guardrails on Wilson's more utopian vision of deliberations by ensuring the creation of a small Council whose four permanent members could be used to guide the League's development.[30]

Smuts had wanted the League to be the "ever visible working order of the great polity of civilisation."[31] The organization, however, was understaffed, underfunded, and unable to act on its own. Despite some successes, the League required a state's ongoing buy-in to its processes to function. Without serious, sustained deliberations, the idea of a trans-governmental institution withered on the vine when challenged. Isolationists ensured that the United States never joined the League of Nations, and those countries that did continued to rely on direct diplomacy as their primary mechanism of international relations. Japan left the League in 1933 when it did not recognize their sovereignty over newly conquered Manchuria; Hitler left a few months later when Britain and France vetoed his plan to rebuild Germany's military. Economic sanctions in 1935—league members finally decided that they needed a stick after all—then failed to stop Italy's invasion of Ethiopia.[32]

The *raison d'être* of League of Nations was to stop state aggression, and its failure to do so made it a marginalized institution by the late 1930s. Japan invaded China; Germany invaded Poland; Russia invaded Finland. The globe was soon engulfed in a conflict more terrible than the First World War. By the end of 1945, more than 70 million would be dead. More than a third of these deaths were civilians who died from starvation and disease. Almost six million Jews were killed in the Holocaust. Eleven million others were killed as part of the Nazi's genocidal policy. Amidst this devastating war, allied governments signed on to a *Declaration of United Nations* to maintain the peace between sovereign nations (Figure 2.3). The depth of the war's atrocities led for calls to widen the proposed organization's mandate to both prevent war *and* uphold human rights.[33]

The United Nations

The United Nations began as a formal declaration of mutual support by Allied leaders in January 1942. The document not only focused on the task at hand, "complete victory . . . against savage and brutal forces seeking to subjugate the world,"[34] but also made a commitment to uphold a slightly earlier agreement between the United States and United Kingdom to work toward the "establishment of a wider

Figure 2.3 A United States Office of War Poster from 1943 that celebrated the United Nations

The Western Roots of Global Governance   25

and permanent system of general security" after the conclusion of hostilities.[35] The United Nations became the formal name of the Allied Forces, and discussions between government officials of what a post-war future might look like were ongoing throughout the rest of the war. With victory assured in the spring of 1945, delegates from the 46 nations who signed the United Nations Declaration met in San Francisco to work out the details of a new international organization.

The failures of the League of Nations to stop foreign aggression weighed heavily on the delegates and much of their energy was spent on creating an administrative structure that could keep rogue states in-line.[36] State sovereignty remained unquestioned—after all the delegates represented their country and its interests at the conference—and much of the discussion was about how to build a League of Nations-like organization that could be more decisive and consequential than its predecessor. The United Nations would thus be an intergovernmental organization like the League of Nations, but delegates decided that only two-thirds majority was needed to take action rather than the League's unanimity. The delegates also set up a standing International Court of Justice, included the World Bank into their governance system, and made it easier to raise troops from member states for peacekeeping missions. The most controversial decision was to install a Security Council whose five permanent seats would go to the United States, Soviet Union, China, France, and the United Kingdom. Each would have veto power over any UN action.[37]

Although the veto rights were only grudgingly accepted by most delegates as necessary to ensure that the most powerful post-war states participated in the organization, many felt that the Security Council was necessary to guide the organization.[38] For some, the council was seen as the best hope to fulfill the League's dream of liberal internationalism.[39] Smuts, now the Prime Minister of South Africa, was a leading voice of this group. Like others of his generation who had witnessed so much warfare, he was now more pessimistic about the organic development of a commonwealth of nations matching his Classical and Christian ideals.[40] Smuts' vision differed in detail from others, but all had a commitment to exporting liberalism to thwart the development of authoritarian regimes. Individual freedoms needed to be protected, state power needed to be reduced, and governments should only rule by consent.[41] Smuts thought that imperialism would play an important role in transforming what he saw as backward countries, while others insisted that empires, by their very nature, were illiberal institutions that needed to be disbanded.

Despite their methodological disagreements, the champions of liberal internationalism believed that the League had failed because it had not incorporated a commitment to individual rights in the face of tyranny. They successfully campaigned to have Smuts speak early in the conference. He took the opportunity to argue that the Allies had won a moral crusade and the United Nations (UN) must stand for human rights:

> We have fought for justice and decency and for the fundamental freedom and rights of man, which are basic to human advancement and progress and peace. Let us, in this new Charter of Humanity, give expression to this faith

26 *The Western Roots of Global Governance*

in us, and thus proclaim to the world and to posterity, that this was not a mere brute struggle of force between the nations.[42]

Good had triumphed over evil, and, for the liberal internationalists, there was now a second chance to spread the West's "higher grade of Evolution" to the rest of the world.[43]

The final version of the *Charter of the United Nations* took a stand in its preamble:

> [T]o reaffirm faith in fundamental human rights, in the dignity and worth of the human person, in the equal rights of men and women and of nations large and small.[44]

A commitment to human rights was also found throughout the rest of the UN Charter, such as in Article 55(c) where all members pledge to work toward the "observance of human rights and fundamental freedoms of all without distinction to race, sex, language, or religion."[45]

Others in San Francisco supported human rights not so much for the specific planks of the liberal philosophy but because the language put the focus on an individual's relationship with the state. The conceptualization of the individual as a discrete entity was itself a Western construct fundamental to liberal philosophy.[46] While all groups define the self as both independent and relational, an emphasis on the individual as being bounded, stable, and separate from their social context had developed in the West over the last 500 years.[47] The "dividual" in Melanesia and India is one example of an alternative conceptualization wherein an individual is seen to a significant degree as being constituted by their relationships with others.[48] By relying on a more Western idea of the individual, the United Nations' founding documents downplayed the dense, dynamic web of inter-relationships that form one's identity and shape their actions. In so doing, the messiness of daily life could be simplified, once again, to nested relationships between individuals, states, and the world.

The focus on the individual in the framing of the United Nations was also a pragmatic choice for many delegates. They saw the Second World War as another example of ethnic conflict and feared that a focus on minority rights would only exacerbate tensions.[49] Following Hobbes, some delegated envisioned nation-building as a zero-sum game of trust between a people and their government.[50] Protection of human rights was part of the social contract, and, if effectively done, would help to erase the tribalism that led to instability. Minority rights were antithetical to this vision, as there should only be one people—the "French" or the "Chinese"—under one government. Following this line of reasoning, the state's responsibility was to erase these differences not through campaigns of racial purity as was done in Nazism, but through education, assimilation, and other non-violent means. The United Nations' goal, in their minds, should be to set the ceiling to which states should aspire. The mechanisms to reach those human rights goals would however be the sole purview of sovereign nations.

The culmination of these efforts was the *Universal Declaration of Human Rights*, a non-binding pledge that "the inherent dignity and of the equal and inalienable rights of all members of the human family is the foundation of freedom, justice and peace in the world."[51] Adopted in 1948, the Declaration was unanimously supported in the United Nations by all of the countries that cast a vote and was chaired by Eleanor Roosevelt, the wife of a former United States President. Its 30 articles were a paean to western liberalism—the right to asylum, freedom from torture, free speech, the right to education—that echoed many of the sentiments of the United States Declaration of Independence and Constitution that were discussed in Chapter 1. When Jan Smuts passed away two years later, he must have believed that the clutch of Western ideals that he held dear would indeed "guide the future civilization for ages to come."[52]

Dissent within the United Nations was nonetheless already palpable in the deliberations and voting of the *Universal Declaration of Human Rights*. Communist China and the Soviet Union, for example, pushed for more non-discrimination language in the declaration, openly calling out member nations like the United States and South Africa for the racist policies occurring within their borders. Some of the more influential voices on the committee drafting the declaration were from colonies that had just gained their independence. They put forward a condemnation of colonialism that was only narrowly defeated. Women on the committee made changes to make the text of the Declaration more gender inclusive; non-Western nations stressed how their own traditions should also be seen as commiserate with the Declaration's ideals.[53] These vocal critiques were generally not against the Declaration's conceptualization of the individual, universal human rights, and the roles of institutions in upholding these rights. They were highlighting the yawning gap between ideals and practice to call into question the Victorian narrative of Western superiority that had legitimized imperialism.[54]

Other concerns with the project of liberal internationalism were becoming visible. When the Declaration was approved, for example, Saudi Arabia had abstained because the delegates felt that some of the articles conflicted with Islamic legal traditions.[55] In the decades that followed, concerns would continue to rise about how religious freedom could be maintained amidst a universalist ethos.[56] A related objection was submitted by the American Anthropological Association during deliberations on the *Universal Declaration of Human Rights*. They argued that "respect for the cultures of differing human groups"[57] was essential and:

> Standards and values are relative to the culture from which they derive so that any attempt to formulate postulates should grow out of the beliefs or moral codes of one culture must to that extant detract from the applicability of any Declaration of Human Rights to Mankind as a whole.[58]

Their full-throated appeal to cultural relativism questioned both the idea of a social contract between an individual and the state and the notion that a global civilization based on shared values was obtainable or even desirable.

28 *The Western Roots of Global Governance*

Perhaps the greatest test to the United Nations' vision was, and remains, Israel. After World War I, the British had taken over Palestine from the Ottoman Empire as part of a League of Nations mandate until the region could stand on its own.[59] Jews had begun migrating into the region in significant numbers in the late nineteenth century, and immigration surged with British promises to make a Jewish homeland in Israel. By the end of World War II, 31% of the population was Jewish. The rest were overwhelmingly Arabs—largely Muslim but with a significant Christian minority—who had also been promised their own state. Violence erupted, the British asked the United Nations to solve their problem in 1947, and the UN's proposed solution of an Arab State, Jewish State, and a partitioned Jerusalem led to waves of violence in Palestine and across the Middle East.[60] Israel's conflicts over sovereignty, religious freedom, and human rights were a microcosm of the aspirations and limitations of the Westphalian solution that has continued to thwart United Nations peacekeeping efforts.

A Changing World

It is difficult to overstate the degree that the world has changed since the formation of the United Nations. The number of sovereign states has almost tripled. Immigration patterns have also diversified, rapidly changing the ethnic make-up of many Western nations. Global exports have increased almost exponentially, supply chains for even the most mundane now snake around the world, and new technologies like personal computers, cell phones, and the internet have made massive amount of information almost instantaneously available.[61] These and many other post-World War II changes are part of an accelerating 500-year-old wave of globalization that began with the European Voyages of Exploration.

One way to think of globalization is as complex connectivity, a condition created by a dense network of intense interactions and interdependencies between disparate people that is brought about through the flow of goods, ideas, and people.[62] Connectivity has waxed and waned over the course of human history, embroiling groups together into cultural horizons that stretched across broad regions. Earlier eras of globalization were associated with an interrelated suite of societal changes that echo contemporary ones.[63] Today's globalization is nonetheless unprecedented in the number, span, and depth of long-distance interactions. The interrelated societal trends associated with globalization are therefore now far more pronounced, disrupting state and corporate attempts to channel interactions in a manner of their choosing.[64]

The first trend is *time–space compression*, an acceleration of long-distance economic, political, and social processes that shrinks one's experience of space and time.[65] The world therefore feels smaller with time–space compression, and complex connectivity between groups means that changes in one place can have swift ramifications across a broad region. A second trend is *deterritorialization*, the sense that a place seems only tenuously connected to its local, geographically fixed, context.[66] Linked to the idea of time–space compression, deterritorialization occurs because of foreign influences on a plethora of local practices.

The third trend, *standardization*, occurs as people try to bridge increasingly fluid geographic and cultural boundaries. Common ways of envisioning the world like the metric system are needed to facilitate long-distance interactions and to make the actions of all parties in a transaction comprehensible.[67] *Unevenness* nonetheless occurs because long-distance interaction networks are neither geographically ubiquitous nor equal in their effects to all parties.[68] Hollywood, for example, enjoys considerable global influence, but box office smashes in one region can bomb in another.

As flows of ideas, objects, and people increase, a degree of *homogenization—* our fifth globalization trend—occurs as individuals come to rely on a similar suite of practices, attitudes, and products.[69] McDonalds, for example, is a globally recognized brand that has changed how people eat, and there have also been widespread convergence of ideas on beauty and sickness. *Heterogeneity* occurs at the same time as foreign elements from throughout an interaction network blend together in local settings.[70] McDonalds tweaks its menu based on local tastes, and surrounding restaurants do their own take on fast food. *Re-embedding of local culture*, the seventh trend seen in globalization, is a reassertion of local traditions in response to the corrosive effects of global flows. These traditions, often presented as a counterweight to ground individuals within heritage communities, are sometimes newly invented evocations of an idealized past.[71] The final trend is *vulnerability*. Complex complexity leads to interdependence because of the numerous, deeply embedded connections between various groups.[72] A Russian invasion of Ukraine roils international stock markets, and an illness in China quickly becomes a global pandemic.

Standardization *and* unevenness, homogenization *and* heterogenization: these and other trends illustrate the dynamic, often contradictory, nature of globalization in action. Complex connectivity is knitting together people, places, objects, and ideas in ways that often do not respect state governments and their boundaries.[73] As the state's ability to dictate the terms of the long-distance interactions of its citizens has weakened, so has the power of the United Nations to govern world affairs through these states. The institutions associated with the United Nations, such as the International Monetary Fund and UNICEF, are similarly debilitated by their state-centered organization.[74] Rather than changing their *modus operandi*, these institutions have tended to double down on the idea that global governance is about organizing the relationship between recognized sovereign states.

To manage dynamic global conditions, many other international government organizations (IGOs) have arisen that often mimic the ideological structure of the United Nations. The European Union, formed in 1993, is an example of a political and economic union that, among other provisions, creates a single market and allows the free movement of goods and people between member states. OPEC, founded in 1960, is a union of oil producing nations that sets production targets and influence prices. The Group of Seven (G7) is an organization of some of the wealthiest states that sometimes works closely with the UN-associated International Monetary Fund; the Group of Twenty (G20) is more often seen as a rival UN that includes only the most powerful states. Premised on the idea of sovereign

30   *The Western Roots of Global Governance*

states, each organization works for the benefit of its members, routinely creating conflict with other IGOs.

The United Nations and other IGOs have also been joined on an already crowded international stage by transnational companies. The number of companies operating in more than one state has ballooned from about 7,000 in 1970 to more than 100,000 today.[75] The largest of these companies—General Motors, Exxon, and Nestle—generate revenues that dwarf those of many countries. By going transnational, these firms can diversify assets, find new markets, and acquire talent, giving them their own "feet on the ground" to navigate uncertainty. Corporate structures have Western roots in both Roman law and as early tools of British and Dutch colonialism.[76] They emerge from the same intellectual foundations as the nation-state and, on multiple occasions, have blatantly served state interests abroad.[77]

Although their internal organizations differ in detail, each corporation is generally seen as an autonomous actor with its own resources that works for the benefit of its shareholders.[78] In most countries, corporations are defined as legal persons that can enter contracts, be sued, and own property.[79] As these organizations take over infrastructure typically associated with state governments like roads, prisons, and communication networks, calls have grown to treat to them as foreign powers whose aims can often run counter to a host state's interests.[80] Rather than offering a new model for global governance, transnational corporations are acting as rival states, weakening nation-states from within and even forming their own partnerships with the World Bank, the United Nations, and other international groups.[81]

Another reaction to accelerating globalization has been the explosive growth of non-governmental organizations (NGOs).[82] NGOs are neither governments nor commercial enterprises and instead focus on a wide range of economic, political, social, and environmental issues.[83] The largest NGOs, such as Oxfam, World Vision, and the Bill and Melinda Gates Foundation, make significant impacts in the world's poorer states. Although their organizations vary, most NGOs are incorporated, affording these organizations the same legal protections that companies are given. NGOs are also increasingly seen as state-like actors in their own right, even as many work closely with both governments and transnational corporations. By taking over many of the responsibilities for the health, environmental quality, and other critical aspects of their citizen's lives, NGOs can also erode both a state's institutional development and its integration into the global economy.[84]

In 2013, Thomas Hale, David Held, and Kevin Young published *Gridlock: Why Global Cooperation Is Failing When We Need It Most*.[85] The book argues that countries today are the victims of their earlier successes. Although the United Nations and its associated intergovernmental agencies prevented global war, these coordination efforts created a "self-reinforcing interdependence" that makes leaders unable to effectively solve the problems that arise from increased complex connectivity.[86] They argue that the surging number of transnational corporations and NGOs that take over duties commonly associated with sovereign states have only added to the gridlock. The book identified post-war trends causing collective action problems from increased transaction costs to entrenchment of institutional missions. The authors' subsequent book sought to pathways through this gridlock, most often by aligning state interests, mobilizing domestic constituencies on issues of concern, and shielding organizations from undue political influence.[87]

The recommendations of reform from the *Gridlock* authors are joined by others who identify an array of useful institutional tweaks that can be implemented without a major haul of global governance.[88] Their suggestions would likely allow the world to better work together in the short-term. However, I suggest that more radical change is needed to enhance collective action over the long-term. Today's self-reinforcing interdependence is also a product of too many actors using the same basic playbook. States, transnational companies, and NGOs tend to follow the same deeply rutted path in their organization, decision-making, and interactions that is anchored in Western conceptualizations of the individual, state, social contracts, and sovereignty. As complex connectivity rapidly rises, these conceptualizations become increasingly unmoored from a reality that is better characterized as dense, dynamic webs of cross-cutting interactions.[89] To shore up the status quo in the hopes of solving a pressing issue like climate change—perhaps by clarifying a state' sovereignty claims or reinforcing an individual right—is to pin one's hope on institutions build to navigate a very different world.

A Fork in the Road

When diplomats gathered in Westphalia in 1648, they sought the best option for peace by putting different ideas on the table. At other tables in 1776, the Founding Fathers debated various ideas on how to best organize a federalist government. More ideas were put on more tables when the League of Nations formed, and again in the deliberations about the United Nations. Each time, people put down ideas that they thought would work and, each time, these came from a Western canon of ideas and examples. Over time, a consensus developed for effective global governance based on the ideas of human universals and multi-lateral accords between sovereign states. Those in power agreed on the soaring rhetoric of where they wanted society to go, even while squabbling over the best ways to get there.

Twenty years ago, Kofi Annan recognized that the world was at a fork in the road. He argued that "radical changes" should be considered for global governance and warned that, "history is a harsh judge: it will not forgive us if we let this moment pass."[90] Born in a British colony in West Africa, Annan knew first-hand how much the world had changed. Accelerating globalization and decolonization had made the world's collective action challenges more daunting, and the established tools to solve our problem were becoming less effective. Even the United Nations' foundational ideas—nation-states, sovereignty, universal human rights ideas—were being widely questioned. It was finally time to move beyond Hobbes, Kant, the Bible, and Greek city-states. Annan wanted to forge a Peace of Westphalia fit for the twenty-first century, a governance model that would also look outside of the Western canon for inspiration.[91] Nothing happened.

Our collective action problems have only grown larger since 2003. Trust in government has plummeted in many societies in the twenty-first century, for example, and ownership and usage rights have become even more convoluted.[92] Even communication technology, seen as an elixir of global cooperation in the

32   *The Western Roots of Global Governance*

early 2000s, has turned against us, with Twitter, Facebook, and other platforms spurring greater polarization.[93] Every barrier to successful collective action seems to be rising quickly. At times, it is difficult not to become overcome with despair. We have waited too long at the fork in the road. We are destined for gridlock, helpless in the face of belligerent states, the next pandemic, and vanishing rain forests. When I lose hope in these moments, I think about the challenges that we have endured over the last 100,000 years.

Weak and slow, humanity survived past the last Ice Age because of our ability to cooperate with each other. We have come up with a dizzying array of answers to the challenges of working together, including during times of fragmentation and institutional change. The scale of today's collective action problem is unprecedented: how do we get eight billion people to agree to do anything? But today's seemingly insurmountable problems are also a testament to thousands of years of collective success. Often, people worked together in ways that can now seem unimaginable simply because 500 years of Western thinking about global governance has limited our ideas of the possible. We therefore think of neighborhood organizations in an Indus Valley Civilization city, segmentary tribe organization in pre-Colonial Africa, and today's threatened common property regimes in highland Laos only as interesting curiosities of a by-gone era, rather than as examples for how global society could be better organized. It is long past time to open our eyes to other possibilities.

Notes

1 See Lawrence Peter (2015) *The United Nations: History and Core Ideas* (New York: Palgrave Macmillan).
2 See Thomas Munck (1990) *Seventeenth Century Europe: State, Conflict, and the Social Order in Europe, 1598–1700* (Basingstoke: Macmillan).
3 See Derek Croxton (2013) *Westphalia: The Last Christian Peace* (New York: Palgrave MacMillan).
4 See Thomas Hobbes (1651) *Leviathan or the Matter, Forme and Power of a Commonwealth Ecclesiasticall and Civil* (London: Andrew Crooke); and David Hume (1740) *A Treatise of Human Nature* (London: Noon).
5 For a richer understanding of this period, see Beat A. Kümin and C. Scott Dixon (2020) *Interpreting Early Modern Europe* (Oxon: Routledge).
6 Most of these conversations were about different variations on monarchies. For example, see Jean-Jacques Rousseau (1762) *Du Contrat Social; ou, Principes du droit Politique* (Amsterdam: Marc Michel Rey); and Edmund Burke (1790) *Reflections on the Revolution in France* (London: J. Dudeley).
7 See William Dalrymple (2019) *The Anarchy: The Relentless Rise of the East India Company* (New York: Bloombury); and Nick Robbins (2006) *The Corporation that Changed the World: How the East India Company Shaped the Modern Multinational* (New York: Pluto Press).
8 Some of this literature was critical of European imperialism, see Sankar Muthu (2013) *Enlightenment Against Empire* (Princeton: Princeton University Press).
9 See Immanuel Kant (1795) *Zum ewigen Frieden. Ein philosophischer Entwurf* (Koningsberg: F. Nicolvius).
10 See Zeev Maoz (1998) Realist and Cultural Critiques of the Democratic Peace: A Theoretical and Empirical Re-Assessment. *International Interactions* 24(1): 3–89.

The Western Roots of Global Governance   33

11 See Peter H. Wilson (2017) *Warfare in Europe 1815–1914* (London: Taylor & Francis).

12 See Stephen Gill (2015) At the Historical Crossroads—Radical Imaginaries and the Crisis of Global Governance. In *Critical Perspectives on the Crisis of Global Governance*, edited by Stephen Gill, pp. 181–199 (New York: Palgrave MacMillan); and Adelle Blackett (2001) Global Governance, Legal Pluralism and the Decentered State: A Labor Law Critique of Codes of Corporate Conduct. *Indiana Journal of Global Legal Studies* 8(2): 401–447; and Manuel Castells (2005) Global Governance and Global Politics. *PS: Political Science & Politics* 38(1): 9–16.

13 See Ian Goldin (2013) *Divided Nations: Why Global Governance Is Failing and What We Can Do About It* (Oxford: Oxford University Press); and Antonio L. Rapa (2011) *Globalization: Power, Authority, and Legitimacy in Late Modernity* (Singapore: Institute of Southeast Asian Studies).

14 See Thomas Hale, David Held, and Kevin Young (2013) *Gridlock: Why Global Cooperation Is Failing When We Need It Most* (Cambridge: Polity Press); and Thomas Hale and David Held (2017) *Beyond Gridlock* (Cambridge: Polity Press).

15 See Eric Fawcett and Hanna Newcombe, eds. (1995) *United Nations Reform: Looking Ahead After Fifty Years* (Toronto: Science for Peace); Emad Mayer-Mruwat (1998) United Nations: Critiques and Reforms. *Journal of Third World Studies* 15(1): 221–237; and Thomas G. Weiss (2016) *What's Wrong with the United Nations and How to Fix It*, third edition (Cambridge: Polity Press).

16 See "In Annan's Words: Fork in the Road" *New York Times*, September 23, 2003.

17 See Stephen Wertheim (2011) The League that Wasn't: American Designs for a Legalistic-Sanctionist League of Nations and the Intellectual Origins of International Organization, 1914–1920. *Diplomatic History* 35(5): 797–835.

18 For example, see John Stuart Mills (1859) *On Liberty* (London: John W. Parker and Son); and Herber Spencer (1884) *The Man Versus the State* (London: Williams and Norgate).

19 See Woodrow Wilson (1917) *Constitutional Government in the United States* (New York: Columbia University Press).

20 For Kant, see (1795) *Zum ewigen Frieden. Ein philosophischer Entwurf* (Koningsberg: F. Nicolvius); and (1797) *Die Metaphysik der Sitten* (Koningsberg: F. Nicolvius). Madison's views are found in *Federalist Papers No. 47* (1788, New York: New York Packet).

21 Woodrow Wilson's 1912 campaign speech from which this is quoted was republished in his 1913 book *The New Freedom: A Call for the Emancipation of the Generous Energies of a People* (New York: Doubleday & Page).

22 See the Preface of Wilson (1913).

23 For a brief discussion of Wilson's (and others') racism within the context of internationalism, see Steve Fuller (2016) Making Moral Judgments from a World-Historic Standpoint: The Case of Woodrow Wilson. *Society* 53(2): 315–318.

24 See P.B. Blackenberg (1951) *The Thoughts of General Smuts*, p. 169 (Capetown: Juta and Company), also see Jan Smuts (1918) *The League of Nations: A Practical Suggestion* (London: Hodder and Staughton).

25 See Jan Smuts (1926) *Holism and Evolution*, p. 210 (New York: Macmillan).

26 See Smuts (1926), p. 317.

27 See Smuts (1926), pp. 142–144.

28 See Joseph Kochanek (2012) Jan Smuts: Metaphysics and the League of Nations. *History of European Ideas* 39(2): 267–286 and Francis W. Bush (1984) Jan Smuts and His Doctrine of Holism. *Ultimate Reality and Meaning* 7(4): 288–297.

29 For more on the intellectual foundations of the league, see Stephen Wertheim (2011); and Sakiko Kaiga (2021) *Britain and the Intellectual Origins of The League of Nations, 1914–1919* (Cambridge: Cambridge University Press).

34 *The Western Roots of Global Governance*

30 For an ultimate organization of the League of Nations, see Martyn Housdan (2011) *The League of Nations and the Organization of Peace* (Harlow: Pearson) and Ruth B. Hening (2010) *The League of Nations* (London: Haus Histories).

31 See Smuts (1918), p. 8.

32 For a history of the League of Nations, see Housdan (2011) and Hening (2010).

33 See Robert C. Hilderbrand (1990). *Dumbarton Oaks: The Origins of the United Nations and the Search for Postwar Security* (Chapel Hill: University of North Carolina Press).

34 See Various (1942) *Declaration of the United Nations*, https://avalon.law.yale.edu/20th_century/decade03.asp, accessed on September 3, 2022.

35 See Franklin D. Roosevelt and Winston S. Churchill (1941) *The Atlantic Charter*, https://avalon.law.yale.edu/wwii/atlantic.asp, accessed on September 3, 2022.

36 See Stephen C. Schlesinger (2004) *Act of Creation: The Founding of the United Nations; A Story of Superpowers, Secret Agents, Wartime Allies and Enemies, and Their Quest for a Peaceful World* (Cambridge: Westview Press). For a personal account of the deliberations, see Clark Mell Eichelberger (1977) *Organizing for Peace: A Personal History of the Founding of the United Nations* (New York: Harper & Row).

37 For the organization of the United Nations, see Sam Daws, Paul Graham Taylor, and Sara Lodge, eds. (2016) *The United Nations* (Abingdon: Routledge, Taylor & Francis Group).

38 See Mark Mazower (2009) *No Enchanted Place: The End of Empire and the Ideological Origins of the United Nations* (Princeton: Princeton University Press).

39 See Mazower (2009).

40 See Jan Smuts (1944) *Towards a Better World* (New York: World Books).

41 See Stanley Hoffmann (1985) The Crisis of Liberal Internationalism. *Foreign Policy* 98: 159–177; and Razee Sally (1998) *Classical Liberalism and International Economic Order: Studies in Theory and Intellectual History* (London: Routledge).

42 See (1945) *Documents of the United Nations Conference on Institutional Organizations, San Francisco* vol. 1, pp. 425.

43 See Smuts (1926), pp. 142–144.

44 See United Nations Charter (1945) www.un.org/en/about-us/un-charter, accessed on September 3, 2022.

45 See United Nations Charter (1945).

46 See Clifford Geertz (1974) From the Native's Point of View: On the Nature of Anthropological Understanding. *Bulletin of the American Academy of Arts and Sciences* 28(1): 26–45.

47 See Melford E. Spiro (1993) Is the Western Conception of the Self 'Peculiar' within the Context of the World Cultures? *Ethos* 21(2): 107–153 and Vivian L. Vignoles, Ellinor Owe, Maja Becker, Peter B. Smith, Matthew J. Easterbrook, Rupert Brown, Roberto González, et al. (2016) Beyond the 'East–West' Dichotomy: Global Variation in Cultural Models of Selfhood. *Journal of Experimental Psychology* 145(8): 966–1000.

48 See Mattison Mines (1994) *Public Faces, Private Voices: Community and Individuality in South India* (Berkeley: University of California Press) and Marilyn Strathern (1988) *The Gender of the Gift: Problems With Women and Problems With Society in Melanesia* (Berkeley: University of California Press).

49 J. Cooper (2008) *Raphael Lemkin and the Struggle for the Genocide Convention* (New York: Palgrave McMillan).

50 See Hobbes (1651).

51 See the *Universal Declaration of Human Rights* (1948), www.un.org/en/about-us/universal-declaration-of-human-rights, accessed on September 3, 2022.

52 See W.K. Hancock (1962) *Smuts: The Sanguine Years, 1870–1919*, p. 198 (Cambridge: Cambridge University Press).

53 See Rebecca Adami (2019) *Women and the Universal Declaration of Human Rights* (New York: Routledge); and Johannes Morsink (2011) *The Universal Declaration of Human Rights: Origins, Drafting, and Intent* (Philadelphia: University of Pennsylvania Press).

The Western Roots of Global Governance   35

54 See discussion in Roland Burke (2010) *Decolonization and the Evolution of International Human Rights* (Philadelphia: University of Pennsylvania Press).

55 Saudi Arabia has continued to wrestle with the relationship between universal human rights and Islam. See Andrew Hammond (2012) *The Islamic Utopia: The Illusion of Reform in Saudi Arabia* (London: Pluto).

56 See Linde Lindkvist (2017) *Religious Freedom and the Universal Declaration of Human Rights* (New York: Cambridge University Press).

57 Executive Board (1947) Statement of Human Rights. *American Anthropologist* 49(4): 539–543, p. 539.

58 Executive Board (1947), p. 542.

59 See League of Nations (1924) *The Establishment in Palestine of the Jewish National Home: Memorandum* (London: Whitefriars Press).

60 See Rotem Giladi (2017) Negotiating Identity: Israel, Apartheid, and the United Nations, 1949–1952. *The English Historical Review* 132(559): 1440–1472; John Quigley (2016) *The International Diplomacy of Israel's Founders: Deception at the United Nations in the Quest for Palestine* (New York: Cambridge University Press); and Ofra Friesel (2018) Fifty Years Since the 1967 Annexation of East Jerusalem: Israel, the United States, and the First United Nations Denunciation. *Journal of the History of International Law* 1: 89–123.

61 See Stephan Leibfried and Michael Zürn, eds. (2005) *Transformations of the State?* (Cambridge: Cambridge University Press); Jon Shefner and Arch G Woodside, eds. (2015) *States and Citizens: Accommodation, Facilitation and Resistance to Globalization* (Bingley: Emerald Publishing Limited); and W. M. Spellman (2020) *A Concise History of the World Since 1945: States and Peoples*, second edition (London: Red Globe Press).

62 See John Tomlinson (1999) *Globalization and Culture* (Chicago: University of Chicago Press).

63 See Justin Jennings (2010) *Globalizations and the Ancient World* (New York: Cambridge University Press).

64 See Leslie Sklair (2006) Competing Conceptions of Globalization. In *Global Social Change: Historical and Comparative Perspectives*, edited by Christopher Chase-Dunn and Salvatore J. Babones, pp. 59–78 (Baltimore: John Hopkins University Press).

65 See David Harvey (1989) *The Condition of Postmodernity* (Cambridge: Blackwell).

66 See Arjun Appadurai (1990) Disjuncture and Difference in the Global Cultural Economy. *Theory, Culture, and Society* 7: 295–310; and Anthony Giddens (1990) *The Consequences of Modernity* (Stanford: Stanford University Press).

67 Benedict R. Anderson (1991) *Imagined Communities: Reflection of the Origin and Spread of Nationalism*, second edition (New York: Verso); and Richard Wilk (1995); Learning to Be Local in Belize: Global Systems of Common Difference. In *Worlds Apart: Modernity Through the Prism of the Local*, edited by Daniel Miller, pp. 110–133 (New York: Routledge).

68 See Immanuel Wallerstein (1979) *The Capitalist World-Economy* (Cambridge: Cambridge University Press); Eric R. Wolf (1982) *Europe and the People Without History* (Los Angeles: University of California Press); and Harvey (1989).

69 See John B. Thompson (1995) *The Media and Modernity: A Social Theory of the Media* (Cambridge: Polity Press); and Tomlinson (1999).

70 See Thomas Friedman (1999) *The Lexus and the Olive Tree: Understanding Globalization* (New York: Farrar, Strauss and Giroux); and Akhil Gupta and James Ferguson (2002) Beyond "Culture": Space, Identity, and the Politics of Difference. In *The Anthropology of Globalization: A Reader,* edited by Jonathan Xavier Inda and Renato Rosaldo, pp. 65–80 (Malden: Blackwell).

71 See Eric Hobsbawm and Terrence Ranger, eds. (1983) *The Invention of Tradition* (Cambridge: Cambridge University Press); and Linda Green (2002) Notes on Mayan Youth and Rural Industrialization in Guatemala. In *The Anthropology of Globalization: A Reader*, edited by Jonathan Xavier Inda and Renato Rosaldo, pp. 101–20 (Malden: Blackwell).

36 *The Western Roots of Global Governance*

72 See Ulricke Beck (1992) *Risk Society: Towards a New Modernity* (London: Sage); and Thomas Hyland Eriksen (2007) *Globalization* (New York: Berg).

73 For a discussion of some of these contradictions, see Dennis Conway and Nik Heynen, eds. (2014) *Globalization's Contradictions: Geographies of Discipline, Destruction, and Transformation* (London: Routledge).

74 See Chris McGreal (2015) 70 years and half a trillion dollars later: what has the UN achieved? September 7th edition. *The Guardian*, www.theguardian.com/world/2015/sep/07/what-has-the-un-achieved-united-nations, accessed on September 3, 2022.

75 See Tim Bartley (2018) Transnational Corporations and Global Governance. *Annual Review of Sociology* 44(1): 145–165.

76 See Robert Harris (2020) *Going the Distance: Eurasian Trade and the Rise of the Business Corporation, 1400–1700* (Princeton: Princeton University Press).

77 One of the most well-known examples of early transnational corporations serving state interests is the political economies of Honduras and Guatemala during the early twentieth century. O. Henry famously called these "Banana Republics" because of the outsized influence of American fruit companies (*Cabbages and Kings*, 1904, New York: Doubleday & Page). Also see, Peter Chapman (2007) *Jungle Capitalists: A Story of Globalisation, Greed and Revolution* (Edinburgh: Canongate, 2007).

78 See David Gindis (2020) Conceptualizing the Business Corporation: Insights from History. *Journal of Institutional Economics* 16(5): 569–577.

79 See Ira Bashkow (2014) What Kind of a Person Is the Corporation? *Political and Legal Anthropology Review* 37(2): 296–307.

80 Adrienne LaFrance (2021) FacebookLand. *The Atlantic,* September Issue, www.theatlantic.com/magazine/archive/2021/11/facebook-authoritarian-hostile-foreign-power/620168/, accessed on September 3, 2022.

81 See Benedicte Bull and Desmond McNeill (2007) *Development Issues in Global Governance: Public-Private Partnerships and Market Multilateralism* (Florence: Routledge).

82 See Kim D. Reimann (2006) A View from the Top: International Politics, Norms, and the Worldwide Growth of NGOs. *International Studies Quarterly* 50: 45–67.

83 See Göran Sonnevi, Walter W. Powell, Richard Steinberg, and Göran Sonnevi (2006) *The Nonprofit Sector: A Research Handbook*, Second edition (New Haven: Yale University Press).

84 See Diogo Pinheiro, Jeffrey M. Chwieroth, and Alexander Hicks (2015) Do International Non-Governmental Organizations Inhibit Globalization? The Case of Capital Account Liberalization in Developing Countries. *European Journal of International Relations* 21(1): 146–170.

85 See Thomas Hale, David Held, and Kevin Young (2013).

86 See Thomas Hale, David Held, and Kevin Young (2013), p. 3.

87 See Hale and David Held (2017).

88 For example, see chapters in Stephen Gill (2015) *Critical Perspectives on the Crisis of Global Governance: Reimagining the Future* (Basingstoke: Palgrave Macmillan); and Marek Rewizorski, Karina Jędrzejowska, and Anna Wróbel, eds. (2020) *The Future of Global Economic Governance Challenges and Prospects in the Age of Uncertainty* (Cham: Springer International Publishing).

89 See Ann-Marie Slaughter (2004) Disaggregated Sovereignty: Towards the Public Accountability of Global Government Networks. *Government and Opposition* 39(2): 159–190; Ann-Marie Slaughter (2017) *The Chessboard and the Web: Strategies of Connection in a Networked World* (New Haven: Yale University Press), and Jean L. Cohen (2012) *Globalization and Sovereignty: Rethinking Legality, Legitimacy, and Constitutionalism* (Cambridge: Cambridge University Press).

90 See Fork in Road speech, *New York Times* (2003).

91 See Kofi A. Annan and Nader Mousavizadeh (2013) *Interventions: A Life in War and Peace* (New York: Penguin Books).

92 For trust, see the annual United Nations survey titled "Trust in Public Institutions: Trends and Implications for Economic Security," www.un.org/development/desa/dspd/2021/07/trust-public-institutions/, accessed on September 3, 2022. For rising collective action problems more generally, see Mica Panić (2011) *Globalization: A Threat to International Cooperation and Peace?* (New York: Palgrave Macmillan).

93 See LaFrance (2021).

3 Dividing Sovereignty

In the spring of 1655, Louis XIV, the 16-year-old King of France, supposedly met the French Parliament still in his hunting clothes. Parliament was once again contesting his attempts to raise taxes, suggesting that to do so might cripple the state. "L'Etat?", the king sniffed, "L'Etat, c'est moi." "The State is me," perhaps the most famous quote in French history, is almost certainly part of an apocryphal story.[1] Yet the sentiment is in keeping with the personality of a man who would soon turn a modest hunting lodge into the Palace of Versailles and commission more than 300 official self-portraits. In his youth, he chose the sun as his emblem—he would be the light around which all revolved—and then worked tirelessly, although ultimately unsuccessful, to achieve total control over all aspects of French life during the seven decades of his reign.[2] When we think of absolute sovereignty, our minds often drift back to centuries-old monarchs like Louis XIV.

Unlimited, undivided, and unaccountable authority are the absolutist claims of a government's hold over its citizens that can sound anachronistic to the contemporary reader. As discussed in the previous chapter, the concept was nonetheless accepted with considerable zeal across the political spectrum throughout Europe during the Enlightenment and remains the prevailing legal conceptualization of state power today. Few leaders may thunder from the pulpit about their country's "supreme, irresistible, absolute, uncontrolled authority" over its citizens as Blackstone did at the eve of the American Revolution.[3] China's long-waged campaign to deny statehood to Taiwan is nonetheless based on the same conceptualization of absolute sovereignty, as is the world's 40-year hesitance to accept Northern Cyprus' independence. In the diplomatic world, recognizing a state means recognizing its absolute sovereignty. There are no almost-states, and the only sovereignty is absolute.

The idea of absolute sovereignty developed during the Enlightenment as an answer to violence. It was a law-and-order response not just to the seventeenth-century wars of religion but also to the pernicious uses of force to settle scores by warlords, posses, and duelers in Europe and elsewhere. Just sovereignty, backed by law and in the service of the people, was seen as the *only* way to forestall chaos. The perceived consequences of its absence were memorably invoked in a 1621 sermon:

> [T]ake Sovereignty from the face of the earth, and you turn it into a Cockpit. Men would become cut-throats and Cannibals one unto another. Murder,

DOI: 10.4324/9781003373322-3

adulteries, incests, rapes, robberies, perjuries, witchcrafts, blasphemies, all kinds of villainies, outrageous and savage cruelty, would overflow all Countries. We should have a very hell upon earth, and the face of it covered with blood, as it was once with water.[4]

Governments must therefore have a monopoly on violence, as they would on collecting taxes, telling time, and, more than four centuries later, speaking at the United Nations.

Few people have ever thought that sovereignty is truly absolute in practice. Hugo Grotius, the sixteenth-century Dutch thinker who invented the idea, noted many exceptions to absolute rule,[5] and those who debated the organization of the League of Nations more than 100 years ago often questioned the concept.[6] Subsequent writers have cataloged a long list of ways that sovereignty is curtailed from binding international law to lending restrictions.[7] Everyone therefore knows that a state's sovereignty is limited, divided, and accountable in many ways today. Absolute sovereignty, nonetheless, remains enshrined in state constitutions, intergovernmental organizations, and international law. Leaders, lawyers, and diplomats appreciate the simplicity of one nation, one government, and one legal system. We may not have absolute sovereignty, but we should strive for it.

Sovereignty, as many have argued, is an idea produced by daily practice.[8] Claims of authority associated with sovereignty endure because they are deeply held "social facts" that unconsciously guide behavior.[9] Yet shifts in practice *are* possible that, over time, can change social facts, especially in cases like absolute sovereignty where there is a widening gap between a deeply held concept and daily reality. Brexit, the Russo-Ukrainian War, Walt Disney World's special tax status: many of today's most gripping news stories are about sovereign debates. We tend to hear the faint echoes of that 1621 sermon when we read these stories—with its specter of "a very hell on earth"—and feel compelled to choose absolute sovereignty over chaos. Global collection action problems, after all, have been seen as international relations problems for 400 years. But what if absolute sovereignty is the problem?

Many scholars have argued that absolute state sovereignty has become detrimental to global governance,[10] with some offering tentative ways that sovereignty can be best restructured.[11] David Lake, for example, suggests that subordinate relationships between states should be codified in law,[12] and John Agnew argues that we need to unbundle sovereignty from territoriality.[13] As we remain standing at Kofi Annan's fork in the road, many of the potential global governance paths that could be followed nonetheless remain largely unrecognized. This and subsequent chapters discuss some of the alternatives to our current world order that have long been ignored by leaders because they fall outside of the Western cannon of possibilities. These paths, both ancient and more contemporary, reveal an incredible variety of ways of dividing sovereignty.

This chapter begins our explorations of alternative mechanisms of global governance by outlining how other kinds of sovereignty were employed to manage inter-group relations within large populations. To highlight how much was lost by focusing on Western examples, we start our journey by returning to the eastern

40 *Dividing Sovereignty*

woodlands of the United States. When the Founding Fathers were ignoring Native advice to consider the organization of the Haudenosaunee Confederacy for their fledgling republic, they were also missing another opportunity to learn from the Iroquois about governance. This lost lesson in divided sovereignty might prove useful for better managing today's dynamic, hyper-connected world.

Iroquois Kings and Matriarchs

In 1710, "The Four Indian Kings" traveled from New York to London to meet Queen Anne of Great Britain. The men were important Indigenous leaders sent to ask for aid against the French. Three of the men were Mohawk, one of the Iroquois-speaking nations of the Haudenosaunee Confederacy, including Tee Yee Neen Ho Ga Row who was dubbed the "Emperor of the Six Nations." The London press followed their visit with great enthusiasm and the Queen commissioned official portraits (Figure 3.1).[14] The European reimagining of the visitors and their roles in Native American society is clear in the reporting—some depictions show the men dressed in the crowns and gowns of British royalty—but for our purposes, it is important that the Mohawk and their Mohican neighbors chose four men to represent their nations in London. Canasatego and the other Haudenosaunee delegates that talked to Colonists in Pennsylvania three decades later were

Figure 3.1 (Left) Tee Yee Neen Ho Ga Row (left) and Sa Ga Yeath Qua Pieth Tow (right) were two of the Mohawk delegates to the Queen of England who were dubbed "The Four Indian Kings" by the London Press

Dividing Sovereignty   41

also male, as were the delegates sent to speak to other nations.[15] To the outside world, the face of the Iroquois was a man.

Europeans who traveled among the Iroquois in the early eighteenth century, in contrast, described a village life that was often dominated by women.[16] The Jesuit Joseph François Lafitau, for example, witnessed what he called a "gyneocracy" where:

> Nothing is more real than this superiority of the women. . . . All real authority is vested in them. The land, the fields and their harvest all belong to them. They are the souls of the Councils, the arbiters of peace and of war. They have charge of the public treasury. To them are given the slaves. They arrange marriages. The children are their domain, and it is through their blood that the order of succession is transmitted.[17]

Seen from different vantage points, the Iroquois were either male- or female-dominated. Some of this confusion about Iroquois society stems from rapid culture change and the biases and blinders of European observers.[18] Yet current research suggests that the Iroquois governance before the European was predicated on a divided sovereignty that ran along gender lines.

As briefly discussed in the first chapter, the Iroquois, defined here by their shared language group, began settling into villages in the Lake Ontario region at the beginning of the first millennium AD. Maize had arrived in the region some 500 years earlier, but it was only when the plant became more of a staple crop that people began to settle down.[19] The first houses were nonetheless lightly built and frequently moved, as people remained mobile.[20] This mobility was tied in part to seasonal rounds of hunting and gathering that remained an important part of Iroquois subsistence,[21] yet it also reflected a cross-culturally seen desire to maintain household autonomy amidst a change to larger, more permanent collectives.[22] After a few decades of experimentation, the Iroquois arrived at a solution to the social challenges of settling down: the longhouse, a bark-covered, pole-framed structure with a central row of hearths and communal storage at either end.[23]

The longhouse was the physical manifestation of a clan-based matrilineal and matrilocal social organization. Related women and their families lived together, sharing hearths in a structure that would sometimes grow to more than 100 meters long by the fifteenth century CE as population densities in the region increased.[24] Women owned the longhouse and most of its contents, along with agricultural tools, seeds, and the rights to the communally held agricultural lands around it.[25] A matron "reigned supreme within the long house"[26] and "it would not be healthful"[27] for a man to disobey a matron's order regarding household affairs. Since the longhouse, especially in the first centuries after their introduction, could be the entirety of both the village and the clan, Lafitau was correct to emphasize women's power at home.

Exogamous marriage rules meant that men married into a clan and move into the village of their wives. They kept their clan affiliation elsewhere and maintained these relationships by visiting neighboring communities more frequently.[28]

42 *Dividing Sovereignty*

In seeking marriage partners, raiding, brokering peace, and other activities, men tended to be the links between clans. Smoking pipes became popular, bodily ornamentation grew more elaborate, and sweat lodges were introduced over time to support the intimate negotiations carried out by men.[29] To formalize relationships between communities, the women of a longhouse began to appoint male chiefs (often a civil and war chief) charged with represented their clan in external affairs.[30] These chiefs could be removed from office by the women, and made important decisions only via consensus after considerable community input.[31] The broader tribal nation identities that these chiefs engendered were often effervescent, in that the strength of feeling Seneca or Mohawk waxed and waned depending on situations.

By the beginning of the fifteenth century, an Iroquois system of governance had thus developed wherein women's interest and power were more directed to the inner working of the clan and men's interest and power were more directed outward to the relationships between clans, nations, and foreign groups.[32] Most major decisions were a matter of discussion between all members of a community, but Iroquois society was premised on dividing sovereignty between matrons and chiefs. An unexpected consequence of this sovereignty division occurred in the late fifteenth century when a spike in violence led to the creation of much larger villages that included multiple clans.[33]

The clan and the village were no longer the same, meaning that some villages now had multiple chiefs who were also charged with integrating "a settlement composed of multiple small communities . . . learning to live together."[34] At the same time as men's role inside the village were changing, there were greater needs to reinforce supra-clan identities—clans were now more readily seen as members of tribal nations, and the relationships between nations were formalizing into confederacies—demanding both a wider circulation of men across the region and the creation of wider governance structures.[35] The Haudenosaunee translates to the "People of the Longhouse," reflecting a sentiment that as Iroquois collectives got larger, more and more people gathered together within the same metaphorical longhouse. Clans nonetheless remained the primary social unit of Iroquois life, and women's power continued to shape the daily activities that took place in and around longhouses.

Tee Yee Neen Ho Ga Row was likely chosen to lead the diplomatic mission to London in 1710 AD by a council of Haudenosaunee chiefs who deliberated before reaching a unanimous decision to engage the Queen directly by sending representatives from their group. These men had almost certainly been part of earlier discussion with the men and women of their communities (often speaking with each gender sequentially). Men *were* the face of supra-clan deliberations, entrusted to interact with Europeans. Yet to call male-led groups like tribal councils, a higher level of government is only true in the sense that its deliberations encompassed a larger collective. The Iroquois valued the clan's autonomy over everything else, and chiefs were cautious not to interfere with what could be seen as internal affairs.[36] Their sovereignty emanated outward from the clan, while the matron reigned within it.

Indus Merchants and Clan Leaders

When the engineers of the British East India Company were orchestrating a system of railroads through the Indus Valley of present-day Pakistan in the 1850s, they faced a stone shortage. Track ballast was scare in the fluvial region, and so they mined the baked mud bricks found in mounds that towered over the plain.[37] Subsequent excavations revealed that some of these sites belonged to an Indus Valley Civilization (3300–1300 BC) that would soon become well known for its art, architecture, and technology.[38] British leaders at the time, however, felt that there was little to learn from the region's long-abandoned cities. The colonizers thought that they were bringing progress to South Asia, and many may have even enjoyed the symbolism of their tracks being built on top of the region's past glories. Unbeknownst to them, they were turning their backs on archaeological evidence of a 4000-year-old system of divided sovereignty that just might help improve global governance in the twenty-first century.

The great cities of the Indus Valley Civilization began with the weakening of the spring monsoon rains after 5000 BC that allowed the valley's river channels to stabilize.[39] By the beginning of the fourth millennium BC, the first settlements formed in the valley, often composed of discrete clusters of households.[40] The best excavated of these settlements, Harappa, shows a sequence of development that led over the next 2,000 years to at least seven gated neighborhoods. Each of the neighborhoods was organized into blocks of houses, with each house composed of bedrooms facing an interior courtyard.[41] At its peak, the site sprawled across 150 hectares and contained a permanent population of some 40,000 people.[42] Much of this growth happened during the second half of the third millennium, a time when other settlements in the Indus Valley were also rapidly urbanizing.[43] Indus Valley Civilization cities, along with smaller towns, share Harappa's emphasis on walls, gates, and neighborhoods.[44]

More people living in one place led to greater resource intensification—year-round cropping, for example, and intensive dairying[45]—as well as increasing occupation specialization. Bangles, beads, pottery motifs, seals, and other objects were increasingly used to signal group identities across and between settlements.[46] As sites grew, they appear to have been initially organized along kinship relations. Genetic and isotopic evidence from burials demonstrates that women in the same cemetery at Harappa were more closely related than the men,[47] suggesting possible matrilocality and the guiding role of established families in the coordination of the city's neighborhoods.[48] Some animal motifs on seals also appear to relate to house blocks,[49] and the symbols' persistence over time, when combined with the multigenerational occupation of many houses, suggests lineage heads continued to organize neighborhood politics as settlements grew (Figure 3.2).[50]

Blood and marriage ties in Indus Valley Civilization cities, however, yielded over time to more clan-based identity based on residential proximity, occupation, and daily practices.[51] Isotopic evidence from burials suggests that city leaders developed a foster program that encouraged the immigration of young children to cities so that they could be better acculturated into these groups by an early

44 Dividing Sovereignty

Figure 3.2 An Indus Valley Civilization seal depicting a two-horned bull with an inscription. Some seal motifs may have been linked to clans

age.[52] Some seals and inscriptions served the needs of a settlement's corporate groups,[53] small public buildings were used, at least in the city of Mohenjodaro, as civic spaces,[54] and neighborhoods retained connections to particular villages.[55] Although the political organization of the clans remains unknown, there was an emphasis on their autonomy and collective decision-making.[56] People often maintained relationships to rural kin,[57] but to live in the city meant membership in a clan there that shaped where you lived, what you did, and with whom you interacted.

A focus on corporate identity helps create what Gregory Possehl called a "faceless culture, without the kind of aggrandizement of the individual that we associate with archaic states."[58] Wealth differences were actively suppressed,[59] and there is also no evidence for palaces and centralized governments.[60] Rooting identity at the neighborhood level and minimizing political interference from above helped to preserve a clan-based sovereignty within urbanizing settings. Coordination *between* neighborhoods, however, was made more difficult by clan divisions. This was a particular concern for those involved in the manufacture of goods from shell, talc, stone, and other material. As the "technological virtuosity" of their manufacturing techniques increased over time,[61] workers required enhanced and sustained coordination between specialists living in different neighborhoods, as well as regular long-distance connections to different regions. They therefore needed to work more and more *across* clan divides. The mechanisms that had long structured daily life in the Indus Valley were interfering with industry.

Leaders solved this impasse by carving out a space beyond the neighborhood. By the end of the third millennium BC, for example, a coalition of business interests at Harappa refurbished and expanded gateways. They created plazas adjacent to the gates where some industries now concentrated.[62] There are more tablets, seals, and weights in these locations, as well as mold-made credit tokens that are found across neighborhoods.[63] Some seal motifs, at least at Mohenjodaro, were also now being produced in different parts of the city, suggesting that their use was no longer tied to the clan affiliations of different neighborhoods.[64] The relationship between neighborhoods and gateway plazas remains unclear, but the latter's position within settlements suggests an outward orientation that contrasts to the more inward orientation of the neighborhoods. In smaller settlements, there are similar manufacturing enclaves with mercantile orientations that were linked to Indus Valley cities through kin (and other) affiliations.[65]

In 1979, the Chinese government began establishing Special Economic Zones in their country that were geared primarily toward manufacturing goods for export. The zones were given a more free-market orientations, along with significant autonomy to organize their outward-oriented affairs.[66] The outward-facing manufacturing locales that developed in Indus Valley Civilization settlements are reminiscent of these Special Economic Zones, in so much as they were allowed to play by different rules than the rest of society. The critical difference is that there was no Indus Valley authority that granted an exemption to its sovereign rights. Instead, merchants, and those who manufactured their goods, set up their own institutions to govern a space—both physical and imagined—*beyond* the neighborhood. Since the members of this merchant-based sodality were also members of clans, residents navigated a divided sovereignty as goods were made, distributed, and consumed across the Indus Valley.

Chiefs and Oppida

In 58 BC, Julius Cesar began a war to defeat what he considered to be the barbarian hordes. For eight years, he battled confederations of Celtic language speakers in present-day England, France, Belgium, Germany, and Switzerland. Cesar wrote his *Commentarii de Bello Gallico* amidst the military campaigns as a justification for the war and his place in Roman Society.[67] He called the Gaul confederations, "*civites*," in his book and to defeat each one he targeted their *oppidum*, a central

46 *Dividing Sovereignty*

place that was often enclosed by massive walls. Although not intended as an ethnography, *Bello Gallico* is our best first-hand account on Gallic society. Gaul was Europe before it became the West, a long-neglected contemporary to a Roman Civilization that would later enthrall Enlightenment thinkers. The oppida held within them our final lesson in how sovereignty can be divided.

Bello Gallico describes a nested sociopolitical structure in Gaul that build up from households to extended families, *pagus* (clans), and, finally, civitas (confederation). Patron–client relationships arranged each level of the structure, with leaders expected to show largess to the families that they served.[68] Relationships at the pagus and civitas levels were inherently oppositional and dynamic as leaders strove to convince (and sometimes compel) extended families and clans to become their clients. Time and time again, Cesar remarks on how leaders struggled to create and hold together coalitions of warriors to repel Roman advances. The "kings" that Cesar faced might better resemble the "Big Men" of the Pacific whose power rested on their ability to rally a largely independent people to come together to achieve a common goal.[69]

The origins of the oppida can be traced back to at least the sixth century BC when trends toward greater social stratification in this part of Europe led to the construction of what have been called "princely sites" across the regions. These often-fortified settlements were arranged around the palaces of elite rulers who were normally laid to rest in sumptuous burials that celebrated the virtues of warfare.[70] Written descriptions of this era are scant, but those that remain suggest the existence of a similar sociopolitical structure to what was recorded 200 years later during the Gallic Wars.[71] Civites, however, did not exist. The "princes" of the era lived in settlements measuring only a few hectares in area, and laid claim, at best, to a few thousand clients. They ruled, via charisma and force of arms, over a clan and were incapable of extending their dominance further. Political change was quick, and sometimes violent, as the fortunes of leading families rose and fell.

By the fourth century BC, most of the princely centers were abandoned with the populations dispersed into isolated farmsteads.[72] The reasons for this decentralization were many, but one concern appears to have been the "excessive coercive power" of princes amid a context of "increasing social inequalities."[73] When centralization reoccurred in the third century BC, the major settlements, as well as the concomitant societies arranged around them, tended to be bigger. These settlements—the oppida of Late Iron Age Gaul—vary considerably in their size, history, and composition.[74] Manching, for example, was a 380-hectare oppidum in southern Germany that began as a small settlement. The site was a major production and redistribution center that housed temples serving the different groups that lived in and visited the site.[75] Titleberg in southern Luxembourg was 43 hectares and is known for its 10-hectare space that was used for public assembly.[76]

The oppida are perhaps best defined by what they were not: princely sites. Oppida were often located away from existing settlements so that "communities could gather without infringing on existing power relationships."[77] Elites, like almost all the rest of the population, lived most of the year in the countryside. Their patron–client relationships with surrounding families in the countryside likely formed the clan affiliations noted by Cesar. When families visited the oppida, they may have gathered in clan-based neighborhoods inside the settlement proper, where they tended to their group's fields, houses, workshops, and cemeteries.[78] The basic unit of settlement nonetheless remained the enclosed farmstead,[79] with people while visiting the oppida striving to maintain the same daily rhythms that structured their lives in the countryside. They broke from this rhythm to participate in the deliberations and festivities that united the clans in an oppidum's public buildings and open spaces.[80]

Oppida were often fortified—their high, well-built ramparts are sometimes seen as their defining feature.[81] The sites served as fortresses during the Gallic Wars, but researchers now emphasize the symbolic role played by many of these constructions.[82] The fortifications tend to be over-engineered, ostentatious, and never completed. The walls were testament to the ability of the clans to work together toward a common goal, as well as to the civitas-level leadership that emerged during the episodes to guide ongoing construction.[83] Leaders were also needed to adjudicate conflict, ensure access to long-distance resources, and prepare feasts.[84] In most cases, task-specific leadership appears to have been pulled from clan leaders and other elite. Their jobs were more to convince than to command the clans whose members were temporarily under their directions to achieve a mutually agreed upon goal.[85]

The limits of civitas' sovereignty are illustrated by the plight of Vercingetorix, the chief antagonist in Cesar's *Bello Gallico* (Figure 3.3).[86] A clan leader, Vercingetorix was chosen to organize his confederation's defenses against Cesar's advances. He then attempted to unite the Gauls, almost defeating the Romans in the Battle of Alesia. His story is not just one of military prowess but also one of endless persuasion. He had to repeatedly convince the tribes to fight together, even as they faced a common enemy. Civites were loose confederation of clans, as-needed organizations held together by the periodic shared activities that occurred at oppida. At best, Vercingetorix may have held absolute sovereignty over his clan, but he could not speak for those outside of his clan. Other clan leaders chose to follow him into battle and expected to retain their sovereignty when the fighting was over.

Several scholars suggest that the Gauls are an example of a society against the state.[87] The princely sites of two centuries earlier had failed, at least in part, because the leaders of the time attempted to extend sovereignty across clans. The oppida were designed to maintain clan sovereignty while providing occasional opportunities for greater coordination across clans. When Vercingetorix led the Gallic forces at Alesia, he held sway over an army composed of many clans. In earlier times, other leaders stood astride ramparts coordinating the clans' latest improvement to their oppida or met together in assembly halls at the center of the sites to coordinate external affairs. There were thus moments of civitas-level (and above) sovereignty that were tightly constrained in space and time. Most of one's life in ancient Gaul, however, was lived in a world organized around autonomous clans.

48 *Dividing Sovereignty*

Figure 3.3 Henri-Paul Motte's late-nineteenth-century imagining of Vercingetorix preparing to surrender to Julius Caesar

Dividing Sovereignty

Absolute sovereignty is a state's claim to ultimate authority over its citizens. Unlimited, undivided, and unaccountable are the claims that are the bedrock of the modern political order.[88] Constitutions are built on the concept of absolute sovereignty. It structures many international treaties, underlines our banking system, and shapes the contour of international law. Like it or not, it can feel like we are stuck with absolute sovereignty. When we see it wobbling in today's fast-paced, hyper-connected world, the tendency is therefore to double down on the concept. We *need* absolute sovereignty to maintain order in a world that seems ready to tear apart at the seams. The only alternative—hear again the faint echoes of that fiery 1621 sermon about a world bathed in blood—is chaos. Or is it?

Absolute sovereignty is a conceptual straitjacket originally designed to reign in the violence of seventeenth-century Europe. It was a top-down solution to replace what was in most places a more decentralized political system organized around local lords who lived on largely self-sufficient country manors. Asserting absolute sovereignty was a means of both getting the elite to fall in line with the monarchy and popularizing the ideas of a commonwealth for the population at large. In fits and starts, Europe moved away from a *de facto* system of divided sovereignty wherein the monarch was largely concerned with international affairs.

The seventeenth-century handwringing about sovereignty was thus in part about a manor system in decline and the anxiety about the future. Today, we have similar anxieties about what is happening with our current world order of nation-states that emerged from those seventeenth-century deliberations on the nature of sovereignty.

Our three case studies demonstrate political systems of divided sovereignty that successfully guided pluralistic societies for centuries. Around the shores of Lake Ontario, the Iroquois nations were structured around a system of internally oriented clan matriarchs and externally oriented chiefs. Clans also organized life in Indus Valley Civilization neighborhoods, but merchants carved out their own space to conduct their business. Among the Gauls, leaders of larger groups arose on as-needed bases, bolstered by central places that served as an occasional gathering place for a region. Many other cases could be drawn of divided sovereignty from the ancient and contemporary world.[89] These examples were not unsuccessful attempts by weak leaders at forming a proper government. Divided sovereignty *was* their governance bedrock. It was how their world worked, and, like the reader today, individuals in these societies would have struggled to imagine other possibilities.

I am not suggesting, here and in the chapters that follow, that we should replace our global governance system with one from our case studies. Iroquois, Indus Valley Civilization, or Gallic sovereignty are products of their own histories, climates, and cultural milieus and are therefore ill-fitted to today's conditions. There are nonetheless pages from their playbooks that might suggest news approaches to some of the daunting global collective action challenges that we face. The Iroquois, for example, resolved the free-rider problem via the architectural form of the longhouse, an emphasis on direct democracy, and a politician (the matriarch) firmly anchored in the community. Taking just these pages from the Iroquois would focus our attention back to the local, emphasizing how built forms can encourage people—and their politicians—to cultivate a greater sense of responsivity to one's community as they contemplate more global affairs.

In another example, people living in Indus Valley Civilization cities recognized that the flow of exotica into their settlements could exasperate equity and use rights concerns, so merchants and craft specialists moved some production out of established neighborhoods. The cities thus found success by shifting some socially corrosive activities outside of the sphere of everyday life. Finally, the Gauls recognized that people had little appetite for standing national leaders so they pioneered a government-by-demand system built from periodic assembly with elements that might serve us well today. Most importantly, these case studies demonstrate writ large that dividing sovereignty led *not* to chaos but to enduring prosperity.

From a historical, cross-cultural perspective, absolute sovereignty is an uncommon aspiration. There were, of course, past claims of such power, but in practice, the power of those who made this claim tended to be more about a link to the divine that was tightly circumscribed around individuals and their court.[90]

50 *Dividing Sovereignty*

Sometimes blithely ignored even a few kilometers away, these rulers were not so much weak as working within a limited field of action. Louis XIV's apocryphal "L'Etat, c'est moi" papered over the limits of sovereignty, as did Blackstone's thundering speeches. Sovereignty is, and always has been, divided. Embracing the concept's divisibility allows us to more seriously entertain alternatives to the current structure of global governance, such as the segmentary states discussed in the next chapter.

Notes

1 The story first appears in Charles Pinot Duclos' *Secret Memoirs on the Reigns of Louis XIV and Regency of Louis XV*. Although supposedly based on the collected memoirs of those serving in Louis XIV's court, documents relating to the story and quote have never been found. See his *Contes de Charles Pinot Duclos* (1880, Paris: A. Quantin).

2 See Phillip Mansel (2019) *King of the World: The Life of Louis XIV*. (Chicago: The University of Chicago Press); and John Jeter Hunt (2002) *Louis XIV and the Parlements: The Assertion of Royal Authority* (Manchester: Manchester University Press).

3 See William Blackstone (1765–1769) *Commentaries on the Laws of England,* vol. 1, p. 32 (London: Clarendon Press).

4 See Robert Bolton (1635) *Two Sermons Preached at Northampton at Two Several Assizes There*, p. 10 (London: J. Richardson). The sermon was delivered in 1621. Other examples of the fears of lost sovereignty can be found in Don Herzog (2020) *Sovereignty RIP* (New Haven: Yale University Press).

5 See Edward Keene (2002) *Beyond the Anarchical Society: Grotius, Colonialism, and Order in the World Political Economy* (Princeton: Princeton University Press).

6 As World War I was ending, President Woodrow Wilson commissioned a series of studies that became known as *The Inquiry*. Among them was this one that identified ten types of polities that did not have absolute sovereignty: W.W. Willoughby and C.G. Fenwick (1974) *The Inquiry Handbooks*, vol. 16 (originally publishes as *Types of Restricted Sovereignty and of Colonial Autonomy*) (Ann Arbor: Scholarly Resources).

7 See Stephen D. Krasner (1999) *Sovereignty: Organized Hypocrisy* (Princeton: Princeton University Press); Stephen D. Krasner, ed. (2001) *Problematic Sovereignty: Contested Rules and Political Possibilities* (New York: Columbia University Press); and Daniel Loick (2019) *A Critique of Sovereignty*. Translated by Amanda DeMarco (London: Rowman & Littlefield).

8 See Michel Foucault (1980) *Power/Knowledge* (New York: Pantheon); Charles Tilley (1990) *Coercion, Capital and the European State*, AD 990–1990 (Cambridge: Blackwell); Jean Comaroff and John Comaroff (1991) *Of Revelation and Revolution*, vol. I (Chicago: University of Chicago Press); and Daniel Philpot (2001) *Revolutions in Sovereignty: How Ideas Shaped Modern International Relations* (Princeton: Princeton University Press).

9 See John Searle (1995) *The Construction of Social Reality* (New York: Free Press).

10 See Thomas G. Weiss (2016) *What's Wrong with the United Nations and How to Fix It* (Malden: Polity Press).

11 See John Hoffman (1988) *Sovereignty* (Minneapolis: University of Minnesota Press); and Hansen Blom (2006) Sovereignty Revisited. *Annual Review of Anthropology* 35(1): 295–315.

12 See David A. Lake (2003) The New Sovereignty in International Relations. *International Studies Review* 5(3): 303–323.

13 See John Agnew (2005) Sovereignty Regimes: Territoriality and State Authority in Contemporary World Politics. *Annals of the Association of American Geographers* 95(2): 437–461.

Dividing Sovereignty 51

14 See Eric Hinderaker (1996) The 'Four Indian Kings' and the Imaginative Construction of the First British Empire. *The William and Mary Quarterly* 53(3): 487–526.

15 See Timothy J. Shannon (2008) *Iroquois Diplomacy on the Early American Frontier* (New York: Viking).

16 See Reuben G. Thwaites, Reuben, G., ed. (199) *The Jesuit Relations and Allied Documents: Travels and Explorations of the Jesuit Missionaries in New France, 1610–1791* (Cleveland: Burrows Brothers Company).

17 See Joseph François Lafitau (1979 [1724]) *Customs of the American Indian*, trans. William Fenton and Elizabeth Moore, pp. 66–67, 69 (Toronto: The Champlain Society).

18 See Martha Harroun Foster (2007) Lost Women of the Matriarchy: Iroquois Women in the Historical Literature. *American Indian Culture and Research Journal* 19(3): 121–140; and Nancy Shoemaker (2000) The Rise or Fall of Iroquois Women. *Journal of Women's History* 2(3): 39–57.

19 See Gary W. Crawford, David G. Smith, and Vandy E. Bowyer (1997) Dating the Entry of Corn (Zea mays) to the Lower Great Lakes Region. *American Antiquity* 62(1): 112–119; and Roman G. Harrison and M. Anne Katzenbergh (2003) Paleodiet Studies Using Stable Carbon Isotopes from Bone Apatite and Collagen: Examples from Southern Ontario and San Nicholas Island, California. *Journal of Anthropological Archaeology* 22(3): 227–244.

20 See John L. Creese (2013) Rethinking Early Village Development in Southern Ontario: Towards a History of Place-Making. *Canadian Journal of Archaeology* 37: 185–218; and Ronald F. Williamson (2014) The Archaeological History of the Wendat to A.D. 1651: An Overview. *Ontario Archaeology* 94: 3–64.

21 See Jenneth E. Curtis (2014) Migration and Cultural Change: The Northern Iroquoian Case in South-Central Ontario. *Journal of World Prehistory* 27: 145–195.

22 See Justin Jennings (2021) *Finding Fairness: From Pleistocene Foragers to Contemporary Capitalists* (Gainesville: University Press of Florida).

23 See Mima Kapches (1990) The Spatial Dynamics of Ontario Iroquoian Longhouses. *American Antiquity* 55(1): 49–67; and Dean R. Snow (1994) *The Iroquois* (Malden: Blackwell).

24 See John L. Creese (2016) "Extending the Rafters": Assemblage Theory and the Iroquoian Longhouse. In *Household Archaeology—A Transatlantic Comparative Approach*, edited by Claude Chapdelaine, Adrian L. Burke, and Karim Gernigon. Proceedings of the International Symposium, October 24–25, 2014. Université de Montréal, *P@lethnology* 8: 11–32.

25 See Lewis Henry Morgan (1881) *Houses and House-Life of the American Aborigines Contributions to North American Ethnology*, vol. 4 (Washington, DC: United States Geographical and Geological Survey of the Rocky Mountain Region); Judith K. Brown (1970) Economic Organization and the Position of Women among the Iroquois. *Ethnohistory* 17(3/4): 151–167; Elisabeth Tooker (1984) Women in Iroquois Society. In *Extending the Rafters: Interdisciplinary Approaches to Iroquoian Studies*, edited by Michael K. Foster, Jack Campisi, and Marianne Mithun, pp. 109–123 (Albany: State University of New York).

26 See Brown (1970), p. 136.

27 See Morgan (1881), p. 66.

28 See Bruce G. Trigger (1976) The *Children of Aataensic: A History of the Huron People to 1660*, vol. 2 (Montreal: McGill-Queen's University Press); Bruce G. Trigger (1990) *The Huron: Farmers of the North* (Chicago: Holt, Rinehart, and Winston); and Gail D. MacLeitch (2011) *Imperial Entanglements: Iroquois Change and Persistence on the Frontiers of Empire* (Philadelphia: University of Pennsylvania).

29 See Robert I MacDonald and Ronald F. Williamson (2001) Sweat Lodges and Solidarity: Archaeology of the Hubert Site. *Ontario Archaeology* 71: 21–78; and John D. Creese (2016) Emotion Work and the Archaeology of Consensus: The Northern Iroquoian Case. *World Archaeology* 48(1): 14–34.

52 *Dividing Sovereignty*

30 See Trigger (1990) and Snow (1994).

31 Magee (2008), p. 121; Brown (1970), p. 156.

32 See Brown (1970); Elizabeth Tooker (1970) Northern Iroquois Socio-Political Organization. *American Anthropologist* 72: 90–97; Tooker (1984); Trigger (1976); Trigger (1990); Tooker (1984); Englebrech (2002); Georges E. Siou (1999) *Huron-Wendat: The Heritage of the Circle* (Vancouver: University of British Columbia Press); and John L. Steckley (2014) *The Eighteenth Century Wyandot: A Clan-Based Study* (Waterloo: Wilfred Laurier Press).

33 See Jennifer Birtch (2016) Relations of Power and Production in Ancestral Wendat Communities. In *Household Archaeology—A Transatlantic Comparative Approach*, edited by Claude Chapdelaine, Adrian L. Burke, and Karim Gernigon. Proceedings of the International Symposium, October 24–25, 2014. Université de Montréal, *P@lethnology* 8: 31–48.

34 See Jennifer Birch and Ronald F. Williamson (2015) *The Mantle Site: An Archaeological History of an Ancestral Wendat Community*, p. 163 (Lanham: Rowan & Littlefield).

35 See Lewis Henry Morgan (1851) *League of the Ho-dé-no-sau-nee or Iroquois* (New York: Sage); Englebrech (2003); and Trigger (1990).

36 See Trigger (1990) and Snow (1995).

37 See Rita P. Wright (2010) *The Ancient Indus: Urbanism, Economy, and Society* (New York: Cambridge University Press).

38 See Sir John Marshall (1931) *Mohenjo-daro and the Indus Civilization* (London: Probsthain).

39 See Tawseef Ahmad Mir (2017) Revisiting Floods and Civilization in North-Western Indian Subcontinent during 4th to Mid 2nd-Millennium BC in Archaeological Perspective. *Archaeologies: Journal of the World Archaeological Congress* 13(2): 344–354; Liviu Giosan, Peter D. Clift, Mark G. Macklin, Dorian Q. Fuller, Stefan Constantescu, Julie A. Durcan, Thomas Stevens, Geogg A. T. Duller, Ali R. Tabrez, Kavita Gangal, Ronojoy Adhikari, Anwar Alizai, Florin Fillip, San VanLaningham, and James P. M. Syvitski (2012) Fluvial Landscapes of the Harappa Civilization. *Proceedings of the National Academy of Science* 109(26): E1688–E1694; Vandana Prasad, Anjum Farooqui, Anupam Sharma, Binita Phartiyal, Supriyo Chakraborty, Subhash Bhandari, Rachna Raj, and Abha Sing (2014) Mid-Late Holocene Monsoonal Variations from Mainland Gujarat, India: A Multi-Proxy Study for Evaluating Climate Culture Relationship. *Paleogeography, Paleoclimatology, Paleoecology* 397: 38–51.

40 Jonathan Mark Kenoyer (2011) Changing Perspectives of the Indus Civilization: New Discoveries and Challenges. *Purātattva: Journal of the Indian Archaeological Society* 41: 1–18; and Giosan et al. (2012).

41 See Jonathan Mark Kenoyer (2005) Bead Technologies at Harappa, 3300–1900 BC: A comparative summary. In *South Asian Archaeology 2001*, edited by Catherine Jarrige and Vincent Lefévre, pp. 157–170 (Paris: Editions Recherche sur les Civilisations-ADPF); Jonathan Mark Kenoyer (2010) Measuring the Harappan World: Insights into the Indus Order and Cosmology. In *The Archaeology of Measurement: Comprehending Heaven, Earth, and Time in Ancient Societies*, edited by Iain Morley and Colin Renfrew, pp. 106–121 (New York: Cambridge University Press); and Rita P. Wright (2010).

42 See Jonathan Mark Kenoyer (2000) Wealth and Socioeconomic Hierarchies of the Indus Valley Civilization. In *Order, Legitimacy, and Wealth in Ancient States*, edited by Janet Richards and Mary Van Buren, pp. 88–109 (New York: Cambridge University Press).

43 See M. Rafique Mughal (1997) A Preliminary Review of Archaeological Surveys in Punjab and Sindh: 1993–1995. *South Asian Studies* 13: 241–249; and Rita P. Wright, Rita P. Joseph Schuldenrein, Muhammed Afzal Khan, and M. Rafique Mughal (2005a) The Emergence of Satellite Communities along the Beas Drainage: Preliminary Results from Lahoma Lal Tibba and Chak Purbane Syal. In *South Asia Archaeology 2001*, edited by Catherine Jarrige and Vincent Lefévre, pp. 327–335 (Paris: Éditions Recherche sur les Civilizations-ADPF); and Adam S. Green and Cameron A. Petrie

(2018) Landscapes of Urbanization and De-Urbanization: A Large-Scale Approach to Investigating the Indus Civilization's Settlement Distributions in Northwest India, *Journal of Field Archaeology* 43(4): 284–299.

44 See Jonathan Mark Kenoyer (2020) The Indus Tradition: The Integration and Diversity of Indus Cities. *Purattatva* 50: 19–33.

45 See Laura J. Miller (2003) Secondary Products and Urbanism in South Asia: The Evidence for Traction at Harappa. In *Indus Ethnobiology: New Perspectives From the Field*, edited by Steven A. Weber and William R. Belcher, pp. 251–326 (Lanham: Lexington Books); Laura J. Miller (2004) Urban Economies in Early States: The Secondary Products Revolution in the Indus Civilization. Unpublished Ph.D. dissertation, New York University; Steven A. Weber (1999) Seeds of Urbanism: Paleoenthobotany and the Indus Civilization. *Antiquity* 73(282): 813–826; and Steven A. Weber (2003) Archaeobotany at Harappa: Indications for Change. In *Indus Ethnobiology: New Perspectives from the Field*, edited by Steven A. Weber and William R. Belcher, pp. 175–198 (Lanham: Lexington Books).

46 See Kenoyer (2000).

47 See Brian E. Hemphill, John R. Lukacs, and Kenneth A. R. Kennedy (1991) Biological Adaptions and Affinities of Bronze Age Harappans. In *Harappa Excavations 1986–1990: A Multidisciplinary Approach to Third Millennium Urbanism*, edited by Richard H. Meadow, pp. 137–182 (Madison: Prehistory Press); Kenneth A. R. Kennedy (2000) *God-Apes and Fossil Men: Paleoanthropology in South Asia* (Ann Arbor: University of Michigan Press); and Jonathan Mark Kenoyer, T. Douglas Price, and James H. Burton (2013) A New Approach to Tracking Connections Between the Indus Valley and Mesopotamia: Initial Results of Strontium Isotope Analyses from Harappa and Ur. *Journal of Archaeological Science* 40(5): 2286–2297.

48 See Wright (2010), p. 264.

49 See Jonathan Mark Kenoyer (1998) *Ancient Cities of the Indus Valley Civilization* (Karachi: Oxford University Press and the American Institute of Pakistan Studies); and Jonathan Mark Kenoyer and Richard H. Meadow (2008) The Early Indus Script at Harappa: Origins and Development. In *Intercultural Relations Between South and Southwest Asia: Studies in Commemoration of E. C. L. During Caspers (1934–1996)*, edited by Eric Olijdam and Richard H. Spoor. pp. 124–131. BAR International Series 1826 (Oxford: Archaeopress).

50 See Wright (2010), p. 270.

51 See Adam S. Green (2020) Debt and Inequality: Comparing the "Means of Specification" in the Early Cities of Mesopotamia and the Indus Civilization. *Journal of Anthropological Archaeology* 60: 101232; Jonathan Mark Kenoyer (2010) Measuring the Harappan World: Insights into the Indus Order and Cosmology. In *The Archaeology of Measurement: Comprehending Heaven, Earth, and Time in Ancient Societies*, edited by Iain Morley and Colin Renfrew, pp. 106–121 (New York: Cambridge University Press); and Gwen Robbins Schug (2020) Ritual Urbanism and the Everyday: Mortuary Behavior in the Indus Civilization. In *The Bioarchaeology of Urbanization*, edited by Tracy K. Betsinger and Sharon N. DeWitte, pp. 49–72 (New York: Springer).

52 See Valentine, Benjamin (2016) More than Origins: Refining Migration in the Indus Civilization. In *A Companion to South Asia in the Past*, edited by Gwen Robbins Schug and Subhash R. Walimbe, pp. 187–204 (New York: Wiley); and Benjamin Valentine, George D. Kamenov, Jonathan Mark Kenoyer, Vasant Shinde, Veena-Mushrif-Tripathy, Erik Otarola-Castillo, and John Krigbaum (2015) Evidence for Patterns of Selective Urban Migration in the Greater Indus Valley (2600–1900 BC): A Lead and Strontium Isotope Mortuary Analysis. *PLoS One* 10(4): 1–20.

53 See Walter A. Fairservis (1992) *The Harappan Civilization and Its Writing: A Model for the Decipherment of the Indus Script* (New York: E.J. Brill); and Asko Parpola (1994) *Deciphering the Indus Script* (New York: Cambridge University Press).

54 See Adam S. Green. (2018). Mohenjo-Daro's Small Public Structures: Heterarchy, Collective Action and a Re-Visitation of Old Interpretations With GIS and 3D Modelling. *Cambridge Archaeological Journal* 28(2): 205–223.

54 *Dividing Sovereignty*

55 See Parikh Danika and Cameron A. Petrie (2019) 'We are Inheritors of a Rural Civilization': Rural Complexity and the Ceramic Economy in the Indus Civilisation in Northwest India. *World Archaeology* 51(2): 252–272; Rita P. Wright et al. (2005a); Rita P. Wright, Joseph Schuldenrein, Muhammed Afzal Khan, and S. Malin-Boyce (2005b) The Beas River Landscape and Settlement Survey: Preliminary Results from the Site of Vainiwal. In *South Asian Archaeology 2003*, edited by Ute Franke-Vogt and Hans-Joachim Weisshaar, pp. 101–110 (Aachen: Linden Soft).

56 See Adam S. Green (2021) Killing the Priest-King: Addressing Egalitarianism in the Indus Civilization. *Journal of Archaeological Research* 29: 153–202.

57 See Schug (2020).

58 See Gregory E. Possehl (1998) Sociocultural Complexity Without the State: The Indus Civilization. In *Archaic States*, edited by Gary M. Feinman and Joyce Marcus, pp. 261–291 (School of American Research, Santa Fe).

59 Robin Coningham and Mark Manuel (2009) Priest-Kings or Puritans? Childe and Willing Subordination in the Indus. *European Journal of Archaeology* 12(1–3):167–180; and Paul Rissman (1988) Public Displays and Private Values: A Guide to Buried Wealth in Harappan Archaeology. *World Archaeology* 20(2): 209–228.

60 See Adam S. Green (2021).

61 See Massimo Vidale and Heather M.-L. Miller (2000) On the Development of Indus Technical Virtuosity and Its Relation to Social Structure. In *South Asian Archaeology 1997*, edited by Maurizo Taddei and Guiseppe De Marco, pp. 115–132 (Rome: Istituto Italiano per L'Africa e L'Oriente).

62 See Richard H. Meadow and Jonathan Mark Kenoyer (1997) Excavations at Harappa 1994–1995: New Perspectives on the Indus Script, Craft Activities, and City Organization. In *South Asia Archaeology 1995*, edited by Raymond Allchin and Bridget Allchin, pp. 139–172 (New Delhi: Oxford and IBH Publishing); Heather M. L. Miller (2008) Issues in the Determination of Ancient Value Systems: The Role of Talc (Steatite) and Faience in the Indus Civilization. In *Intercultural Relations Between South and Southwest Asia: Studies in Commemoration of E. C. L. During Caspers (1934–1996)*, edited by Eric Olijdam and Richard H. Spoor, pp. 145–157. BAR International Series 1826 (Oxford: Archaeopress); and Wright (2010).

63 See Jonathon Mark Kenoyer (2008) Indus and Mesopotamian Trade Networks: New Insights from Shell and Carnelian Artifacts. In *Intercultural Relations Between South and Southwest Asia: Studies in Commemoration of E. C. L. During Caspers (1934–1996)*, edited by Eric Olijdam and Richard H. Spoor, pp. 19–28. BAR International Series 1826 (Oxford: Archaeopress); and Rajesh P.N. Rao (2018) The Indus Script and Economics: A Role for Indus Seals and Tablets in Rationing and Administration of Labor. In *Walking With the Unicorn: Social Organization and Material Culture in Ancient South Asia,* edited by Gregg M. Dennys, Jamison Frenez, Randall W. Law, Massimo Vidale, and Richard H. Meadow, pp. 518–525 (Oxford: Archaeopress).

64 See Adam S. Green (2016) Finding Harappan Seal Carvers: An Operational Sequence Approach to Identifying People in the Past. *Journal of Archaeological Science* 72: 128–141.

65 See Brad Chase (2018) Family Matters in Harappan Gujarat. In *Walking with the Unicorn: Social Organization and Material Culture in Ancient South Asia,* edited by Gregg M. Dennys, Jamison Frenez, Randall W. Law, Massimo Vidale, and Richard H. Meadow, pp. 104–19 (Oxford: Archaeopress); and Brad Chase (2010) Social Change at the Harappan Settlement of Gola Dhoro: A Reading from Animal Bones. *Antiquity* 84: 528–543.

66 See Yue-man Yeung, Joanna Lee, and Gordon Kee (2009). China's Special Economic Zones at 30. *Eurasian Geography and Economics* 50(2): 222–240.

67 See Julius Cesar (2006) *Commentarii de Bello Gallico*, edited by H.J. Edwards (London: Dover).

68 Also see Nico Roymans (1990) *Tribal Societies in Northern Gaul: An Anthropological Perspective* (Amsterdam: Universiteit van Amsterdam).

Dividing Sovereignty 55

69 See Tom Moore and David González-Álvarez (2021) Societies Against the Chief? Reexamining the Value of Heterarchy as a Concept for Studying European Iron Society. In *Power From Below: The Dynamics of Political Complexity in the Archaeological Record*, edited by T.L. Thurston and Manuel Fernández-Götz, pp. 125–156 (New York: Cambridge University Press).

70 See Manuel Fernández-Götz (2014a) *Identity and Power: The Transformation of Iron Age Societies in Northern Gaul* (Amsterdam: University of Amsterdam); Chris Gosden, Peter Hommel, and Courtney Nimura (2019) Making Mounds: Monuments in Eurasian Prehistory. In *Enclosing Space, Opening Ground: Iron Age Studies From Scotland to Mainland Europe*, edited by Tanja Romankiewiz, Manuel Fernández-Götz, Gary Lock, and Oliver Büchsenschütz, pp. 141–152 (London, Oxbow Books).

71 See John Collis (2014) Urbanisation in Temperate Europe in the Iron Age: Mediterranean Influences or Indigenous? In *Paths to Complexity: Centralisation and Urbanisation in Iron Age Europe*, edited by Manuel Fernández-Götz, Holger Wendling, and Katja Winger, pp. 15–22 (Oxford: Oxbow Books).

72 See Stephen Fichtl (2018) Urbanization and Oppida. In *The Oxford Handbook of the European Iron Age*, edited by Colin Haselgrove, Katharina Rebay-Salisbury, and Peter S. Wells (Oxford: Oxford University Press), 10.1093/oxfordhb/9780199696826.013.13.

73 See Fernández-Götz (2014a), p. 140, also see Bettina Arnold (2021) "And Make Some Other Man Our King": Labile Elite Structures in Early Iron Age Europe. In *Power from Below: The Dynamics of Political Complexity in the Archaeological Record*, edited by T.L. Thurston and Manuel Fernández-Götz, pp. 106–124 (New York: Cambridge University Press).

74 See John Collis (1984) *Oppida: Earliest Towns North of the Alps* (Sheffield: Department of Prehistory and Archaeology); Stephen Fichtl (2005) *La ville Celtique: Les Oppida de 150 av. J- C. à 15 ap. J.-C.* (Paris: France); Gregory Woolf (1993) Rethinking the Oppida. *Oxford Journal of Archaeology* 12(2): 223–234.

75 See Holger Wendling and Katja Winger (2014) Aspects of Iron Age Urbanity and Urbanism at Manching. In *Paths to Complexity: Centralisation and Urbanisation in Iron Age Europe*, edited by Manuel Fernández-Götz, Holger Wendling, and Katja Winger, pp. 132–139 (Oxford: Oxbow Books).

76 See Fernández-Götz (2014a).

77 See Moore and González Álvarez (2021), p. 137.

78 See Manuel Fernández-Götz and Raquel Liceras-Garrido (2019) Iron Age Societies at Work: Towns, Kinship, and Territory in Historical Analogy. In *Historical Ecologies, Heterarchies, and Transtemporal Landscapes*, edited by Celeste Ray and Manuel Fernández-Götz, pp. 195–214 (New York: Routledge); Lisa Lodwick (2019) Farming Practice, Ecological Temporality, and Urban Communities at a Late Iron Age Oppidum. *Journal of Social Archaeology* 19(2): 2016–228; Tom Moore (2017a) Alternatives to Urbanism? Reconsidering Oppida and the Urban Question in Late Iron Age Europe. *Journal of World Prehistory* 30: 281–300; Tom Moore (2017b) Beyond Iron Age "Towns": Examining Oppida as Examples of Low-Density Urbanism. *Oxford Journal of Archaeology* 36(3): 287–305.

79 See Alzbeta Danielisova (2014) Oppida, Production and Social Status-Complexity of the Late La Tene Period in Central Europe. In *Paths to Complexity: Centralisation and Urbanisation in Iron Age Europe*, edited by Manuel Fernández-Götz, Holger Wendling, and Katja Winger, pp. 76–83 (Oxford: Oxbow Books).

80 See Manuel Fernández-Götz (2014b) Reassessing the Oppida: The Role of Power and Religion. *Oxford Journal of Archaeology* 33(4): 379–394.

81 See Fichtl (2018) and Woolf (1993).

82 See Axle G. Polsluschny (2019) Does Fortified Always Equate to Defensive? Some Thoughts on the Fortification Systems of the Glauberg Hillfort. In *Enclosing Space, Opening Ground: Iron Age Studies From Scotland to Mainland Europe*, edited by Tanja Romankiewiz, Manuel Fernández-Götz, Gary Lock, and Oliver Büchsenschütz, pp. 9–18 (London, Oxbow Books); and Petra Goláňová, Mária Hajnalová,

56 *Dividing Sovereignty*

Lenka Lisá, Peter Milo, Libor Petr, Markéta Fránková, Jan Kysela, Patrik G. Flammer, Romana Kočárová, and Peter Barta (2020) Investigating the Complex Story of One Ditch-A Multidisciplinary Study of Ditch Infill Provides Insight into the Spatial Organisation Within the Oppidum of Bibracte (Burgundy, France). *PLoS One* 15(4): e0231790–e0231790.

83 See Manuel Fernández-Götz and Dirk Krausse (2017) Urbanization Processes and Cultural Change in the Early Iron Age of Central Europe. In *Eurasia at the Dawn of History: Urbanization and Social Change*, edited by Manuel Fernández-Götz and Dirk Krausse, pp. 319–335 (Cambridge: Cambridge University Press).

84 See Manuel Fernández-Götz (2019) A World of 200 Oppida: Pre-Roman Urbanism in Temperate Europe. In *Regional Urban Systems in the Roman World, 150 BCE-250 CE*, edited by Luuk de Light and John Bintliff, pp. 35–66 (Leiden: Brill); and Fernández-Götz and Krausse (2017).

85 See Moore and González Álvarez (2021).

86 See Paul M. Martin (2000) *Vercingétorix: Le Politique, le Stratège.* (Paris: Perrin).

87 For the term, see Pierre Clastres (1987) *Society Against the State: Essays in Political Anthropology* (New York: Zone Books). Moore and González Álvarez (2021); and Manuel Fernández-Götz (2019) are among the scholars that take inspiration from Clastres.

88 See Mark LeVine and Mathias Mossberg (2014) *One Land, Two States: Israel and Palestine as Parallel States* (Oakland: University of California Press).

89 See Donald I. Ray (1996) Divided Sovereignty: Traditional Authority and the State in Ghana. *Journal of Legal Pluralism and Unofficial Law* 28(37–38): 181–202; Spencer W. McBride, Brent M. Rogers, and Keith A. Erekson, eds. (2021) *Contingent Citizens: Shifting Perceptions of Latter-Day Saints in American Political Culture* (Ithaca: Cornell University Press); and T.L. Thurston and Manuel Fernández-Götz, eds. (2021) *Power from Below: The Dynamics of Political Complexity in the Archaeological Record* (New York: Cambridge University Press).

90 See David Graeber and Marshall Sahlins (2017) *On Kings* (Chicago: HAU Books).

4 Building Up and Standing Down

The world is littered with the acronyms of international organizations—the UN, EU, OPEC, NATO, OAS, and AU. There are hundreds of them, each serving overlapping constituencies and often working at cross-purposes to each other. The frenetic growth of these organizations since the First World War correlates with the rapid extension and penetration of global capitalism.[1] To manage a complex connectivity that frequently subverts national borders, governments, corporations, the wealthy, and interest groups have joined forces to try to better manage global flows to their liking. These organizations *have* seen great success. Wars have been contained, economic volatility dampened, and billions of dollars in aid given. Without the collective action made possible by—more acronyms!—IGOs (inter-governmental organizations), NGOs (non-governmental organizations), and TSNs (transnational corporations), the world would be in a far worse place.

The International Red Cross & Red Crescent Movement, colloquially known as the Red Cross to most readers, was one of the earliest of these organizations. The Red Cross originated in a military engagement in the Austro-Sardinian War, one of the many now nearly forgotten violent confrontations that convulsed late-nineteenth-century Europe. A Swiss businessman named Henry Durant was shocked at the suffering in the aftermath of a battle and worked with local villagers to care for the wounded. Durant wrote a book of his experiences, and then helped organize a conference in 1863 that formed the first iteration of the organization.[2] Through its strict neutrality, wide reach, and considerable resources, the Red Cross has built a trusted name that allays many of the trust, equity, and autonomy fears in the countries where they operate.

The International Red Cross & Red Crescent Movement can rightfully be lauded as a successful answer to the collective action problem of caring for those in need amid armed conflicts and natural disasters. The structure of the organization is nonetheless illustrative of the limits of the Western imagination. The general assembly that meets every two years is made up of representatives from 192 national societies. There is also a governing board that makes decisions in the interim and appoints a secretary general, as well as five constitutional advisory committees. The Red Cross also has a headquarters in Geneva, five regional offices, 50 "country or country cluster" support offices, and three offices to represent the organization in the United Nations, African Union, and European Union.

DOI: 10.4324/9781003373322-4

58 *Building Up and Standing Down*

There are thousands of permanent Red Cross employees, as well as 14 million volunteers in 192 countries.[3]

From its inception, the Red Cross has worked with governments and its organizational structure echoes in many ways that of the League of Nations and United Nations described earlier in the book. Other large international organizations employ a similar governance model.[4] The roots of this common structure are based in centralization, federalization, and confederation systems that have developed within Western traditions.[5] All three models are premised on the idea of having in place robust state, provincial, and local levels of government to facilitate collective action. In a centralized (or "unitary") system, provincial and local governments are subordinate to the state level. In confederations, state and local levels are subordinate to the provincial authorities, and federalist (or "mixed") systems divide power across all three levels.[6]

There are, and should be, rigorous debate on how a more judicious mix of centralized, federal, and confederate features within organizations can lead toward better global governance.[7] A question rarely asked, however, is one of permanence. Do we need all those general assembles, governing boards, secretary generals, and advisory committees? If gridlock is a major problem in global governance,[8] then much of the glut gumming up our system is the standing infrastructures of thousands of international organizations. Losing a few acronyms might be useful, but far more effective would be to quickly scale up to an International Red Cross & Red Crescent Movement—or an Organization of American States or World Federation of Trade Unions—to meet the particular needs of a situation and then scale back down after that situation is resolved. To a significant degree, organizations, like the Red Cross, do just that when they put boots on the ground, swelling their ranks in a location to deal with the latest disaster. Yet the necessity of permanently maintaining a large cohort of bureaucrats to coordinate an organization's efforts remains gospel.[9]

On-demand, made-to-order global governance might sound like a fairy tale dreamed up by those unfamiliar with how the real world works. Yet governance models like this have been used for centuries around the globe to periodically organize large groups of people to fulfill common goals. Sometimes glossed as "segmentary states," their organizational principles offer alternative models for global governance that might be far more effective in dealing with the many conflicts that emerge unexpectantly in today's hyperconnected world.[10] The first of our three case studies in this chapter are the Alur of Uganda. These central African farmers and herders were organized into a welter of overlapping, ever-shifting political structures that confused European observers of the late nineteenth and early-twentieth century. In Western eyes, the region lacked "proper" government. The British therefore installed one—once again failing to see the merits in a non-Western political system of governance.

The Alur of Uganda

When European explorers, missionaries, and soldiers entered the interior of Africa in the late nineteenth century, they were on the lookout for chiefs.[11] They

Building Up and Standing Down 59

had a game plan for how to interact with such individuals, often preparing a kit of various gifts that had been acceptable elsewhere. Mobile hunter-gatherers like the !Kung of the Kalahari had no chiefs, but if there was a hint of hierarchy, someone had to be at the top. If they could not find their chief, they might create one, and then pretend that he was there all along.[12] In some places, however, there were simultaneously too many and not enough chiefs for the population at hand. For decades, this was seen as a problem of legibility and translation: a better understanding of the tribes in question would ultimately reveal the expected underlying structures. Instead, early-twentieth-century ethnographic work uncovered a different kind of governance.[13]

In 1940, Fortes and Pritchard published *African Political Systems*, a highly influential book that divided African political systems into three types.[14] The more egalitarian !Kung were emblematic of one type, while the many chiefs (and they now recognized some as kings) with supreme political authority composed another type. The book also codified "segmentary lineage systems" as a group in between, firmly asserting that large collectives could be sustained without a centralized political authority and standing government via a range of kin-, clan- and ritual-based structuring elements. How these systems worked, however, remained only partially understood. Since segmentary lineage systems were a troubling exception to the evolutionary model of bands, tribes, chiefdoms, and states that had once again become the dominant discourse in anthropology by the mid-twentieth century, they were often ignored or explained away by people working outside of the region.[15]

The work on segmentary systems in Africa nonetheless continued, yielding more refined understandings like this one that is worth quoting at length:

> In societies lacking ranked and specialized holders of political authority the relations of local groups to one another are seen as a balance of power, maintained by competition between them. Corporate groups may be arranged hierarchically in a series of levels; each group is significant in different circumstances and in connection with different social activities—economic, ritual, and governmental. Relations at one level are competitive in one situation, but in another the formerly competitive groups merge in mutual alliance against an outside group. A group at any level has competitive relations with others to ensure the maintenance of its own identity and the rights that belong to it as a corporation, and it may have internal administrative relations that ensure cohesion of its constituent elements. The aggregates that emerge as units in one context are merged into larger aggregates in others, so that a segment that in one situation is independent finds that it and its former competitors are merged together as subordinate segments in the internal administrative organization of a wider overall segment that includes them both. The wider segment is in turn in external competitive relations with other similar segments, and there may be an entire series of such segments.[16]

As this passage indicates, understanding how segmentary lineage systems operate was so difficult for outsiders because the overall structure of society could change

60 *Building Up and Standing Down*

drastically from year to year. An institution might vanish in months, with formerly rival leaders now working together as subordinates on a new project. Making sense of what was happening required both an extended stay to see all the moving parts and some local people one could trust to explain what was happening.

Aidan Southall spent 22 months among the Alur of Uganda from 1949 to 1951 trying to understand how, in his words, their "segmentary state" functioned prior to direct colonial administration in 1914.[17] The Alur were, and remain, located along the northern shores of Lake Albert. A variety of ethnic groups, such as the Lwo, Okebo, Madi, and Lendu, were organized under an Alur identity umbrella, forming a collective of some quarter million people at the turn of the twentieth century. Like all outsiders, Southall's understanding of the Alur segmentary state was a product of his own biases and the agendas of his informants within the changed political structure of the Protectorate of Uganda.[18] He nonetheless mastered some of the local languages and spent time in different Alur villages, moving between groups to try to capture a variety of perspectives on what life had been like in the region a few generations earlier.

In the late nineteenth century, the Alur were organized around a hereditary paramount king whose ritual authority far exceeded his political authority. The Paramount King's power was based on his superior ability to make rain and ensure the fertility of the land and people. To retain his services, people provided animals, crops, and labor. In the seventeenth and eighteenth centuries, people from the Paramount King's line migrated further afield setting up their own segments among different ethnic groups whose members once again brought gifts in exchange for their ritual services by their newly appointed segment kings.[19] As Alur society grew, the segments were connected by a series of shrines that trumpeted the ritual abilities of the royal lineage, and gifts occasionally flowed back to the Paramount King from the leaders of other segments who acknowledged his ultimate ritual authority. Each segment, however, was an independent political actor that was, in turn, composed of a fluctuating set of lineages (Figure 4.1).

The basic building block of Alur society was the lineage.[20] Relatives were expected to look out for each other, and those outside the lineage were seen as less trustworthy. Primary allegiance was therefore to one's kin, and most governance matters were handled within the lineage through customary means. Conflict resolution and other coordination needs between lineages were usually handled by the kings of each of the impacted segment, who formed an ever-changing suite of staff and resource "power triangles" to deal with the problem at hand.[21] Those who failed to comply with a decision risked the king's wrath, since an "afront to his stool" could be met with the plundering of resources by other lineages who answered the king's call to restore order.[22] Even a friendly visit of the king to one's territory was feared because of the crippling gift demands made to sustain his court during its time spent among lineage members.

Much of Alur government, though fleeting and problem-specific above the lineage level, was guided by a suite of common practices backed by tradition. There was a basic blueprint to how marriage disputes and other typical collective action problems should be resolved, a cross-cutting royal lineage that facilitated desired

Building Up and Standing Down 61

Figure 4.1 A 1892 drawing from the London Illustrated News of the Buganda capital in a kingdom neighboring the Alur. The Buganda shared the Alur's emphasis on connections between a ceremonial capital and outlying regions

62   *Building Up and Standing Down*

actions across segments, and an ultimate ritual authority that, when pressed, could adjudicate conflicts and coordinate affairs that could not be adequately managed at the segment or lineage level. The resulting governance system created a supra-Alur identity held by thousands of people who lived very different lives and rarely, if ever, came together in one place. Southall called the Alur a state because when needed its leaders temporarily created a society-spanning, command-and-control apparatus that would be the envy of any despot. Adapting to circumstances, the Alur had the capacity to quickly form, rejig, and disband hierarchies between segments.[23]

Alur political organization was just one of many kinds of segmentary lineage systems known from late-nineteenth and early-twentieth-century Africa.[24] In some groups like the Tiv, everyone was seen as belonging to the same all-encompassing descent group. Others emphasized shared territory to reinforce a collective identity. All these groups nonetheless worked via a shifting landscape of effervescent power triangles that emerged to meet particular challenges of collective action.[25] Swiftly building up problem-orientated governments and then standing them down created a staccato rhythm of politics that contrasts sharply with the steady drone of fluorescent lights and clicking keyboards in today's standing bureaucracies with which we are more familiar. Africa's flexible governance models might be seen as exceptions to a general rule, except that these forms were documented elsewhere during Europe's Age of Discovery.

The Aymara of the Lake Titicaca Basin

When the Spaniards arrived in the Andes in the early sixteenth century, they heard tales of great Aymara kingdoms in the Lake Titicaca Basin that had variously fought and allied with the Inca. Some like the Lupaqa remained in power, with their leaders claiming 20,000 households of pastoralists, farmers, and fisherfolk under their command.[26] The Spanish studied the organization of these kingdoms to tax households more effectively. They found, however, only loose confederations of nested kinship groups that shared a common territory, language, and ethnic identity.[27] The smallest units above the nuclear family, as well as the largest and everything in between, were called *ayllus*. Ayllu organization was an inconvenience for Spanish administrators who had hoped to use Indigenous political structures for their benefit—the Aymara kings, it seemed, had no real kingdom to command.[28]

The nested ayllus of the Lupaqa, like the other Aymara kingdoms, were organized as moieties that at each level paired together two ayllus that complimented, and sometimes competed against, each other. The leaders of the ayllus at the varying levels of Lupaqa society claimed that their positions were hereditary, with the dual kings of the Lupaqa maximal ayllus emphasizing their position within long, unbroken lines of Lupaqa-wide rulers.[29] Their claims to authority were maintained by hosting feasts, gift redistributions, ancestor venerations, and other ritually charged events. As one moved up the ayllu scale, however, leaders became less involved in day-to-day activities. Their power, though recognized, laid increasingly dormant. Aymara paramount leaders only became visible when a conflict between lower ayllus needed to be resolved or a rare ritual performed,[30] often in specially designated settlements that served as aggregation/defensive sites for a diffused, and often mobile, population.[31]

Elizabeth Arkush argues that the Aymara Kingdoms were organized in a manner broadly similar to Africa's segmentary lineage system and follows other researchers in questioning their status as kingdoms or states as traditionally conceived.[32] If Lupaqa, Collas, Canas, and other kingdoms existed in the Lake Titicaca Basin, they were manifested for only fleeting moments of time, such as to celebrate a shared god or to fight off the Inca invasion. Polity-wide government emerged to confront a specific collective action problem, and then disappeared when that the problem was resolved. Aymara paramount leaders were thus on-demand kings for maximal ayllus that were rarely brought together. The "capitals" of the kingdoms normally catered only to a few local ayllus; their "kings," most days, almost indistinguishable from the dozens of other leaders who were ostensibly ranked below them.

Archaeological projects specifically designed to find Aymara Kingdoms in the archaeological record in the centuries preceding the late-fifteenth-century Inca expansion have failed to find much of a state infrastructure.[33] Ana Luz Alejandra Sejas Portillo, for example, set out to better understand the operation of the Quillacas-Azanaques Confederation in Southern Bolivia.[34] An Aymara kingdom of more than 10,000 households, the confederation had a royal family in the Colque Guarache who negotiated on behalf of their subjects with the Inca and were recognized by early Spanish authorities.[35] Sejas Portillo's survey documented as many as a dozen Quillacas-Azanaques aggregation centers that featured plazas, accessible above ground sepulchers, and cooking and serving wares associated with feasting. Often, she could distinguish a house or small set of houses near the plaza with more imports and other high-status goods. These were likely the home of second tier ayllu leaders who helped coordinate the affairs of those living in the center and surrounding hamlets. Yet Sejas Portillo found no evidence for a primary hub that orchestrated confederation politics. A higher tier *was* there when needed, but only local- and mid-level governance was visible.

Arkush attempted to find the archaeological signature for the Colla kingdom that hugged the northern shore of Lake Titicaca. There are more ethnohistoric records for the Colla. Not only do we know the names of kings, but we also know their capital at the time of the Spanish Conquest and the names and location of the geographic segments that made up the kingdom. Archaeological research, however, determined that their capital was only founded during the Inca era, and Arkush, like Sejas Portillo, struggled to find clear evidence for the maximal ayllus discussed in the records. At the aggregation sites, Arkush could nonetheless trace the rough contours of more minimal ayllus expressed in small neighborhoods defined by walls and geographic features, and the sites often featured tombs, plazas, and other integrative features for the community. She also found a third-order center, Lamparaquen, mimicking a general pattern across this part of the basin for defended mid-level centers that "must have been the seats of political power and smaller satellites that must have held a subordinate position."[36]

64 *Building Up and Standing Down*

Throughout the Lake Titicaca Basin, the basic pattern is the same as in these two examples. Although art styles and overall settlement clustering sometimes mimic the political boundaries of the kingdoms as they are known from ethnohistoric records, we find no evidence on the ground for a standing political organization with such features as a palace, storerooms, or an administrative complex. Aymara kings clearly existed—multiple independent sources discuss their antiquity (Figure 4.2)—but their royal lineage, and the maximal ayllus that they directed, were on call for when situations demanded a higher level of collective action than was normally required.

There are many ways to define a state.[37] In this book, we have tended toward one that emphasizes recognition of sovereignty by its citizens and foreign leaders.[38] Definitions like this one sidestep the "how" of politics, to focus on the resulting understanding of a collective unit that bridges internal differences. Southall called the Alur a state because at times the segments came together into a single polity. Hundreds of thousands of people could effectively be seen, however fleetingly, as subjects beholden to the desires of a centralized government—another common feature of state definitions.[39] The Aymara ayllus in the centuries prior to the Spanish Conquest, in turn, can also be seen as the foundation of occasional states, although it appears that they came together even more rarely than the Alur. The smaller scale ayllus that governed everyday actions were the building blocks for larger ayllus, with the feasts and other reoccurring events at aggregation centers setting the rules of the game for how ayllus could be arranged into bigger and bigger units. The Aymara had a ready-to-assemble state, but most days they did not need one.

Figure 4.2 A roll-out drawing of a Colonial-era cup depicting (center, upper register) the encounter between the Inca emperor on the left and one of the Colla kings on the right

Kandy and the Galactic Polities of Southeast Asia

A mandala is a cosmogram in the Buddhist and Hindu tradition, a map both of how the cosmos is organized and how one should navigate it.[40] The typical mandala is geometric with a center point surrounded by concentric circles composed of other points. The center is the holiest of holies—often representing Meru, the mountain of the gods and the center of the universe—with the sacred yielding to the more profane as one moves away from the center. Throughout much of the second millennium CE, the kings of Southeast Asia modeled their kingdoms as mandalas, placing their palaces at the center of the universe. They were the *Chakravartin* who made the "spiritual realm manifest on earth," a living conduit to the divine.[41] The Portuguese, and later the Dutch and British, were fascinated by the displays of deference accorded to many of the rulers of southeast Asia, as well as the violence that could be meted out at their command (Figure 4.3).[42] The kings they met seemed to hold more absolute power than those who reigned over Europe.

The kingdoms of Southeast Asia have nonetheless been described as heterarchical.[43] Hierarchies abounded in communities that were often strictly divided by caste and class, but this ranked social order was created in parallel processes of "emboxment" that linked sets of households together through personal ties.[44]

Figure 4.3 Philip Baldaeus' drawing of the reception of Dutch General Gerard Hulft by King Rajasinghe II of Kandy in 1656

66   *Building Up and Standing Down*

Since kings lacked the "administrative machinery to directly exploit or control their lands,"[45] their power was profoundly personal. Each often maintained the right to appoint provincial rulers, placing family and allies into leadership roles that might be rotated on an annual basis. These leaders, who regularly visited the capital and its ritually charged buildings, needed to assert their own sacred centrality in their respective provinces to obtain the emboxed labor and resources desired by the king. Yet they too lacked the administrative machinery to control a population living in small, self-sufficient villages. The combination of emboxment, multiple sacred centers, and village autonomy encouraged factionalism. Rival factions, juggling to keep together their own shifting coalitions, always threatened to topple the monarch.[46]

"What emerges," Stanley Tambiah wrote on these kingdoms, "is a galactic picture of a central planet surrounded by differentiated satellites, which are more or less 'autonomous' entities held in orbit and within the sphere of influence of the center."[47] Regions tended to have abutting "galactic polities," creating a situation where the gravitational pull of one capital might, over time, overtake that of another. A satellite province could also aspire to the spiritual gravitas of a capital, while a capital might one day lose its connection to the divine because of royal (in)action. The end results were political mandalas in constant flux due to "the dynamics of pulsation and changing spheres of influence."[48] Similar galaxies in a state of flux were found at lower levels of society. Their basic form nonetheless remained the same at each level—mandalas with a sacred center encircled by entities under its thrall[49]—because this was how a society *should* be organized in the minds of both those in power, their political rivals, and the population at large.[50]

Since kingdoms were the spiritual realm manifested on earth, a ruler's primary concern was to retain their center's galactic pull.[51] The capital's architecture and layout often mimicked the organization of the cosmos. The thirteenth-century compound of Sukhothai in present-day Thailand, for example, had the king's palace, a temple, and monastery that was encircled by three ramparts with gates in the four cardinal directions.[52] Spiritual potency, if the capital was properly arranged and rituals were properly followed, would then flow outward through the gates, connecting the capital to its provincial "children."[53] The flow of labor, resources, and exotica into the capital during regular visits and annual ceremonies were in recompense for the work done to maintain cosmic order. These were also the gifts that were then transformed into temples, sumptuous clothing, and opulent feasts that reaffirmed the king's status as a divine conduit to the gods.[54]

One of the better understood kingdoms is Kandy in what is now Sri Lanka. Kandy was a satellite province that broke from another kingdom in the fourteenth century and lasted almost 400 years before succumbing to the British in 1815.[55] A powerful adversary—the king's forces wiped out Portuguese, Dutch, and British armies that invaded Sri Lanka's mountainous interior[56]—Kandyan rulers presided over a galactic system with the help of a vanishingly small state bureaucracy. The king had one minister in the seventeenth century, bloating to four by the time of British conquest. These ministers were overshadowed in the capital by the dozens of people in the service of the king who attended to his bath, cracked a whip as he walked, and carried his Golden Arms. The system of governance worked by what Ralph Pieris calls regional and functional devolution.[57] The king, in theory, owed most of the land and, in return for use rights, a person was required to provide a small grain tax as well as the *rājakāriya* (king's duty). Those from different provinces paid their duty through several months of labor doing a specialized activity that was learned intergenerationally within their communities, such as pottery making, weaving, or road building. Provincial leaders ensured the coordination of these activities, as well as the proper housing and feeding of the laborers.[58]

By outsourcing most aspects of governance, the rulers of Kandy could focus on maintaining the gravitational pull that kept the provinces in their orbit. Much of this work was concerned with improving the generative potency of the capital. Each king embarked on new royal projects. They added a garden, tore down and rebuilt a palace, or even put in a lake.[59] This was existentially necessary work that was said to benefit all, with perhaps none as important as the King's caring for the Buddha's tooth. Allegedly taken from the ashes of the Buddha when he was cremated in 543 AD, the tooth was acquired by the Kingdom of Kandy at the end of the sixteenth century. The tooth was seen as a living object that required an entourage as large as the sovereign.[60] The proper care of the tooth was often a point of contention, as was every aspect of daily and annual rituals in Kandy.[61] When everything was in proper order, the king could amass tens of thousands of laborers and soldiers within a matter of days to do his bidding. Provincial leaders nonetheless stood ready to proclaim themselves the true Chakravartin, and it was easy for a far-off province to be lured into the pull of a rival power.[62]

The Kingdom of Kandy was a chimera for European colonizers. The polity would melt away during their military advances, and then a few weeks later they would find themselves trapped by a force of more than 10,000 soldiers.[63] The colonizers marveled at a king who had hundreds of attendees, but only four full-time administers, two of whom were concerned solely with his person and the operations of the capital city.[64] Devolved governance would not be seen as that unusual to the colonizers—they were familiar with weak kings and court intrigue—but they would have also seen this structure in terms of a degeneration from an ideal form. They failed to recognize that effective, large-scale collectives could be sustained by leaving almost all government functions in local, and to a lesser extent, provincial hands. A center's galactic pull, with its regular connections between elites, allowed a state to quickly form on command to rebuild a palace or fight off an enemy, and then shrink to leave behind only a king, his retinue, and, in the case of Kandy, a tooth.

Building Up and Standing Down

The world faces difficult collection action problems that require coordination between millions, if not billions, of people. To achieve this coordination, we require big organizations. The problems that we face, however, are varied and surprising in their impacts. We know, for example, that global pandemics will

68 *Building Up and Standing Down*

occur again. COVID-19 has its trajectory—genetic mutations, shifting medical advice, and changing cultural perceptions—and monkey pox has a different one. Globe-spanning organizations like the International Red Cross & Red Crescent Movement therefore need to continually adapt to new challenges.

With tools forged by Western academics and politicians over the last 300 years, the Red Cross created an organizational structure that has adapted to today's interconnected and everchanging world by mixing elements of centralization, federalization, and confederation. An organization, in their minds, that is not an organization at all. Within the Red Cross' website, there is a discussion of the movement and its composition that reads in part:

> It [the International Red Cross & Red Crescent Movement] is not a single organization. It is composed of the International Committee of the Red Cross (ICRC), the International Federation of Red Cross and Red Crescent Societies and the 190 individual National Societies. Each has its own legal identity and role, but they are all united by seven Fundamental Principles.
>
> These principles are humanity, impartiality, neutrality, independence, voluntary service, unity and universality. Each component of the Movement is committed to respect and uphold them.[65]

The Red Cross' innovative mixture of Western governance traditions provides considerable autonomy to its constitute parts and has been widely emulated. Their solution nonetheless adds parallel, standing bureaucracies, further filling the global stage with more actors, each with their own "legal identity and role." Not being an organization seems to only add more clutter. Is there a better way?

This chapter's three case studies provide examples of what have sometimes been glossed as "segmentary states" by anthropologists and archaeologists. The term usefully emphasizes the segments that can come together into a political whole but fails to capture the temporal rhythms of these organizations. In each case, there was an accepted leader ready to organize the segments into collective action. There was also a basic blueprint for how the segments should come together, as well as feasts, festivals, and other mechanisms to maintain a polity-wide identity and sense of mutual obligation. Alur, Aymara, and Kandyan communities knew that their polity *could* become a state in the sense of a centralized decision-making apparatus with defined territory, subject populations, and a monopoly on legitimate violence,[66] but for months, and even years, the state was largely latent, waiting to be called into being.

The feature that our case studies lacked was permanence. We tend to think of the "state" as "a 'real-concrete' agent with will, power, and activity of its own."[67] It is a fixed entity, external to individuals, housed in buildings, and codified in law. States, however, are better seen as sets of institutions, agreed-upon rules of the game that help to structure daily activities.[68] For us, a brick-and-mortar courthouse is needed to reinforce these rules, as is a judge's bench and the clerk's call to order. We need all those police officers with guns. To maintain order, to collect

Building Up and Standing Down 69

revenue, and to defend territory, we have come to feel that standing bureaucracies and extensively built infrastructure are required.

Nation states as conceived of today can alleviate many collective action challenges like free riders, the expectation for equity, and trust. Yet one of the problems that routinely derail collective action *is* permanence.[69] People are more amenable to participating in a larger organization when the benefits to them are clear and the organization is short-lived. The group in this chapter figured out how to make a state only when they needed it. One of the most striking aspects of our case studies is the almost vanishingly small size of their standing state-level governments. Most days, an outside observer would struggle to find much evidence for the institutions that cross-cut local groupings.

The primary work of governing for the rulers in our case studies was about maintaining the social and cosmological relationships that could bring segments together when required. We see some of this work occurring in the figures associated with this chapter: traveling along a wide road to a palace compound (see Figure 3.1), witnessing a leader with a majestic headdress (see Figure 4.2), and offering supplication at a ceremony (see Figure 4.3). The Alur, Aymara, and Kandy governments, in our eyes, seem weakly developed. They are often classified as "early," "archaic," or "inchoate" states by scholars,[70] the initial stages of the more robust government structures of today. We should see these instead as alternatives to these more familiar structures that might lead toward better mechanisms of global governance.

The case studies were each built around kin-based units that were the primary unit of action. Through reciprocal ties, units were paired with each other, creating a larger "us" that could be used when needed. Similar ties were made across a polity, connecting a nested set of leaders who progressively spent more time signaling their potential positions of political power than on governing daily activities. One way of looking at the case studies is to see what will not work today—kinship is unlikely to form the glue for an international organization and few CEOs will lay prostrate on the ground at a world court. How segments were constituted in the past and how those relationships were maintained, however, is less important than the more general understanding that segmentary states have effectively organize collectives of tens of thousands of people for centuries. Collectives of tightly organized segments with a notional, though well-recognized, central authority are thus a possible, and perhaps even desirable, way to meet coordination demands while preserving a greater degree of local autonomy.

The glue that binds the International Red Cross & Red Crescent Movement together are both its international committee and federation, and the movement's seven fundamental principles of humanity, impartiality, neutrality, independence, voluntary service, unity, and universality. Our case studies also emphasize the importance of shared values, yet demonstrate that agreed-upon prescriptions for action can allow for a build-to-order governance system that may strike many readers as impossible. As with absolute sovereignty, we assume that the only alternative to chaos is a standing government, so we spend much of our time

70 Building Up and Standing Down

debating about what that government should look like. Segmentary states shift our attention to the lower levels of governance and the links between them. With a strong enough foundation of local ties, we can foster the development of far more nimble intergovernmental organizations that build up to address a collective action challenge and then stand down.

Notes

1 See Karen Gram-Skjoldager, Haakon A. Ikonomou, and Torsten Kahlert (2020) *Organizing the 20th-Century World: International Organizations and the Emergence of International Public Administration, 1920–1960s* (London: Bloomsbury Academic); Akira Iriye (2002) *Global Community: The Role of International Organizations in the Making of the Contemporary World* (Berkeley: University of California Press); and Jacob Katz Cogan, Ian Hurd, Ian Johnstone, and Brian Langille (2016) *The Oxford Handbook of International Organizations* (Oxford: Oxford University Press).

2 See Caroline Moorehead (1999) *Dunant's Dream: War, Switzerland, and the History of the Red Cross* (New York: Carroll & Graf).

3 See www.ifrc.org for information on the structure and size of the International Red Cross & Red Crescent Movement.

4 See essays in Brian Frederking and Paul F. Diehl, eds. (2015) *The Politics of Global Governance: International Organizations in an Interdependent World*. Fifth Edition (Boulder: Lynne Rienner Publishers).

5 Two classics of comparative governance are Alfred C. Stepan (2001) *Arguing Comparative Politics* (Oxford: Oxford University Press); and Michael Stewart (1964) *Modern Forms of Government: A Comparative Study*. Third edition (London: George Allen & Unwin). Both books largely look at the suite of possible governments that emerge from Enlightenment debates.

6 One way to look at the debates about the merit of different governance systems is to see how they play out in a single nation. For the United States, James A. Morone (2016) *By the People: Debating American Government*. Second edition (New York: Oxford University Press).

7 See Ngaire Woods (1999) Good Governance in International Organizations. *Global Governance* 5(1): 39–61.

8 See Thomas Hale, David. Held, and Kevin Young (2013) *Gridlock: Why Global Cooperation Is Failing When We Need It Most* (Cambridge: Polity Press).

9 For example, see Kenneth W. Abbott and Duncan Snidal (1998) Why States Act Through Formal International Organizations. *The Counseling Psychologist* 42(1): 150–176.

10 Almost everyone in the world is now subject to some form of global governance, see Sophie Harmon and David Williams, eds. (2013) *Governing the World: Cases in Global Governance* (New York: Routledge).

11 See Johannes Fabian (2000) *Out of Our Minds Reason and Madness in the Exploration of Central Africa* (Berkeley: University of California Press); and Frank McLynn (1992) *Hearts of Darkness: The European Exploration of Africa* (London: Hutchinson).

12 See Liva Palagashvili (2018) African Chiefs: Comparative Governance Under Colonial Rule. *Public Choice* 174: 277–300; and Robert W. Harms (2019) *Land of Tears: The Exploration and Exploitation of Equatorial Africa* (New York: Basic Books).

13 See Gerhard Lindblom (1920) *The Akamba in British East Africa: An Ethnological Monograph* (Uppsala: Appelberg); Robert S. Rattray (1923) *Ashanti* (Oxford: Ahsherford); E. E. Evans-Pritchard (1947) *The Nuer: A Description of the Modes of Livelihood and Political Institutions of a Nilotic People* (Oxford: Clarendon Press); A. R.

Building Up and Standing Down 71

Radcliffe-Brown and Cyril Daryll Forde (1950) *African Systems of Kinship and Marriage* (London: Oxford University Press).

14 See Meyer Fortes and E. E. Evans-Pritchard (1940) *African Political Systems* (London: Oxford University Press).

15 For example, see Elman Service (1975) *Origins of the State and Civilization: The Process of Cultural Evolution* (New York: Norton).

16 See John Middleton and David Tait (1970) Introduction. In *Tribes Without Rulers*, edited by John Middleton and David Tait, pp. 1–31 (Routledge, New York), p. 6.

17 See Aidan W. Southall (1956) *Alur Society: A Study in Process and Types of Domination* (London: W. Heffer & Sons); Aidan W. Southall (1970) The Illusion of Tribe. *Journal of Asian and African Studies* 5(1–2): 28–50; and Aidan W. Southall (1999) The Segmentary State and the Ritual Phase in Political Economy. In *Beyond Chiefdoms: Pathways to Complexity in Africa* edited by Susan Keech McIntosh, pp. 31–38 (Cambridge: Cambridge University Press).

18 For a contextualization of Southall's work, see Adrian J. Browne (2018) The Alurization of Aidan Southall—Contested Ethnonymic Traditions in North-Western Uganda. *History in Africa* 45: 221–245.

19 Also see Okete J.E. Shiroya (1982) Alur Culture and Society c. 1650–1850. *Journal of Eastern Research and Development* 12: 13–20.

20 For a general discussion of trust in African lineages, see Jacob Moscona, Nathan Nunn, and James A. Robinson (2017) Keeping It in the Family: Lineage Organization and the Scope of Trust in Sub-Saharan Africa. *American Economic Review: Papers & Proceedings* 107(5): 565–571.

21 See Peter Robertshaw (2010) Beyond the Segmentary State: Creative and Instrumental Power in Western Uganda. *Journal of World Prehistory* 23(4): 255–269.

22 See Aidan W. Southall (1988) The Segmentary State in Africa and Asia. *Comparative Studies in Society and History* 30(1): 52–82.

23 See Southall (1970).

24 See remaining chapters in Middleton and Tait (1970).

25 For a discussion of how lineages come together and fall apart in the general region, see Parker Shipton (2009) *Mortgaging the Ancestors: Ideologies of Attachment in Africa* (New Haven: Yale University Press).

26 See John V. Murra (1968) An Aymara Kingdom in 1567. *Ethnohistory* 15(2): 115–151.

27 The ayllu structure of Aymara communities in the Inca, Colonial, and Republican era have been discussed by many authors including Thomas A. Abercrombie (1998) *Pathways of Memory and Power: Ethnography and History Among Andean People* (Madison: University of Wisconsin Press); Juan Albarracín-Jordan (1996) *Tiwanaku: Arqueología Regional y Dinámica Segmentaria* (La Paz: Plural Editores); Thérèse Bouysse-Cassagne (1987) *La Identidad Aymara: Aproximación Histórica (Siglo XV, Siglo XVI)* (La Paz: Hisbol); Tristan Platt (1987) Entre Ch'axwa y Muxsa: Para una Historia del Pensamiento Político Aymara. In *Tres Reflexiones Sobre el Pensamiento Andino*, edited by T. Bouysse-Cassagne, O. Harris, T. Platt, and V. Cereceda, pp. 61–132 (La Paz: Hisbol); Tristan Platt, Therese Bouysse-Cassagne, and Olivia Harris (2006) *Qaraqara-Charka. Mallku, Inka y Rey en la Provincia de Charcas (Siglos XV–XVII): Historia Antropológica de una Confederación Aymara* (La Paz: Plural) and Thierry Saignes (1986) *En Busca del Poblamiento Étnico de los Andes Bolivianos (siglos XV y XVI)* (La Paz: MUSEF).

28 For a discussion of ayllu organization in Bolivia and how it has changed over the last 400 years, see S. Elizabeth Penry (2019) *The People Are King: The Making of an Indigenous Andean Politics* (New York: Oxford University Press).

29 See Murra (1968).

30 See Thérèse Bouysse-Cassagne (1987) *La Identidad Aymara. Aproximación Histórica (siglo XV, siglo XVI)* (La Paz: Hisbol). Javier Izko (1992) *La Doble Frontera* (La Paz:

72 Building Up and Standing Down

Hisbol-Ceres, La Paz); Platt (1987); and Silvia Rivera Cusicanqui (1978) El Mallku y la Sociedad Colonial en el Siglo XVII: el Caso de Jesús de Machaca. *Avances* 1: 7–27.

31 See Albarracín-Jordan (1996); Izko (1992); Platt (1987), and Claudia Rivera Casanovas (2004) Regional Settlement Patterns and Political Complexity in the Cinti Valley, Bolivia. Unpublished Ph.D. dissertation, University of Pittsburgh, Pittsburgh.

32 See Elizabeth Arkush (2014) "I Against My Brother": Conflict and Confederation in the South-Central Andes. In *Embattled Bodies, Embattled Places: War in Pre-Columbian Mexico and the Andes*, edited by Andrew K. Scherer and John W. Verano, pp. 199–226. (Washington, DC: Dumbarton Oaks).

33 See Elizabeth Arkush (2011) *Hillforts of the Ancient Andes: Colla Warfare, Society, and Landscape* (Tallahassee: University Press of Florida).

34 See Ana Luz Alejandra Sejas Portillo (2019) Local Level Leadership and Centralization in the Late Prehispanic Yaretani Basin, Bolivia. Unpublished Ph.D. dissertation, University of Pittsburgh, Pittsburgh.

35 See Abercrombie (1999); Waldermar Espinoza Soriano (1982) El reino Aymara de Quillaca-Asanaque, siglos XV y XVI. *Revista del Museo Nacional* (Lima) 45: 175–274; and Platt 1987.

36 See Arkush (2014), p. 215; also see Elizabeth Arkush (2018) Coalescence and Defensive Communities: Insights from an Andean Hillfort Town. *Cambridge Archaeological Journal* 28(1): 1–22; Elizabeth Arkush (2017) The End of Ayawiri: Abandonment at an Andean Hillfort Town of the Late Intermediate Period. *Journal of Field Archaeology* 42(3): 241–257; and Elizabeth Arkush and Hugo C. Ikehara (2019) Pucarani: Defensive Monumentality and Political Leadership in the Late Pre-Columbian Andes. *Journal of Anthropological Archaeology* 53: 66–81.

37 For discussions of defining the state in a globalized world, see Clifford Geertz (2004) What Is a State If It Is Not a Sovereign?: Reflections on Politics in Complicated Places. *Current Anthropology* 45(5): 577–593; and James Ferguson and Akhil Gupta (2002) Spatializing States: Toward an Ethnography of Neoliberal Governmentality. *American Ethnologist* 29(4): 981–1002.

38 See Daniel Philpott (1995) Sovereignty: An Introduction and Brief History. *Journal of International Affairs* 48(2): 353–368.

39 Centralization is a common feature of state definitions by archaeologists. See Norman Yoffee (2004) *Myths of the Archaic State: Evolution of the Earliest Cities, States and Civilizations* (Cambridge: Cambridge University Press); Clifford Ando Clifford and Seth Francis Corning Richardson (2017) *Ancient States and Infrastructural Power: Europe, Asia, and America* (Philadelphia: University of Pennsylvania Press); and Joyce Marcus and Gary M. Feinman, eds. (1998) *Archaic States* (Santa Fe: School of American Research Press).

40 See D. Dennis Hudson and John Stratton Hawley (2010) *Krishna's Mandala: Bhagavata Religion and Beyond* (New Delhi: Oxford University Press); and Koichi Shinohara (2014) *Spells, Images, and Maṇḍalas: Tracing the Evolution of Esoteric Buddhist Rituals* (New York: Columbia University Press).

41 See Hendrik Spruyt (2020) *The World Imagined*, p. 256 (New York: Cambridge University Press).

42 See Donald Ferguson (1998) *The Earliest Dutch Visits to Ceylon* (New Delhi: Asian Educational Services); and George D. Winius (1971) *The Fatal History of Portuguese Ceylon: Transition to Dutch Rule* (Cambridge: Harvard University Press).

43 See Joyce White (1995) Incorporating Heterarchy into Theory on Socio-political Development: The Case from Southeast Asia. In *Heterarchy and the Analysis of Complex Societies*, edited by Robert Ehrenreich, Carole Crumley, and Janet Levy, pp. 101–23 (Arlington: American Anthropological Association).

44 See Georges Condominas (1990) *From Lawa to Mon, From Saa' to Thai: Historical and Anthropological Aspects of Southeast Asian Social Spaces* (Canberra: Department of Anthropology, Research School of Pacific Studies, Australian National University).

Building Up and Standing Down 73

45 See Alan Stathern (2007) *Kingship and Conversion in Sixteenth Century Sri Lanka: Portuguese Imperialism in Buddha Land*, p. 28 (New York: Cambridge University Press).

46 This discussion, of course, neither does justice to the variety of polities in early second millennium AD Southeast Asia nor captures the ongoing debate about how these polities might be best characterized. These features, nonetheless, reoccur in many kingdoms. See, for example, the debates published in the *Journal of Southeast Asian Studies* (1984), issue 15(2), that presents the results of a symposium on societal organization in mainland southeast Asia prior to the eighteenth century. A more recent discussion of southeastern Asian political forms can be found in Victor Lieberman (2003) *Strange Parallels: Southeast Asia in Global Context, c. 800–1830* (Cambridge: Cambridge University Press).

47 See Stanley J. Tambiah (1973) *Culture, Thought, and Social Action: An Anthropological Perspective*, p. 261 (Cambridge: Harvard University Press).

48 See Tambiah (1973), p. 261. For other regions, see Stanley J. Tambiah (1976) *World Renouncer and World Conqueror: A Study of Buddhism and Polity in Thailand Against a Historical Background* (Cambridge: Cambridge University Press).

49 See Michael Roberts (2002) The Collective Consciousness of the Sinhalese During the Kandyan Era: Manichean Images, Associational Logic. *Asian Ethnicity* 3(1): 29–46; Deborah E. Tooker (1996) Putting the Mandala in Its Place: A Practice-Based Approach to the Spatialization of Power on the Southeast Asian 'Periphery'—The Case of the Akha. *The Journal of Asian Studies* 55(2): 323–358 and Deborah E. Tooker (2012) *Space and the Production of Cultural Difference Among the Akha Prior to Globalization : Channeling the Flow of Life* (Amsterdam: Amsterdam University Press).

50 Note that the galactic state model has been rightfully criticized for its royalty-centered, top-down perspective, see Nicola Tannenbaum (1993) Galactic Polities, the Asiatic Mode of Production and Peasant-States: Southeast Asian Pre-Modern Polities. *The Australian Journal of Anthropology* 4(1): 45–61; and Donald K. Emmerson (1980) Issues in Southeast Asian History: Room for Interpretation—A Review Article. *The Journal of Asian Studies* 40(1): 43–68. We are nonetheless concerned here with the worldview of royalty and how their concerns impacted governance.

51 The most famous discussion of the spectacle of the court in southeast Asia is Clifford Geertz (1980) *Negara: The Theatre State in Nineteenth-Century Bali* (Princeton: Princeton University Press).

52 See Alexander B. Griswold (1967) *Towards a History of Sukhodaya Art* (Bangkok: Fine Arts Department of the Government of Thailand).

53 See Elizabeth M. B. Gosling (1983) The History of Sukhothai as a Ceremonial Center: A Study of Early Siamese Architecture and Society, vols. I and II. Unpublished Ph.D. dissertation, University of Michigan, Ann Arbor.

54 See Gayathri Madubhani Ranathunga (2013) Influence of Foreign Culture and Hybrid Culture: The Case of the Kandyan Kingdom of Sri Lanka. *International Journal of Costume and Fashion* 13(2): 53–64.

55 For a general history of the kingdom, see Lorna Srimathie Dewaraja (2008) *The Kandyan Kingdom of Sri Lanka, 1707–1782*, second revised edition (Pannipitiya: Stamford Lake); and Nihal Karunaratna (1999) *Kandy, Past and Present*, 1474–1998 A.D. (Colombo: Central Cultural Fund, Ministry of Religious and Cultural Affairs).

56 See Chana Wickremesekera (2004) Military Organisation in Pre-modern Sri Lanka: The Army of the Kandyan Kings. *South Asia: Journal of South Asian Studies* 27(2): 133–151.

57 See Ralph Pieris (1956) *Sinhalese Social Organization: The Kandyan Period* (Colombo: Ceylon University Press Board).

58 Beyond Pieris (1956); see Lorna Srimathie Dewaraja (1972) Revenues of the King of Kandy. *Journal of the Sri Lanka Branch of the Royal Asiatic Society* 16: 17–24.

74 *Building Up and Standing Down*

59 For a discussion of the ideological underpinning of building in the capital, see James S. Duncan (1990) *The City as Text: The Politics of Landscape Interpretation in the Kandyan Kingdom* (Cambridge: Cambridge University Press); and Kapila D. Silva (2011) Mapping Meaning in the City Image: A Case Study of Kandy, Sri Lanka. *Journal of Architectural and Planning Research* 28(3): 229–251.

60 See John Strong (2021) *The Buddha's Tooth: Western Tales of a Sri Lankan Relic* (Chicago: University of Chicago Press); and A. M. Hocart (1931) *The Temple of the Tooth in Kandy*. Memoirs of the Archaeological Survey of Ceylon, vol. iv (London: Luzac and Co.).

61 See Elizabeth Nissan (1988) Polity and Pilgrimage Centres in Sri Lanka. *Man* 23(2): 253–274.

62 See Pieres (1956) for the relative independence of outlying provinces in the Kingdom of Kandy. For court intrigue, see Gananath Obeyesekere (2017) Between the Portuguese and the Nāyakas: The Many Faces of the Kandyan Kingdom, 1591–1765. In *Sri Lanka at the Crossroads of History*, edited by Zoltán Biedermann and Alan Strathern, pp. 161–176 (London: UCL Press).

63 See Channa Wickremesekera (2004) *Kandy at War: Indigenous Military Resistance to European Expansion in Sri Lanka 1594–1818* (Colombo: Vijitha Yapa Publications).

64 See Pieres (1956).

65 See the webpage of the International Committee of the Red Cross, where the movement is described: www.icrc.org/en/movement, accessed on May 23, 2022.

66 For example, Bob Jessop (2022) defines a state as:

> (1) [A] politically organized coercive, administrative and symbolic apparatus endowed with general and specific powers; (2) a clearly demarcated core territory under the more or less uncontested and continuous control of the state apparatus; and (3) a stable population on which the state's political authority and decisions are binding.

in State Theory, in *Handbook on Theories of Governance*, second edition, edited by Christopher Ansell and Jacob Torfing, p. 78 (Northampton: Edward Elgar Publishing).

67 See p. 69 of Phillip Abrahms (1988) Notes on the Difficulty of Studying the State. *Journal of Historical Sociology* 1(1): 58–89.

68 See Douglas C. North (1990) *Institutions, Institutional Change, and Economic Performance* (New York: Cambridge University Press); and Douglas C. North (1991) Institutions. *Journal of Economic Perspective* 5(1): 97–112.

69 See John M. Anderies and Marco A. Janssen (2013). *Sustaining the Commons* (Tempe: Center for the Study of Institutional Diversity, Arizona State University).

70 For example, see Peter Skalník and Henri J.M. Claessen (1978) *The Early State* (The Hague: Mouton); and Joyce Marcus and Gary M. Feinman (1998) *Archaic States* (Santa Fe: School of American Research Press).

5 (Re)Building Consensus

In 1992, Francis Fukuyama published *The End of History and the Last Man*.[1] The Berlin Wall had just fallen, the Soviet Union was crumbling, and democracies were popping up all over the world. The Cold War was over; freedom had won, and Fukuyama proclaimed that we had reached "the end-point of mankind's ideological evolution and the universalization of Western liberal democracy as the final form of human government."[2] For 15 years, his predictions seemed prescient. The number of democratic countries clicked steadily upward, as did the world's Level of Freedom measure (a number based on political rights and civil liberties).[3] Very soon, he thought, shared principles of democracy across countries would hasten the end of global power politics—the League of Nations' dreams of world peace and prosperity would finally be realized a century later.

Fukuyama was wrong. Democratization plateaued in 2007, and by 2010, the number of countries switching to autocracies was surging.[4] Many of the democracies that remain today are under siege from within. Polarization is deepening and every compromise is portrayed as an act of betrayal.[5] Even Fukuyama has lost hope, fearing that "we could be facing the end of the 'end of history.'"[6] Democracy's recent decline is a result of rising levels of populism, misinformation, internal violence, and economic equality that, among other factors, is leading more people to support their country's authoritarian measures.[7] Most of these regimes follow nationalist agendas, cultivating an us versus them mentality among their constituencies to solidify positions of power. The "us" is often narrowly conceived—what a Russian or Mexican should or used to be—and steeped in the rhetoric of a popular sovereignty that gives short-shrift to civil liberties and minority groups that stand in the way of the will of the people.

The tilt to more authoritarian regimes with nationalist agendas is deeply troubling for those interested in improving global governance.[8] With its emphasis on sovereign nation-states as the only legitimate political actors in world affairs, the shift marks a return to a political climate more like when the United Nations was founded. As discussed earlier in this book, a state-orientated governance model was ill-equipped to deal with changing post-World War II political, economic, and social realities. Surging globalization over the last few decades has only widened the disconnect, stymieing the attempts of leaders to wall off their counties from unwanted flows of goods, ideas, and people.[9] Rather than exploring

DOI: 10.4324/9781003373322-5

76 *(Re)Building Consensus*

new possibilities of global governance as we linger at the fork in the road, many governments are increasingly doubling down on a system based on pursuing a nation's narrow interests that was not working before.[10] To solve tomorrow's difficult collective action problems, we need to find better ways to align interests and broker sustainable global solutions.

What is consensus and how is it reached? The dictionary that gets us perhaps closest to answering that question is Merriam-Webster's three-part definition that suggests consensus is (A) a "general agreement" that (B) is "arrived at by most of those concerned" in a (C) spirit of "group solidarity in sentiment and belief."[11] Consensus is thus an *iterative process* of coming to an agreement wherein voices are heard and compromises are made to come to a near unanimous decision.[12] For this process to translate into actions, the deliberating parties need to think of themselves as a group "in sentiment and belief" during and after their conversations. Consensus decision-making was the ideal aspired to for the League of Nations, a meeting of the minds that would act in the world's collective interest.[13] The League, however, failed to keep the peace, and a trip today to the United Nations General Assembly Hall may lead the visitor to question if consensus-seeking is a cover for doing nothing.[14] The interests of delegates tends to remain focused on the countries that they represent—What does Nigeria get from this decision?— and the institution often appears unable to act decisively as a collective body.[15]

One way of improving consensus building and collective action in global governance is to take lessons from past examples that worked. This book already alluded to how the Iroquois reached decisions inside the longhouse and how this decision-making structure was adapted to maintaining their broad confederacy.[16] Iroquois men, and then the women, deliberated for hours before a consensus was reached. The Jesuits and other seventeenth and early-eighteenth-century European observers who sat with them came to marvel at the Iroquois ability to consistently reach a general agreement on even the most difficult of topics.[17] By the end of the eighteenth century, however, conflict over land and rising prejudice led to the rejection of governance examples outside of those found in "civilized" Europe. The Iroquois, along with many other societies, were thus largely ignored when late-nineteenth-century and early-twentieth-century politicians and intellectuals laid down the foundations for today's global order.

This chapter looks at three examples of past consensus-building that resulted in collective action in the Uruk period temple complexes in Mesopotamia, the thing moots of Viking Scandinavia, and the early-twentieth-century exchange chains of interior New Guinea. To begin in Mesopotamia may seem an odd choice—the images of Babylonian and Persian kings astride their worlds seem the opposite of the long deliberations that took place in Iroquois longhouses. This iconography of royal actions hides a more complicated power dynamics,[18] but more importantly we are considering the fourth millennium BC that witnessed the first cities emerge from societies dedicated to relative egalitarianism, collective resources, and wealth redistribution. How these groups came together to build a city can provide insights into how we can better solve some of today's global issues.

The Temple Precincts of Uruk Mesopotamia

In 1943, Thorkild Jacobsen published an article titled "Primitive Democracy in Ancient Mesopotamia."[19] He argued that the monarchies attested to in the historical records were later developments in the region and that the region's first governments were instead organized around a council of elders and general assembly that comprised all standing members—he speculated that it might have been "all adult free men"—of the community.[20] Writing before the advent of radiocarbon dating, Jacobsen was a literary scholar probing the beginning of political institutions before most of the fifth and fourth millennium BC sites that pertained to this period of development had even been excavated. The earliest texts from the region had also not yet been translated, and most of his colleagues thought that Jacobsen was wrong. Mesopotamia, after all, was seen as the birthplace of the Oriental despot, the foils to the Classical democracies that are so integral to the origin stories of Western governance.[21]

Jacobsen built his argument on three points. First, he noted that judicial powers in Babylon and Assyria were "invested in the community as a whole, in an assembly open to all citizens."[22] Wide participation was expected, with the town long deliberating on matters of local importance. Second, Jacobsen argued that in the *Epic of Gilgamesh*, a poem of a legendary early king of Uruk, the ruler needed permission to act first from an assembly of the city's elders and then from an assembly of townsmen. They sat, talked, and rendered a decision. Finally, Jacobsen looked to the gods, suggesting that their decision-making might reflect past practices in Mesopotamia. The gods—and, in this case, goddesses were also included—would embrace and then sit down to eat and drink before "the meeting was ready to settle down to more serious affairs."[23] The decision-maker at most times was a group of 50 gods, but important issues were put in front of all to discuss.

Subsequent researchers have affirmed Jacobsen's assertion based on new literary evidence, adding more nuance as the corpus of translated early Mesopotamian writing expands.[24] Katz, for example, stresses that the general assembly and council of elders should be seen as occasionally conflicting political bodies,[25] while Bartash stresses that a quorum was necessary for the gods to deliberate and that the assembly of 50 gods was charged with elaborating on and implementing the decisions made by an assembly of all gods.[26] There are, of course, many details missing from these texts on how decisions were made, and vigorous debates over the details that do exist. We should also be hesitant to project the literary evidence back almost 1,000 years to when cities like Uruk were first coming into being. These stories nonetheless clearly show that a decision-making process by consensus that involved prolonged discussion within two assemblies was on the minds of later Mesopotamians.

Moreover, archaeological and epigraphic evidence from the fourth millennium BC suggest that democratic institutions likely guided the first centuries of urban life in southern Mesopotamia. After 5000 BC, a drying of the Tigris and

78 *(Re)Building Consensus*

Euphrates deltas allowed for more permanent settlement in the region.[27] The Near Eastern groups that came into the deltas were likely semi-mobile.[28] Families came together at temporary aggregation sites where they lived in spatially discrete clusters—likely "to underscore aspects of descent, lineage, and the family collective" that organized life[29]—and used a shared storage system that was often monitored via a system of seals.[30] Early fourth millennium groups in Mesopotamia were also "strongly egalitarian," using feasts, burials, and other collective events to redistribute wealth and to keep status differences in check.[31] The increasing size and permanence of some sites, however, would challenge the status quo.

Composed of two 15–20 hectare architectural clusters, Uruk was perhaps southern Mesopotamia's largest settlement by the mid-fourth millennium.[32] People likely lived in tripartite buildings composed of a large central room flanked by smaller rooms on each side.[33] Uruk's two clusters were organized around shrines that grew dramatically in size until they became the twin focal points of the city.[34] We know much more about the eastern Eanna Precinct, a walled-off area featuring temples that were grander scale versions of the era's tripartite houses.[35] The precinct expanded the idea of the household to encapsulate the city and surrounding villages, with people periodically filing into the complex for events from the surrounding region.[36] These visitors provided goods and labor to support Eanna and, while there, were feted with food and drink made on the premises.[37] Iconography in Uruk (and elsewhere) changed to support a more corporate, rather than lineage-based, identity,[38] and the settlement grew to 250 hectares by the end of the fourth millennium BC. As many as 50,000 people lived in the city.[39]

The world's first writing comes from the Eanna Precinct (Figure 5.1).[40] For our purposes, the most important examples of this writing are the "Standard Professions Lists" found at Uruk and other early Mesopotamian cities.[41] "Conscious attempts" to structure a temple complex's affairs,[42] the list gave specific roles to people while working for the temple who likely spent much of the year doing a wide variety of tasks within their own households.[43] There were dozens of occupations listed, such as bakers, potters, jewelers, and cooks, as well as a group of higher offices linked to participation in an assembly and charged with organizing the precinct's affairs.[44] Individuals were clearly ranked, with most people simply seen as general laborers.[45] Everyone nonetheless took rations and were consistently portrayed as being in service to their gods.[46] The supra-household hierarchy that emerged within the precincts, as well as the considerable wealth generated there, was hived off from the more household- and neighborhood-orientated decision-making that guided daily life.[47]

Combining the literary, archaeological, and epigraphic evidence provides a tentative picture of consensus building during the first centuries at Uruk and other southern Mesopotamian cities during the late fourth millennium BC. Emphasis was placed on coming together in a special place, where everyone worked toward achieving a common goal that was celebrated in that place's art and architecture. They also ate and drank together, were given roles in a collective project, and accepted rations for their work in that project. The details of deliberations remain unknown—a general and administrative assemble seems likely with the former meeting periodically and the other convening more regularly—but what is clear

Figure 5.1 A tablet from southern Mesopotamia, circa 3000 BC, that records a possible ration distribution of barley and emmer wheat from a temple precinct

from our Uruk example is that their government-by-assembly worked by aligning interests and efforts long before discussions took place. Those who came to the Eanna Precinct were already invested in making their collective work, as were the Vikings of Scandinavia.

The Things of Viking Scandinavia

For more than 300 years, a 43-cm-diameter iron ring hung on a door in a church in Sweden.[48] The ring's almost 250 runes were long assumed to date to Christianity's adoption in the region during the eleventh century that ended the Viking Age (~700–1100 AD). A re-translation of the runes in the 1970s, however, demonstrated that it dated to some 300 years earlier. The object was a Norse oath ring, likely from the nearby assembly site of Hälsinger, that reminded participants to respect the common laws and customs that were associated with the periodic gatherings at the location.[49] In repurposing the ring, the church had coopted the sacred associations of the long-standing site to insert a new religion into the core of Viking political and jural decision-making.[50] For the Christian faithful, civilization had finally come to Europe's last redoubt of paganism.

80 (Re)Building Consensus

The ritually charged assembly sites of Scandinavia were known as *things*. Typically, they were prominent places on the landscape that were on common land and along well-traveled transportation corridors.[51] A thing site could be re-visited for centuries, standing dormant until "activated" as the physical manifestation of shared Viking laws and traditions to guide the deliberations of those who gathered.[52] Although Scandinavians still regularly traveled to things in the first centuries of the second millennium, Christianity reshaped critical aspects of the assembly, as did the strengthening monarchies that supplanted much of the thing's legislative authority. The era's rich corpus of written records is nonetheless a critical resource since earlier Old Norse rune inscriptions like those on the Hälsinger oath ring are rare.[53] Combining these later written sources with archaeological data and evidence from Nordic verse can provide a rich understanding of the changing role played by things in Viking governance.[54] We thus know how Vikings built consensus, even between groups that, at the moment, hated each other.

Thing-like assemblies were used by Germanic groups by at least the first century AD, and then likely imported into Scandinavia by the mid-first millennium AD to resolve conflicts between groups.[55] By the twelfth century, there were hundreds of Viking thing sites.[56] Most of these were local places of assembly to deal with within-group concerns. Higher-level assemblies adjudicated issues that could not be resolved locally or that involved a larger group of people. The highest-level things might be used only once in a generation, with people traveling for days to gather. There were two types of meetings: the *althings* where all eligible individuals were expected to attend and representative assemblies that, though potentially witnessed by all, brought together only a subset of community leaders (Figure 5.2).[57] The democratic nature of the thing should not be overstated.

Figure 5.2 A detail from *Althing in session* by William Gersham Collingwood that was painted around 1897 after his visit to Iceland as part of his fascination with the Viking sagas

The public that could attend was a minority of the population—often it was free men with property holdings—and only a smaller elite group regularly spoke.[58] Yet there was an emphasis on public deliberations in Viking governance with decisions made with the broad agreement of both participants and spectators.

Peace was assured for those traveling to a thing, and travelers were sometimes reimbursed for the expenses incurred during their journey. Since a thing site could be revisited for centuries, the spaces were filled with memories. Signs of past events were readily visible—the fire pits from past feasts or a runestone commemorating an earlier agreement—and often the sites were located near burial mounds and other reminders of one's ancestors.[59] They were sacred nodes on the landscape, routinely featuring regularly refurbished processional routes and markers that guided how they were best approached.[60] Attendees set up camp in prescribed locations or, more rarely, in buildings that were left vacant for much of the year.[61] Benches were sometimes put into place before an assembly, as well as poles and rope to divide the area of deliberation from that of spectators.[62] Attendees feasted, played sports, and traded.[63] Before the onset of Christianity, sacrifices were also made to entice the gods to these events. The gods' thing was perhaps the most important location within their home of Asgard, and they sat with the mortals as they deliberated at the things on earth.[64]

Unlike at Uruk, we have a sense of how assemblies unfolded at Viking thing sites. The law was the people, in the sense that the traditions that guided behavior were seen as constituting the ethnic identity of the group that came together at a local thing.[65] They were thus prescribed ways of speaking, with those on both sides of an argument—we know much more about how judicial cases unfolded— expected to present their cases with reference to the gods, ancestors, the law, and traditions to support their positions. There appears to have been a quorum of participation for a thing to be valid, as well as high vote thresholds to make decisions binding. In the earliest written Norwegian laws, for example, local things required all participants to agree on the decision of the assembly, while the regional things required three-quarter agreement.[66] Spectators could not join in the discussion of participants but were supposed to shout their dissent or support during deliberations. The decisions made by the assembly were expected to be honored, and those in attendance were expected to serve as witnesses.

Thing sites were initially designed to reinforce a more egalitarian collective. Sites like Bjarkøy in Norway, for example, had a tight arrangement of equal-sized sod houses that encircled the open space used for assemblies.[67] The material remains at Bjarkøy and other early thing sites also reflect few status differences, and the architectural arrangement meant that people in conflict would need to live next to other for the couple of weeks that a thing was in session.[68] The egalitarian ethos of the spaces continued even as status differences widened in Viking society over time—individuals might return each year at Midsummer to the same hearth at a thing that had been used by their family for generations. This stability stood in contrast to the "fragmented, fluid, and constantly contested" political environment of Viking leaders vying for power.[69] Many moved between halls in their territory, attempting to attract and retain followers through their generosity

82   *(Re)Building Consensus*

and prowess in warfare. Leaders also routinely participated in things, where time and time again they would stress their right to rule within an institution originally structured to sustain egalitarian relationships.[70]

The thing moots of Viking Scandinavia maintained order during a time when violence always seemed on the verge of spiraling out of control. Things were effective in consensus-building, in part, because of their framing of deliberations. There was an entrenched rhythm to assemblies that shaped society—moments when important members of communities put down their arms and, for days, moved along prescribed corridors to a sacred center.[71] Together, they rebuilt the thing for each event. They also ate, drank, told stories, and made sacrifices, "activating" the site so that the living, dead, and the gods could gather. These actions reminded attendees of their shared identity and primed them to think of the collective good when making their deliberations. Their focus when they began the assembly was therefore already on reaching decisions that were both acceptable to as many participants and spectators as possible and in keeping with Norse laws and tradition. This framing continued after an assembly, with agreements etched in stone and iron. A similar commitment to consensus-building was encountered by Australian gold miners when they ventured into the highlands of New Guinea in the 1930s.

The Exchange Chains of Early-Twentieth-Century Highland New Guinea

In 1926, news of a gold strike in Edie Creek began a rush to the interior of New Guinea.[72] Prospectors moved deeper into the highlands in the 1930s, a region marked as unexplored on maps and colored by the fantasies and nightmares of Western authors.[73] These men, and a few women, climbed into a region of startling cultural diversity—a medley of hunter-gatherers, horticulturalists, and intensive agriculturalists who spoke hundreds of languages. Some were curious about these groups,[74] especially the anthropologists that soon followed.[75] The indigenous population of New Guinea was nonetheless seen as a "stone age" people, a window into past lifeways that was of little practical utility to those seeking to improve contemporary politics.[76] Yet vast networks of collective action had developed in parts of this region through exchange chains, linking together previously isolated and hostile groups without the benefit of a centralized authority.

New Guinea polities were kin-related and small, often numbering in the low hundreds. Men and women tended to live separately, with politics seen as a male affair dominated by "Big Men" who competing for prestige and supporters.[77] Big Men sought status largely through prowess in warfare and resource exchanges. War was therefore endemic throughout much of New Guinea in the early twentieth century,[78] and a leader who could coordinate defense within and between villages was highly valued.[79] Resource exchanges, through mortuary feasts, bride-wealth payments, and other events that drew together groups,[80] occurred in parallel to warfare and were another means for a Big Men and his supporters to display "in concrete form their otherwise invisible individual and collective power."[81]

Although some were despots who ruled by force, most Big Men attained their position through relationship-building both within their community and with other Big Men who alternated between being enemies or allies. Much of a Big Man's time was spent visiting with other to build trust and reach consensus on political actions.[82]

Of particular interest to us are two wide-ranging exchange systems, the *moka* and *tee* cycles used by Enga, Melpa, and Gawigl speakers of the western highlands.[83] At the time of European contact, the region was densely settled by farmers who subsisted off sweet potatoes and bred pigs for consumption and exchange.[84] Evidence from archaeology, oral history, and plant genetics suggest that sweet potatoes were introduced into the region a few centuries ago, leading to population pressure and conflict over arable land.[85] The moka and tee cycles were the culmination of efforts to channel the ensuing warfare between groups into a system of competitive, albeit often friendly, exchanges that emphasized mutual benefit over parochial concerns. Violence did not disappear, but it was substantially curbed as Big Men focused their energies on building financial chains that brought shell, tree oil, axes, salt-packs, birds, and, especially, pigs into their communities.

Both the moka and tee cycles worked through the same principle of presenting a main gift that is worth more than the one received as an initiatory gift.[86] To not lose prestige, a gift had to be returned—Strathern calls the back and forth between gift-givers "alternating disequilibrium"[87]—setting up a closely watched cycle of exchanges between partners that can foster peace or incite war. Gift-giving was, and remains, an important means of maintaining relationships between individuals in the Western highlands of New Guinea, and Wiessner and Tumu's oral history project among the Enga suggests that the moka and tee cycles likely began with each household finding its own exchange partners. Conflicts ensued between their efforts, however, and most men had little time and ability to make wide-ranging connections. Big Men therefore stepped in, refining the exchanges so that they were headlined by a few major events dominated by a handful of well-connected players. Smaller events, nonetheless, continued, banking gifts that eventually made their way into the moka and tee cycles. Live pigs became the most highly regarded gift in these cycles. They would be attached to stakes on the ground for presentation (Figure 5.3), their histories of ownership underlining the wide exchange networks that linked communities.

The differences between the moka and tee cycles were considerable—tee exchanges could be an order of magnitude larger in terms of the number of pigs exchanged, they involved more people coming from further away, and the tee's position of Great Kamongo who coordinated the cycle was becoming hereditary.[88] Yet for our purposes, they both can be seen as large public festivals that brought together families for a few days of eating, singing, and dancing. Communities maintained the spaces used for these gatherings; they stockpiled mounds of sweet potatoes to feed attendees, and cared for the pigs that would be led away from the event. Although only a few Big Men might be making exchanges at a moka or tee event, thousands of people were therefore often involved in its preparation.[89] Consensus was needed to make an event happen, and consensus was needed as an

84 *(Re)Building Consensus*

Figure 5.3 Men considering stakes in the ground for pigs before a moka event in the Hagen area of New Guinea. Note the neck ornament, *omak*, that some wear to mark their generosity at past mokas

event unfolded. Since a Big Man's status was based on his ability to bring prestige to others, he was in constant motion maintaining relationships across a vast and varied social network.

The exchange chains that fed the moka and tee cycles were sustained not just by the Big Men's efforts. Circulating cults were also integral to making connections between groups.[90] The Kepele ancestral cult, for example, was popular among Enga speakers.[91] The cornerstone of the cult was a five-day festival that celebrated the equality of all men. Everyone brought one, and only one, pig to the festival. They ate these pigs together amid ceremonies where the youth were initiated, and the ancestors honored. Kepele ritual experts also circulated at other times of the year, and relatives and friends routinely traveled to smaller Kepele events in the cycle. The result was an "atmosphere of cooperation and trust" among the more that 50 Enga polities that participating in the Kepele cult.[92] The participation of men and women in circulating cults like the Kepele bridged divides between communities making the moka and tee cycles possible by both cementing a broader cultural identity and ameliorating the social tensions associated with widening social distances. Of course, the cults also required continued consensus-building to function.

The most famous movie on western New Guinea highland polities, *Ongka's Big Moka*, ends in failure.[93] Ongka is a Big Man who spends a decade convincing others to contribute to a moka. Not enough people come forward with gifts and there are accusations of sorcery. He is forced to postpone—yet again—as the cameras stop rolling. In an atomized and violent region, groups found peace and prosperity centuries before European contact by cultivating a system of competitive generosity. The system worked by channeling the ambitions of leaders away from warfare into widening exchange networks, while at the same time creating an ethos that valued the contributions of every household. Although Big Men were first among equals, they could only achieve and sustain that status by continually demonstrating their value to the collective. Consensus was made possible by exchange systems that dispersed wealth and prestige widely, as well as by circulating cults that narrowed the social distance between and within groups. It was also made possible by a cultural fixation on persuasion. Ongka eventually got his moka, dispersing 600 pigs, 12 cassowaries, 8 cows, 10,000 Australian dollars, a truck, and a motorbike. In his speech, he declared that "I have knocked you down by giving so much."[94] He and his community had won by giving away their wealth, and now his rivals would attempt to do the same.

Achieving Consensus *and* Collective Action

The United Nations has 163 rules for deliberations within the General Assembly.[95] These rules provide a procedural floor—the bare minimum required for the organization to function—while the delegates strive to reach near unanimous decisions through a process of consensus building that involves formal and informal negotiations.[96] Through time, the UN has gotten better at consensus building. To take just one recent example, the Global Compact on Refugees was endorsed in 2018 by the General Assembly by a vote of 181 in favor, two against, and three abstentions. The compact, "a blueprint for governments, international organizations, and other stakeholders to ensure that host communities get the support they need and that refugees can lead productive lives,"[97] was the result of two years of intense negotiations.[98] In terms of creating a vision statement that countries could rally around, it was a great achievement for the United Nations.

Yet the Global Compact on Refugees is also a reflection of the recent failures of the UN. The compact is a non-binding agreement, a statement on what the world *ought* to be doing. One of the two nations that voted against the agreement was the United States, the UN's host country and its largest funder. On the eve of the vote, the United States issued a statement that, in bold letters, laid down the nation's rationale for opposing the compact:[99]

> **We** [the United States] **believe the Compact and the process that led to its adoption, including the New York Declaration, represent an effort by the United Nations to advance global governance at the expense of the sovereign right of States to manage their immigration systems in accordance with their national laws, policies, and interests.**

86 (Re)Building Consensus

Nationalism trumped global governance in the calculus of the United States. Many of the other delegates who voted for the Compact because of its spirit also shared the U.S. concerns on infringement—the primary reason why the compact was a compact, rather than a binding treaty, was because so many nations expressed sovereignty concerns.[100]

The UN has created an immigration blueprint that few are likely to follow. The Compact is illustrative of the broader trend today toward political paralysis and inaction in global governance.[101] Even when almost everyone agrees on what the world should do, nations, as well as corporations and individuals, go their own way. Far too frequently, consensus building does not lead to collective action because of self-interest. The case studies in this chapter provide us with examples of consensus-building that put the collective above the individual. They demonstrate that collective action is far easier when there is a strong sense of belonging to a broader group. Everyone entering the Eanna Precinct was there in service to the goddess, the laws discussed at thing moots made the people, and the exchange cycles of highland New Guinea were premised on the idea of ensuring peace and prestige for all who participated. Family, kin, and other kinds of identities were not erased during these interactions, but there was a palpable sense of togetherness created that is largely missing today in the United Nations and other international organizations.

What is striking about all three case studies is the substantial work that went into forming a collective identity long before any deliberations occurred. For Uruk, people took on new jobs for the precinct, laboring together in their shared faith. The Vikings traveled for days along sacred pathways before reconstructing a thing site side by side. The Enga, Melpa, and Gawigl were constantly working to sustain the Moka and Tee cycles, feeding pigs and collecting valuables for years that would eventually be given to others. The assemblies in the case studies then began with days of feasting, songs, and dancing often explicitly celebrating the shared identity that linked participants. They drank, flirted, and laughed in locations designed to minimize social distance. By the time people finally sat down to deliberate, they were primed to accept some personal sacrifices to improve the overall group's well-being.

The Hälsinger oath ring is illustrative of the public commitment to politics in our case studies. There was public commitment to consensus-building in the sense that a large swath of the population participated in decision-making events. They might not have had a voice in the assembly, but they brewed the beer for the temple precinct, staked a pig at a Tee ceremony, or, shouting, bore witness behind the rope. Many would have heard the professed oath of a leader, and many more would be dedicated to the assembly's success because of their intensive personal investment in associated events. There was also public commitment, in a second sense, to decision implementation. Pledged resources were subsequently given in the temple precinct and inscribed into the record; a king confirmed might be enthroned at the next thing with allegiance given; the gifts taken away from a moka made clear that a previous challenge to generosity had been answered.

(Re)Building Consensus 87

Public consensus led to action in closed loops that were baked into how proceedings unfolded. What was said was done, or a leader was replaced.

Our case studies confirm what all of us have experienced regularly: reaching a consensus is not always enough to ensure collective action. The challenges discussed in Chapter 1—a lack of trust, the free rider problem, expectations for equality, impermanence, unclear resource rights—often make it difficult to implement decisions, especially when people see themselves primarily as members of competing groups. A way to foster collective action is to create a shared identity that is forged not just through slogans but through shared experiences. There is considerable societal work that needs to be done before, during, and after deliberation that cannot be hived off and given to a small group of dedicated delegates and aid workers. Books like Fukuyama's *The End of History* comforted us with the idea that global governance would soon be easy.[102] His predictions did not come to pass because so few of us have invested our personal time, labor, and resources in global politics. How can so many get involved in such deliberations? One answer to this question is through a greater commitment to leadership from below.

Notes

1 See Francis Fukuyama (1992) *The End of History and the Last Man* (Free Press: New York).
2 This quote comes from the article that appeared before his 1992 book, Francis Fukuyama (1989) The End of History? *The National Interest* 16: 3–18, p. 3.
3 See Larry Diamond (2015) Facing Up to the Democratic Recession. *Journal of Democracy* 26(1): 141–155.
4 See Vanessa A. Boese, Staffan I. Lindberg, and Anna Lührmann (2021) Waves of Autocratization and Democratization: A Rejoinder. *Democratization* 28(6): 1202–1210.
5 See Thomas Carothers and Andrew O'Donohue, eds. (2019) *Democracies Divided: the Global Challenge of Political Polarization* (Washington, DC: The Brookings Institution); Steven Levitsky and Daniel Ziblatt (2019) *How Democracies Die* (New York: Broadway Books); and Gary Saul Morson and Morton Schapiro (2023) *Minds Wide Shut: How the New Fundamentalisms Divide Us* (Princeton: Princeton University Press).
6 See Meghan Gibson (2022) Francis Fukuyama: We Could Be Facing the End of the "the End of History". *The New Statesman*, March 30th Edition https://www.newstatesman.com/encounter/2022/03/francis-fukuyama-on-the-end-of-the-end-of-history, accessed on February 6, 2023.
7 See David Waldner and Ellen Lust (2018) Unwelcome Change: Coming to Terms with Democratic Backsliding. *Annual Review of Political Science* 21: 93–113; and Stephan Haggard and Robert R. Kaufman (2021) *Backsliding: Democratic Regress in the Contemporary World* (Cambridge: Cambridge University Press).
8 For example, see Eugencia C. Heldt and Henning Schmidtke (2019) Global Democracy in Decline?: How Rising Authoritarianism Limits Democratic Control over International Institutions. *Global Governance* 25(2): 231–254 and Jose Luis de Sales Marques, Thomas Meyer, and Mario Telò (2019) *Cultures, Nationalism and Populism New Challenges to Multilateralism* (Milton: Routledge).
9 See James H. Mittelman (2011) *Contesting Global Order: Development, Global Governance, and Globalization* (London: Routledge).
10 See Rifki Dermawan (2020). The National Interest Concept in a Globalised International System. *Indonesian Journal of International Relations* 3(2): 30–45.

88 (Re)Building Consensus

11 See the definition of consensus here: www.merriam-webster.com/dictionary/consensus, accessed on May 27, 2022. Other definitions give less emphasis on the consensus building process.

12 See Lawrence Susskind, Sarah McKearnan, and Jennifer Thomas-Larmer (1999) *The Consensus Building Handbook: A Comprehensive Guide to Reaching Agreement* (Thousand Oaks: Sage).

13 See Chapter 2.

14 For example, see Claudia Liuzza (2021) The Making and UN-Making of Consensus: Institutional Inertia in the UNESCO World Heritage Committee. *International Journal of Cultural Property* 28(2): 261–284.

15 For a discussion of the factionalism in the United Nations, see Joachim Müller (2006) *Reforming the United Nations: The Struggle for Legitimacy and Effectiveness* (Leiden: M. Nijhoff Publishers); and Enrico Bertacchini, Claudia Liuzza, Lynn Meskell, and Donatella Saccone (2016) The Politicization of UNESCO World Heritage Decision Making. *Public Choice* 167(1–2): 95–129.

16 See Chapters 1 and 3.

17 See Allan Greer, ed. (2019) *The Jesuit Relations: Natives and Missionaries in Seventeenth-Century North America.* Second edition (Boston: Bedford/St. Martin's).

18 For example, see Lori Khatchadourian (2016) *Imperial Matter: Ancient Persia and the Archaeology of Empires* (Oakland: University of California Press).

19 See Thorkild Jacobsen (1943) Primitive Democracy in Ancient Mesopotamia. *Journal of Near Eastern Studies* 2(3): 159–172.

20 See Jacobsen (1943), p. 172.

21 See Edward Said (1978) *Orientalism* (New York: Pantheon).

22 See Jacobsen (1943), p. 165.

23 See Jacobsen (1943), p. 167.

24 For a summary of scholarly approaches to literary sources on early Mesopotamian governance, see Ronald T. Ridley (2000) The Saga of an Epic: Gilgamesh and the Constitution of Uruk. *Orientalia* 69(4): 341–367.

25 See Dina Katz (1987) Gilgamesh and Akka: Was Uruk Ruled by Two Assemblies? *Revue D'assyriologie et D'archéologie Orientale* 81(2): 105–114.

26 See Vitali Bartash (2010) Puhru: Assembly as a Political Institution in "Enuma Elish". In *Babel und Bibel 4. Proceedings of the 53e Rencontre Assyriologique Internationale*, edited by Leonid Kogan, pp. 1083–1109 (Winona Lake: Eisenbrauns).

27 See Douglas J. Kennett and James P. Kennett (2006) Early State Formation in Southern Mesopotamia: Sea Levels, Shorelines, and Climate Change. *Journal of Island and Costal Archaeology* 1: 67–99.

28 See Reinhard Bernbeck (2008) An Archaeology of Multisited Communities. In *The Archaeology of Mobility: Old World and New World Nomadism*, edited by Willeke Wendrich and Hans Barnard, pp. 43–71 (Los Angeles: Cotsen Institute of Archaeology at UCLA); Petr Charvát (2002) *Mesopotamia before History* (London: Routledge), and Susan Pollock (1999) *Ancient Mesopotamia: The Eden That Never Was* (New York: Cambridge University Press).

29 See Peter M. M. G. Akkermans (2013) Living Space, Temporality, and Community Segmentation: Interpreting Late Neolithic Settlement in Northern Syria. In *Interpreting the Late Neolithic of Upper Mesopotamia*, edited by O. P. Nieuwenhuyse, R. Bernbeck, P. M. M. G. Akkermans, and J. Rogasch, pp. 63–75 (Turnhout: Brepols), p. 69.

30 See Kim Duistermaat (2013) Private Matters: The Emergence of Sealing Practices in Neolithic Syria. In *Interpreting the Late Neolithic of Upper Mesopotamia*, edited by O. P. Nieuwenhuyse, R. Bernbeck, P. M. M. G. Akkermans, and J. Rogasch, pp. 315–322 (Turnhout: Brepols); Marcella Frangipane (2007) Different Types of Egalitarian Societies and the Development of Inequality in Early Mesopotamia. *World Archaeology* 39(2): 151–176, and Phillip J. Graham and Alexia Smith (2013) A Day in the Life of an Ubaid Household: Archaeobotanical Investigations at Kenan Tepe, South-Eastern Turkey. *Antiquity* 87: 405–417.

(Re)Building Consensus 89

31 See Frangipane (2007), p. 157, also see Reinhard Bernbeck (2013) Multisited and Modular Sites in the Halaf Tradition. In *Interpreting the Late Neolithic of Upper Mesopotamia*, edited by O.P. Nieuwenhuyse, R. Bernbeck, P. M. M. G. Akkermans, and J. Rogasch, pp. 51–62 (Turnhout: Brepols).

32 See Finkbeiner, Uwe (1991) *Uruk: Kampagne 35–37, 1982–1984. Die archäologishe Oberflächenuntersuchung* (Survey). (Baghdad: Deutches Archäologisches Institut Abteilung Baghdad).

33 For what settlements looked like just before urbanization in lower Mesopotamia, see Michael Roaf (1984) Tell Madhhur: A Summary Report on the Excavation. *Sumer* 43: 108–167.

34 See Hans J. Nissen (1988) *The Early History of the Ancient Near East 9000–2000 BC* (Chicago: University of Chicago Press); J. N. Postgate (1994) *Early Mesopotamia: Society and Economy at the Dawn of History* (New York: Routledge); and Krystyna Szarzńska (2011) Observations on the Temple Precinct EŠ$_3$ in Archaic Uruk. *Journal of Cuneiform Studies* 63: 1–4.

35 See Peter M. M. G. Akkermans (1989) Tradition and Social Change in Northern Mesopotamia during the Later Fifth and Fourth Millennium B. C. In *Upon This Foundation: The 'Ubaid Reconsidered*, edited by Elizabeth F. Henrickson and Ingolf Thussen, pp. 339–367 (Copenhagen: Museum Tusculanum Press); Postgate (1994); and Hans J. Nissen (2015) Urbanization and the Techniques of Communication: The Mesopotamian City of Uruk during the Fourth Millennium BCE, In *The Cambridge World History. Volume 3, Early Cities in Comparative Perspective, 4000 BCE-1200 CE*, edited by Norman Yoffee, pp. 113–130 (Cambridge: Cambridge University Press).

36 See Hans J. Nissen (2001) Cultural and Political Networks in the Ancient Near East during the Fourth and Fifth Millennium. In *Uruk Mesopotamia and Its Neighbors: Cross-Cultural Interactions in the Era of State Formation*, edited by Mitchell S. Rothman, pp. 149–179 (Santa Fe: School of American Research Press); and Jason Ur (2014) Households and the Emergence of Cities in Ancient Mesopotamia. *Cambridge Archaeological Journal* 24(2): 249–268.

37 See Jill Goulder (2010) Administrators' Bread: An Experiment-Based Re-Assessment of the Functional and Cultural Role of the Uruk Bevel-Rim Bowl. *Antiquity* 84: 351–362; Susan Pollock (2003) Feasts, Funerals, and Fast Food in Early Mesopotamian States. In *The Archaeology and Politics of Food and Feasting in Early States and Empires*, edited by Tamara L. Bray, pp. 17–38 (New York: Kluwer Academic/Plenum); Nissen (2001); and Denise Schmandt-Bessarat (2001) Feasting in the Ancient Near East. In *Feasts: Archaeological and Ethnographic Perspectives on Food, Politics, and Power*, edited by Michael Dietler and Brian Hayden, pp. 391–403 (Washington, DC: Smithsonian Institution Press).

38 See Holly Pittman (1994) Towards and Understanding of the Role of Glyptic Imagery in the Administrative Systems of Proto-Literate Greater Mesopotamia. In *Archives Before Writing: Proceedings of the International Colloquium Oriolo Romano, October 23–25, 1991*, edited by Piera Ferioli, Enrica Fiandra, Gian Giacomo Fissore, and Marcella Frangipane, pp. 177–203 (Torino: Scriptorium).

39 See Finkbeiner (1991).

40 See Hans J. Nissen, Peter Damerow, and Robert K. Englund (1995) *Archaic Bookkeeping: Early Writing and Techniques of Economic Administration in the Ancient Near East* (Chicago: University of Chicago Press).

41 See Hans J. Nissen (1986) The Archaic Texts from Uruk. *World Archaeology* 17(3): 317–334.

42 See Norman Yoffee (2005) *Myths of the Archaic State: Evolution of the Earliest Cities, States, and Civilization*, p. 34 (New York: Cambridge University Press).

43 See Ur (2014).

44 See Nissen (1986).

45 See Vitali Bartash (2018) Age, Gender, and Labour: Recording Human Resources in 3350–2500 BC Mesopotamia. In *What's in a Name?: Terminology Related to the Work*

90 *(Re)Building Consensus*

Force and Job Categories in the Ancient Near East, edited by Agnès Garcia-Ventura, pp. 45–80 (Münster: Urgarit-Verlag).

46 See Camille Lecompte (2018) The Archaic Lists of Professions and Their Relevance for the Late Uruk Period: Observations on Some Officials in Their Administrative Context. In *What's in a Name?: Terminology Related to the Work Force and Job Categories in the Ancient Near East*, edited by Agnès Garcia-Ventura, pp. 81–132 (Münster: Urgarit-Verlag).

47 See Yoffee (2005), and Norman Yoffee (2016) The Power of Infrastructures: A Counternarrative and a Speculation. *Journal of Archaeological Method and Theory* 23: 1053–1065. For a discussion of how efforts to encapsulate Mesopotamian hierarchies failed, see Justin Jennings (2021) *Finding Fairness: From Pleistocene Foragers to Contemporary Capitalists* (Gainseville: Univerity Press of Florida).

48 For more on the Forsa Ring, see Marianne Hem Eriksen (2015) The Powerful Ring: Door Rings, Oath Rings, and the Sacred Place. In *Viking Worlds: Things, Spaces, and Movement*, edited by Marianne Hem Eriksen, Unn Pedersen, Bernt Rundberger Irmelin Axelsen, and Heidi Lund Berg, pp. 73–87 (Oxford: Oxbow Books).

49 For a translation of the Forsa Ring runes, see Stefan Brink (2002) Law and Legal Custom in Viking Age Scandinavia. In *Ordning mot Kaos: Studier av Nordisk Forkristen Kosmolgi*, edited by Andrén Anders, Kristina Jennbert, and Catharina Raudvere, pp. 291–316 (Lund: Nordic Academic Press), p. 98. For the general meaning of the runes, I rely on Nanouschka Myrberg (2008) Room for All? Spaces and Places for Thing Assemblies: The Case of the All-thing on Gotland, Sweden. *Viking and Medieval Scandinavia* 4: 133–157.

50 For an example of the overlap between thing sites and churches, see Marie Ødegaard (2018) Thing Sites, Cult, Churches, Games and Markets in Viking and Medieval Southeastern Norway, c. 800–1600. *World Archaeology* 50(1): 150–164.

51 See Alexandra Sarmack (2017) *Viking Law and Order: Places and Rituals of Assembly in the Medieval North* (Edinburgh: Edinburgh University Press).

52 See Myrberg (2008), p. 152. Note that *thing*, or *ping*, is a term that referred both to a place and an assembly of people.

53 For example, see Terje Spurkland (2005). *Norwegian Runes and Runic Inscriptions*. Woodbridge (Suffolk: Boydell Press). Most runes were found on stones that commemorated significant events.

54 See Peter G. Foote (1984) Things in Early Norse Verse. In *Festskrivt til Ludvig Holm-Olsen pd hans 70-Drsdag den 9, Juni 1984*, pp. 74–83 (Øvre Ervik: Alvheim and Eide); Marianne Hem Eriksen, ed. (2015) *Viking Worlds: Things, Spaces and Movement* (Oxford: Oxbow Books); and Sarmack (2017).

55 See Frode Iversen (2013) Concilium and Pagus: Revisiting the Early Germanic Thing System of Northern Europe. *Journal of the North Atlantic* Special Issue 5: 5–17.

56 See Sarah Semple, Alexandra Sanmark, Frode Iversen, Natascha Mehler, Halldis Hobæk, Marie Ødegaard, and Alexis Tudor Skinner (2021). *Negotiating the North: Meeting-Places in the Middle Ages in the North Sea Zone* (London: Routledge).

57 See Peter G. Foote and David M. Wilson (1970) *The Viking Achievement: The Society and Culture of Early Medieval Scandinavia* (London: Sidgwick and Jackson).

58 See Andrew Dennis, Peter Foote, Richard Perkins, and Richard Perkins (1980) *Laws of Early Iceland: Grágás, the Codex Regius of Grágás, With Material from Other Manuscripts* (Winnipeg: University of Manitoba Press).

59 Anundshög is an example of a thing site that incorporated 1,000 years of activity that included a tumulus, ship burials, henges, and a rune stone. See Alexandra Sanmark and Sarah Semple (2010) "Something Old, Something New": The Topography of Assembly in Europe with Reference to Recent Field Results in Sweden. In *Perspectives in Landscape Archaeology: Papers Presented at Oxford 2003–2005*, edited by Helen Lewis and Sarah J. Semple, pp. 107–119. Bar International Series (Oxford: Archaeopress); and Sarah Semple, Alexandra Sanmark, Frode Iversen, Natascha Mehler,

Halldis Hobæk, Marie Ødegaard, and Alexis Tudor Skinner (2021). *Negotiating the North: Meeting-Places in the Middle Ages in the North Sea Zone* (London: Routledge).

60 See Lotte Hedeager (2011) *Iron Age Myth and Materiality: An Archaeology of Scandinavia, AD 400–1000* (London : Routledge) and Sanmark (2017).

61 The most famous of the temporary camps are the houses made from sod in Iceland. Walls were left intact across generations with a new roof made for each thing moot. See Orri Vésteinsson (2013) What Is in a Booth? Material Symbolism at Icelandic Assembly Sites. *Journal of the North Atlantic* 5: 111–124. The courtyard sites in Western Norway are examples of thing sites that had permanent buildings. See Axle Bruen Olsen (2015) Courtyard Sites in Western Norway. Central Assembly Places and Judicial Institutions in the Late Iron Age. In *Viking Worlds: Things, Spaces, and Movement*, edited by Marianne Hem Eriksen, Unn Pedersen, Bernt Rundberger Irmelin Axelsen, and Heidi Lund Berg, pp. 43–55 (Oxford: Oxbow Books).

62 See Olof Sundqvist (2016) *An Arena for Higher Power: Ceremonial Buildings and Religious Strategies for Rulership in Late Iron Age Scandinavia* (Leiden: Brill).

63 See David Zori, Jesse Byock, Ergill Erlensson, Steve Martin, Thomas Wake, and Kevin J. Edwards (2013) Feasting in Viking Age Iceland: Sustaining a Chiefly Political Economy in a Marginal Environment. *Antiquity* 87(335): 150–165; and Sarmack (2017).

64 See Nanna Løkka (2013) Þing Goða —The Mythological Assembly Site. *Journal of the North Atlantic* Special Issue 5: 18–27.

65 For a general discussion of the link between ethnicity and law in Europe, see Robert Bartlett (1994) *The Making of Europe: Conquest, Consolidation, and Culture Change* (London: Penguin).

66 See L.M. Larson (1935) *The Earliest Norwegian Laws, Being the Gulathing Law and the Frostathing Law* (New York: Columbia University Press).

67 See Inger Storli (2010) Court Sites of Arctic Norway: Remains of Thing Sites and Representations of Political Consolidation Processes in the Northern Germanic World During the First Millennium Ad? *Norwegian Archaeological Review* 43(2): 128–144.

68 See Sarah Semple and Alexandra Sanmark (2013) Assembly in North West Europe: Collective Concerns for Early Societies?" *European Journal of Archaeology* 16(3): 518–542.

69 See Anders Winroth (2014) *The Age of the Vikings*, p. 133 (Princeton, NJ: Princeton University Press).

70 See the article and response for Trine Louise Borake (2019) Anarchistic Action. Social Organization and Dynamics in Southern Scandinavia from the Iron Age to the Middle Ages. *Archaeological Dialogues* 26(2): 61–73.

71 See Sanmark (2017) for a landscape approach to things.

72 For a history of early gold prospecting in New Guinea, see Hank Nelson (2016) *Black, White & Gold: Gold Mining in Papua New Guinea, 1878–1930* (Acton: Australian National University Press).

73 See Chris Ballard (2009) The Art of Encounter: Verisimilitude in the Imaginary Exploration of Interior New Guinea (1725–1876). In *Oceanic Encounters: Exchange, Desire, Violence*, edited by Margaret Jolly, Serge Tcherkézoff, and Darrell Tyron, pp. 221–257 (Canberra: Australian National University Press).

74 For an example of how a prospector saw Indigenous New Guinea, see Michael J. Leahy Michael J. and Douglas E. Jones. 1991. *Explorations into Highland New Guinea, 1930–1935* (Tuscaloosa: University of Alabama Press).

75 For the relationship between early ethnographers and administrators in New Guinea, see J. J. de Wolf and S. R. Jaarsma (1992) Colonial Ethnography: West new Guinea (1950–1962). *Bijdragen Tot de Taal-, Land- En Volkenkunde* 148(1): 103–124.

76 This idea of New Guinea as a relic of the past can be seen in how "Stone Age" was used by early writers. For example, see L. J. Brass (1941) Stone Age Agriculture in New Guinea. *Geographical Review* 31(4): 555–569 and Beatrice Blackwood (1939) Folk-Stories of a Stone Age People in New Guinea. *Folklore* 50(3): 209–242.

92 *(Re)Building Consensus*

77 See Marshall D. Sahlins (1963) Poor Man, Rich Man, Big-Man, Chief: Political Types in Melanesia and Polynesia. *Comparative Studies in Society and History* 5(3): 285–303.

78 See Pierre Lemonnier (1990) *Guerres et Festins: Paix, Échanges et Compétition dans les Highlands de Nouvelle-Guinée* (Paris: Éditions de la Maison des sciences de l'homme).

79 See Paul Roscoe (2008) Settlement Fortification in Village and 'Tribal' Society: Evidence from Contact-Era New Guinea. *Journal of Anthropological Archaeology* 27(4): 507–519.

80 For a general discussion of exchange relationships across highland New Guinea, see D.K. Feil (1987) *The Evolution of Highland Papua New Guinea Societies* (Cambridge: Cambridge University Press).

81 See Paul Roscoe (2017) The Emergence of Sociopolitical Complexity: Evidence from Contact-Era New Guinea. In *Feast, Famine or Fighting?*, edited by Richard J. Chacon and Rubén G. Mendoza, pp. 197–222 (Cham: Springer International Publishing), p. 198.

82 Although "Big Man" is a term widely applied by ethnographers (and by the groups themselves) in New Guinea, leadership positions vary greatly across the island. For an early discussion, see M. J. Meggitt (1967) The Pattern of Leadership among the Mae-Enga of New Guinea. *Anthropological Forum* 2(1): 20–35; and Cherry Lowman-Vayda (1968) Making Big Men. *Anthropological Forum* 2(2): 199–243. Paul Roscoe (2000) has more recently attempted to summarize the literature on leadership in New Guinea in: New Guinea Leadership as Ethnographic Analogy: A Critical Review. *Journal of Archaeological Method and Theory* 7(2): 79–126.

83 See Andrew Strathern (1971) *The Rope of Moka: Big-Men and Ceremonial Exchange in Mount Hagen, New Guinea* (Cambridge: University Press); D. K. Feil (1984) *Ways of Exchange: The Enga Tee of Papua New Guinea* (St. Lucia: University of Queensland Press); and Polly Wiessner and Akii Tumu (1998) *Historical Vines: Enga Networks of Exchange, Ritual, and Warfare in Papua New Guinea* (Washington, DC: Smithsonian Institution Press).

84 For a classic ethnography on this subsistence system in the highlands of western New Guinea, see Roy A. Rappaport (1984) *Pigs for the Ancestors*, second edition (New Haven: Yale University Press).

85 See James B. Watson (1965) The Significance of a Recent Ecological Change in the Central Highlands of New Guinea. *The Journal of the Polynesian Society* 74(4): 438–450; Jack Golson (1981) New Guinea Agricultural History: A Case Study. In *A Time to Plant and a Time to Uproot: A History of Agricultural in Papau New Guinea*, edited by D. Denoon and C. Snowden, pp. 55–64 (Boroko: Institute of Papau New Guinea); and C. Roullier, R. Kambouo, J. Paofa, D. McKey, and V. Lebot (2013) On the Origin of Sweet Potato (Ipomoea Batatas (L.) Lam.) Genetic Diversity in New Guinea, a Secondary Centre of Diversity. *Heredity* 110(6): 594–604.

86 For a discussion of gift-giving in New Guinea, see Rena Lederman (1986) *What Gifts Engender: Social Relations and Politics in Mendi, Highland Papua New Guinea* (Cambridge: Cambridge University Press).

87 See Strathern (1971), p. 11.

88 See Richard Feachem (1973) The Religious Belief and Ritual of the Raiapu Enga. *Oceania* 43(4): 259–285; Polly Wiessner (2009) The Power of One?: Big-Men Revisited. In *The Evolution of Leadership: Transitions in Decision-Making from Small Scale to Middle Range Societies*, edited by Kevin J. Vaughn, Jelmer W. Eerkens, and John Katner, pp. 195–222.

89 For a discussion of interrelated feasting regimes among the Enga, see Polly Wiessner (2001) Of Feasting and Value: Enga Feasts in a Historical Perspective (Papua New Guinea). In *Feasts: Archaeological and Ethnographic Perspectives on Food, Politics and Power*, edited by Michael Dietler and Brian Hayden, pp. 119–143 (Washington, DC: Smithsonian).

(Re)Building Consensus   93

90 See Andrew J. Strathern (1984) Lines of Power. In *Migration and Transformations: Regional Perspectives on New Guinea*, edited by Andrew J. Stathern and Gabriele Stürzenhofecker, pp. 231–256 (Pittsburgh: University of Pittsburgh Press).

91 See Philip J. Gibbs (1978) The Kepele Ritual of the Western Highlands of Papua New Guinea. *Anthropos* 73(3/4): 434–448; and Wiessner (2001).

92 See p. 244 in Polly Wiessner (2002) The Vines of Complexity: Egalitarian Structures and the Institutionalization of Inequality Among the Enga. *Current Anthropology* 43(2): 233–269.

93 The film, first aired in 1974, was directed and produced by Charles Nairn as part of Granada Television's Disappearing World Series. Andrew Strathern, a noted New Guinea anthropologist, served as an advisor for the film.

94 The narrator of the film tells us of Ongka's later success in the last frames of a movie over a shot of the weary Big Man tended to the pigs that he hopes to give away one day.

95 The United Nations Roles of Procedure and Comment for the General Assembly can be found here: www.un.org/en/ga/about/ropga/, accessed on June 7, 2022.

96 See Gert Rosenthal (2017) *Inside the United Nations: Multilateral Diplomacy Up Close* (Abingdon: Routledge).

97 This quote is taken from the United Nation's webpage of the Compact: www.unhcr.org/the-global-compact-on-refugees.html, accessed on June 7, 2022.

98 See Elizabeth G. Ferris and Katharine M. Donato (2020) *Refugees, Migration and Global Governance: Negotiating the Global Compacts* (Abingdon: Routledge).

99 The statement of the United States Mission to the United Nations can be found here: https://usun.usmission.gov/national-statement-of-the-united-states-of-america-on-the-adoption-of-the-global-compact-for-safe-orderly-and-regular-migration/, accessed on June 7, 2022.

100 See the discussion of deliberations in Ferris and Donato (2020).

101 See, for example, chapters in Patrick M. Butchard, ed. (2020) *The Responsibility to Protect and the Failures of the United Nations Security Council* (Oxford: Hart); and Oliver Christian Ruppel, Christian Roschmann, and Katharina Ruppel-Schlichting, eds. (2013) *Climate Change. Volume II, Policy, Diplomacy and Governance in a Changing Environment: International Law and Global Governance* (Baden: Nomos).

102 See Fukuyama (1992). The author thought that the spread of liberal democracies would create a common political ethos that would make global governance easier and more effective.

6 Powering From Below

In 2011, Ryan Lizza published a piece in the *New Yorker* about the seeming incoherence of Barack Obama's foreign policy. It ended with an anonymous quote from one of his advisors who said that the era was not conducive to the "John Wayne expectation for what America is in the world." Instead of heading the pack with guns akimbo, the President was where he needed to be, "leading from behind."[1] The reaction to these last three words was immediate and pointed—the Washington Post thundered, "Leading from behind is not leading. It is abdicating. It is also an oxymoron."[2]—and Obama and White House officials spent the next few months insisting that they were leading from the front after all.[3] Concerns about the president's leadership abilities nonetheless continued into his second term, often paired with warnings of China's rise and America's decline.[4] Few people, however, questioned the idea that proper governance was about being led by *someone*, a lone figure standing for a country who strides across stages to shake hands and sign peace treaties.

This narrow definition of how to guide and influence a group was surprising in that Lizza's article was about global leadership in the wake of the Arab Spring. Beginning in December 2010, the Arab Spring was a series of protests and uprising against authoritarian regimes in northern Africa and the Middle East. The movements were generally acephalous, gaining traction, in part, because there was no leader that could be coopted or removed. Rather than being a different way for an executive to lead, this was power from below—a more diffused groundswell that shaped the immediate actions and long-term goals of the organizations involved. Over the next two years, the people deposed rulers and passed sweeping political reforms. Other protest movements in the West, like Occupy Wall Street and Black Lives Matter, found success by following a similar governance model, emphatically rejecting hierarchical leadership in favor of consensus-building and group decision-making. Although there was still only one kind of leadership among the policy wonks debating Obama's foreign policy, protestors were advancing another model for how the world could work.

Power from below, however, proved effervescent. The Arab Spring abated by the end of 2012, with only Tunisia transitioning to a constitutional democracy. The Occupy movement also failed to generate significant economic reforms, and support for Black Lives Matter is diminishing.[5] The reasons for these movements'

DOI: 10.4324/9781003373322-6

loss of momentum are myriad, but one reason is organizational. Protest movements tend to be of-the-moment, channeling the public's ire in a common direction. Their organizations are often acts of schismogenesis that create an idealized alternative to the regimes that they oppose. In the case of these more recent protests, the promise of power from below, among its other attributes, was distributed responsibility, facilitated communication, and limited social inequality. True believers built small scale utopias, like the autonomous zones erected in several United States cities during the summer of 2021 or—of a different political stripe—the truck convoy protests in the Canadian capital in the spring of 2022,[6] that promptly broke down as much internally as from outside forces.

Power from below is bubbling up more regularly in our increasingly globalized society.[7] Without stability, however, this looks like a recipe only for seething turmoil. Perhaps power from below, like its close cousin "leading from behind," is a governance oxymoron? Both are not. Power is about relationships between people,[8] and scholars today distinguish power-over (asymmetrical relations that compel action) from power-with (the ability of a group to act together to achieve a collective goal).[9] In one sense, power from below is another way of saying popular sovereignty, a government created and sustained by the people. Yet popular sovereignty is typically understood by social contract theory, a power-over perspective wherein individuals submit to a higher authority in return for the protection of certain rights and the maintenance of order.[10] Power-with perspectives, in contrast, often focus on the possibilities of what is sometimes termed "strong democracy." Citizens in these systems govern themselves as much as possible rather than delegating responsibility to representatives.[11]

Western democracies have long expressed ambivalence about popular control over government.[12] As societies grow in size and complexity, representation is seen as necessary in democracies and the representatives need to be insulated from mob rule in their deliberations. Perhaps, James Madison said it best after two years of studying past governance models in the run-up to the framing of the United States Constitution:

> such [strong] democracies have ever been spectacles of turbulence and contention; have ever been found incompatible with personal security, or the rights of property; and have in general been as short in their lives, as they have been violent in their deaths.[13]

Madison was so weary of even representative popular government that he successfully campaigned for the creation of a second, smaller body of aristocrats—the U.S. Senate—that could act independently of the House of Representatives.[14] This was the People and Senate of Rome redux, the reprisal of a tradition of dual house rule that would hold sway in Europe and shape the democracies that emerged over the past 250 years.

As discussed in Chapter 1, Adams, Madison, and the other framers of the United States Constitution did their homework. They looked at only a narrow range of past and present societies, however, in reaching their decision regarding the infeasibility of strong democracies. This chapter re-visits the possibilities of strong democracy from beyond the classic Western cannon, suggesting that stable, power-from-below governance is possible for large collectives. Our case studies take us from the Zulu of nineteenth-century South Africa to the Tlaxcallan of Post-Classic Mexico and Ukraine's fourth millennium BC Cucuteni-Trypillia culture. The political structures of these examples were different, but all shared an emphasis on power-with that fostered sustained, widespread participation in governance. Our case studies demonstrate some of the mechanisms that enable power-from-below governments to thrive, as well as the considerable commitments that these systems required from citizens.

The Zulu Kingdom of Southern Africa

In 1824, Henry Flynn was one of the first Europeans to meet Shaka, the warrior king of the Zulus.[15] Flynn's party landed on the coast of southern Africa, and for two days was guided into the interior to visit his royal residence. They came to a large circular palisade enclosing a ring of bee-hived-shaped thatch huts. The size of the enclosure was overwhelming to the Europeans—excavations at a later royal residence revealed an enclosure containing more than 3,000 huts and measuring 570 meters in diameter[16]—as were the "80,000 natives in their war attire" that marched and danced at Shaka's command.[17] Although Flynn was known to exaggerate,[18] his small group of traders were witnessing a show of strength from a leader who had formed a vast kingdom less than a decade earlier (Figure 6.1).

The nineteenth-century Zulu Kingdom is often held up as an example of centralized state formation.[19] From the vantage point of the royal residence, Zulu society was indeed organized in a pyramid with the king on top, local chiefs in the middle, and everyone else below.[20] In theory, the king was all-powerful. He owned the land, all the cattle, killed at whim, and controlled if, when, and to whom someone could marry.[21] Shaka's early success in warfare encouraged loyalty—booty flowed to the homesteads of his supporters from conquests and

Figure 6.1 The Royal Residence of the Zulu King Cetshwayo, circa 1875

Powering From Below 97

raiding.[22] Consolidation became more difficult as expansions slowed, however, and Shaka needed to create a functioning kingdom out of groups that had been antagonistic to him and to each other.[23] There were now more than 250,000 people in the Zulu Kingdom, divided into hundreds of decent groups. Previous chiefs in the region had combined blood, co-residence, and marriage ties with the threat of violence to solidify their rule across closely related groups.[24] Shaka's newly won kingdom, however, was too large for traditional governance tactics, and violence alone was unlikely to keep the local chiefs by his side.

Prior to the Zulu State's coalescence, the homestead was a self-contained political, economic, symbolic, and legal unit.[25] The heads of these homesteads were each "a little king in his domestic domain, with powers of life or death over those who lived in it."[26] The "little kings" of the homestead had retained considerable power in earlier chiefdoms,[27] and administration "ran in a separate thread" from a chief to each homestead.[28] In the homestead head's eyes, a chief worked for him: the thread could easily be severed if the relationship proved unbeneficial. Chiefdoms therefore tended to remain small in size and short in duration because of the difficulties of weaving many homesteads together into a cohesive polity.[29]

Shaka sought to build off this governance model by pulling together the most influential chiefs of the kingdom into a council. In theory, homestead allegiance would pass from each head to lesser chiefs, then thread through the greater chiefs and king's council to Shaka himself. Shaka's genealogical removal from most groups, however, inhibited trust. He therefore began to replace some leaders with his own kin.[30] By putting his people in power, however, he removed those who others trusted.

To keep his kingdom together, Shaka soon embraced a more revolutionary agenda to make the state everyone's homestead, legitimizing a new societal order with the same flowery language that had asserted a head's right to rule.[31] He expanded mandatory military service to 20 years for all males and made it a prerequisite for marriage that would be arranged by the king. The idea was that young men would pass from their natal homesteads into state facilities that were run, in many cases, by royal women of Shaka's line.[32] The facilities were built to look like homesteads and were conceived as such by Zulu leaders: young men, and the many women brought in to work there, would be coming under the domain of a new homestead head (the king) who demanded their complete fealty.[33] After 20 years of devoted service, they would marry someone from outside of their home region and eventually indoctrinate their children into the direct king to commoner relationship.[34] Within a generation or two, the power of the homestead, and the local chiefs who organized them, would be broken.

Shaka's ambitious plan of social engineering largely failed. Almost everyone still lived and worked within isolated, self-sufficient homesteads during his reign and those who were sent to state facilities tended to return home to marry and live.[35] Only a small percentage of people in the kingdom would ever think of themselves as Zulu,[36] and it appears that Shaka and subsequent kings struggled to provision their facilities through tribute obligation from more distant locales.[37] Homesteads continued to control the means of their own production, and the king,

98 *Powering From Below*

at best, had only a limited monopoly on iron and other desired imports.[38] With little leverage, Shaka resorted to violence and terror to enforce his vision.[39] His support began to evaporate, and Shaka was assassinated in 1828. The 80,000 warriors who performed for Flynn were not only a show of the king's strength, but also a testament to the transformative ambitions that would undo him.

By the time of Mpande's reign from 1840 to 1872, a new balance between the homestead heads, chiefs, and the Zulu king had been achieved.[40] While the ruler's sweeping powers remained notionally intact, Mpande listened to appeals, limited raiding, sought consensus from his council before taking action, and placed less emphasis on the long-term removal of youth from their homesteads.[41] He also focused on concentrating judicial and spiritual authority in his residence, while allowing far more provincial and local independence than Shaka had tolerated. Mpande embraced the idea of a state composed of thousands of different threads, twisting, combining, and turning before they reached him. He sometimes feigned "innocence, weakness, and willingness to co-operate" as he pitted the interests of one coalition against another and fended off encroaching white settlers.[42] Often he would urge chiefs to take action that would both fulfill their personal interests *and* benefit the kingdom. Mpande made Shaka's innovations work by leading from behind, a style of malleable, often subdued, governance that allowed the state to weather many challenges until the king died of old age in his seventies.

Mpande's reign can be viewed as one of inevitable decline in the face of creeping European colonialism. The British defeated the Zulus seven years after his death, and diplomacy and warfare with Boer and British settlers undeniably shaped the history of the kingdom.[43] Mpande's reign, however, can also be seen as an example of how governance structures can successfully adapt to environments where considerable social, economic, and political power remain at the local level. Shaka's attempt to circumvent homestead heads almost brought the Zulu state to ruin, while Mpande's accommodation created a durable polity that could adapt to quickly changing circumstances by giving more people a voice. The Zulus did not need a "strong" leader to survive within the context of nineteenth-century southern Africa; they needed a leader who was willing to recede into the background as other stepped forward. The Tlaxcallan, our next case study, may have not needed a leader at all.

The Tlaxcallan Republic of Mexico

In 1519, The Spanish Conquistador Hernán Cortés found an unlikely ally in Tlaxcallan during his march to Tenochtitlan, the Aztec capital. The tiny state—a group of 100–200,000 people living 100 kilometers from Tenochtitlan—had somehow fought off Aztec advances for decades until it became a lone speck of unconquered territory within a sprawling empire. In a letter to the King of Spain, Cortés described Tlaxcallan's enduring fight against the Aztecs:

> They had tried with all their forces both by day and by night to avoid being subject to anyone, for this province never had been, nor had they ever had

an over-all ruler. For they had lived in freedom and independence from time immemorial.[44]

Cortés met up to 50 representatives in his negotiations with the Tlaxcallan (Figure 6.2). For the Spaniard, their lack of an "over-all ruler" was a flaw to be remedied and he soon elevated a leader to speak for the group. Archaeological and ethnohistoric research is only now beginning to uncover the Tlaxcallan power-from-below government.[45]

Prior to the fifteenth century, the Tlaxcallan region was composed of noble houses that came together into larger confederacies.[46] Each house was anchored by a palace in a confederacy's main settlement, with commoners working the patchwork of fields associated with each house. Genealogy was important among nobles—some land was inherited, and titles tended to remain in the family—but commoners could shift their loyalties from one house to another based on prevailing conditions. The result was that the fortunes of houses, and the shifting confederacies that they formed, waxed and waned.[47] This system of autonomous noble houses was ill-equipped to counter Aztec aggression and a new governance system emerged that was organized around a ruling council that included as many as 200 officials.[48] These officials, likely a mix of hereditary nobles and those who obtained high status through exemplary service to the state, were the ones who

Figure 6.2 A seated Cortés meets a contingent from Tlaxcallan in the Lienzo of Tlaxcala

100 *Powering From Below*

met Cortés, and, after much debate and consensus-building among the council and public at large, agreed to side with the Spaniards.[49]

Some discussions of the "Independent Republic of Tlaxcallan"[50] might be over-zealous in describing it as a polity "of the people, by the people, for the people."[51] Yet by Mesoamerican standards—as well as those of the late-eighteenth-century United States—wealth inequality was muted, and social mobility was striking.[52] Archaeological survey and excavations at the eponymously named capital of Tlaxcallan reveal a settlement organized into at least 20 neighborhoods. Each neighborhood had a plaza associated with temples where elaborate communal feasts took place,[53] public meetings were held, and an open market provided wide access to obsidian, gold, silver, and other luxuries that were normally restricted to elites in other societies in the region.[54] The neighborhoods were likely each organized around a noble house, both long established ones and new ones that catered more to the ballooning population of refugees from the Aztec wars.[55] Palaces are nonetheless hard to identify at Tlaxcallan because there are only minor differences in house size and elaboration across the settlement.[56] Although we know that nobles existed based on a plethora of documents written soon after the Spanish Conquest,[57] Tlaxcallan's elite avoided ostentatious displays of wealth and power to cultivate a collective identity.

Aurelio López Corral and his colleagues at the National Institute of Anthropology and History in Mexico have conducted extensive survey and excavations at the Tlaxcallan capital. Their analysis of objects collected across the site indicates a "low state regulation of artisan production" and:

> [A] notable absence of images of leaders, political figures, governors, or ancestors. What we [the authors] find are themes related to gods, government, festivals, sacrifice, and ritual elements.[58]

Artisans across the settlement thus celebrated the collective and the higher callings for its citizens, subsuming their noble house identities to assert a pan-Tlaxcallan identity in the face of Aztec aggression. The art often emphasized Tezcatlipoca, a god associated with the value of all individuals, and celebrated the grueling two-year initiation rite for leaders that emphasized their responsibility to the state and its people.[59]

Those leaders who were part of the ruling council appear to have met at a complex that was one kilometer removed from the capital. The meeting site, called Tizatlan, was built on a massive platform. Excavations in the 1920s revealed small rooms in the center of the platform, flanked by massive plazas with monumental entrances.[60] Requiring 60,000 m³ of construction fill, Tizatlan was the largest construction in Tlaxcallan.[61] The site was a place for many to gather, with space for common citizens to participate in the deliberations that occurred there. The scope of these deliberations appears to have been largely concerned with external affairs—declaring war, creating alliances, appointing ambassadors—rather than the internal affairs of the noble houses. The ability of the council to choose and remove leaders nonetheless ensured that each of the noble houses worked for the benefit of the broader Tlaxcallan community.[62]

The degree of both social mobility and noble house independence remains unclear. Those like Lane Fargher who emphasize the republican qualities of Tlaxcallan stress the state's egalitarian ethos wherein anyone could aspire to leadership. They see the noble houses as beholden to the council, perhaps even becoming administrative provinces with limited autonomy.[63] Previous scholarship, however, emphasizes the enduring power of nobles in Tlaxcallan to control their own affairs.[64] Both views are likely correct in that the sweeping collective ideals instilled at ceremonies in places like Tizatlan did not completely replace a system based on entrenched elite prerogatives. Prowess in warfare and other exemplary service to the state nonetheless led to positions of power in Tlaxcallan society for both commoners from the region and newcomers.[65] Those living along the margins of the state were also well integrated into the polity's collective ethos and had access to the open markets that connected citizens and redistributed wealth[66]

In our Zulu case study, power from below was the result of a monarch's failed attempts to sideline the region's homesteads. The Tlaxcallan noble houses, in contrast, came together to form a centralized government to which they willingly transferred considerable power. At the same time, nobles gave up many of their elite prerogatives, redistributed wealth widely, and allowed for considerable social mobility. The make-up of the ruling council suggests that every noble house in Tlaxcallan was represented at Tizatlan, and the location's immense, open, plazas hints at participation by the public at large. Similar occasions to discuss matters of state occurred in the neighborhood plazas as the members of a noble house and their leaders feasted and prayed together. Tlaxcallan's power-from-below governance system yielded a "collective action payoff" that was "unrivaled in Terminal Post-Classic Mexico."[67] The noble house structured daily life, but people were willing to die for Tlaxcallan because of the opportunities that the state provided.

The Cucuteni-Trypillia Mega-Sites of Ukraine

In 1979, Linda Ellis went behind the Iron Curtain to learn more about Cucuteni-Trypillia pottery production. The swirling patterns on the pottery were mesmerizing and early—the culture dated to the fifth through fourth millennium BC—but Western scholars were paying scant attention to the region. For the next five years, the young Ph.D. student was engulfed in the "immense energy and efforts" of Eastern European and Russian archaeologists.[68] The book that resulted from her studies, *The Cucuteni-Tripolye Culture: A Study in Technology and the Origins of Complex Society*, was both a presentation of her findings and a summary of 100 years of hard-to-obtain scholarship in Romanian and Slavic languages.[69] Near the end of the book were three figures from V. P. Dudkin's recent aerial survey work that showed what appeared to be three immense circular settlements of hundreds of houses.[70] These massive settlements dated more than 1,000 years before the Great Pyramids of Egypt. Suddenly, Cucuteni-Trypillia was about more than just pottery.

Most of the mega-sites were in Ukraine, a country that began opening to more outside scholars after the break-up of the Soviet Union in 1991. Only in the last ten years, however, has geophysics, paleoenvironmental studies, intensive surface survey, and excavations revealed the full extent and complexity of these settlements.[71] Maidanetske, for example, covered 200 hectares and boasted almost 3,000 houses (Figure 6.3). Three ditches and nine rings of houses surrounded an open plaza; there were gateways, kilns, roads, and nine assembly houses.[72] The settlements look like cities—the oldest in the world by centuries—but they lacked the evidence for social hierarchy and heterogeneity that archaeologists had come to expect in sites of this size. The ensuing debates about what to call these settlements is less interesting to us than how they functioned: Cucuteni-Trypillia mega-sites provide us with another blueprint for power-from-below governance.[73]

The people who lived in the region subsisted off a range of domesticated and wild plants and animals that changed little over two millennia.[74] Each of the sites was occupied for a couple of centuries, and some are at least partially contemporaneous and within a couple of day's hike from each other. Tens of thousands of people would have lived together if all of the houses were occupied at the same time, but the lack of evidence for agricultural intensification and deforestation suggests a more staggered occupation.[75] Lines of wooden houses found at the settlements may have been associated with lineages whose member built and occupied their homes at different times.[76] When a home fell out of use it was often

Figure 6.3 An artist's impression of what Maidanetske would have looked like, circa 3700 BC, after buildings took over the main plaza

Powering From Below 103

burned, sometimes creating a "memory mound" that celebrated a lineage's ancestors.[77] Streets and gaps identify neighborhoods nested within quarters, and there are slight variations in layout and organization to suggest that kin- and village-based groups settled in different neighborhoods.[78] Whether residing or visiting, each person had their place in a Cucuteni-Trypillia mega-site that was maintained across generations.

Neighborhoods often had their own assembly house, with a bigger one serving each quarter. An even larger assembly house can sometimes be found near a mega-site's center.[79] The only assembly house that has been excavated to date is one at Nebelivka that could have fit as many as 1,000 people inside.[80] In most respects, the assembly house looked like a typical home, with many of the rooms mimicking at a much larger scale the architectural layout and fixtures found throughout the site. Yet there is no detritus of daily living, leaving "little doubt that this [the assembly house] is a public building where meetings, and even ceremonies, could have taken place."[81] Attendees likely entered the structure via a monumental doorway that led into a courtyard. They then passed into the house proper, moving through familiar room settings, before coming to the assembly house's distinctive feature: a large patio in the center of the house that boasted a set of drinking cups along one wall. Assembly houses likely served to bridge lineage, neighborhood, and quarter divides by bringing people together to eat, drink, and deliberate within a shared "home."[82]

Assembly houses were only one of the integrative features of Cucuteni-Trypillia's mega-sites. The radial roads funneled visitors and residents toward the open space in the site's center for communal activities; and the surrounding ditches, though perhaps serving a defensive function, acted to delineate the boundaries of their broader community.[83] Building and maintaining these features further reinforced the social bonds between participants. At the same time, community was forged by people doing daily activities that paralleled those that had been done for centuries. Everyone practiced a similar set of house rituals, for example, using a familiar set of figurines and pottery[84] to celebrate the Great Goddess.[85] The view from their house window was also reminiscent of the much smaller settlements from which people came. The parallel construction, inhabitation, and destruction of similar-looking houses were familiar,[86] neighborhoods had the same kilns and other features of old,[87] and ringing houses around a ceremonial core was standard practice.[88] The site *looked* like a big village, and villages were places of kin and mutual aid.

The origin of mega-sites is debated. Defense against raiding may have spurred the ditches and concentric designs of the early settlements in the Cucuteni-Trypillia culture,[89] but the mega-sites that came later seem to be designed originally as places of aggregation that filled in with houses over time.[90] Some scholars suggest that only a small population lived there permanently in the initial phases of mega-sites, perhaps serving as anchors for community members in the surrounding region who made a pilgrimage to the site every year.[91] The radial streets would have allowed groups to converge for a gathering in the center of the mega-site, before adjourning to their respective quarters, neighborhoods, and

104 *Powering From Below*

houses.[92] Despite some differences in layout, they all reflect a social organization predicated on cyclically bringing people together and splitting them apart. The encroachment of the central space and the buffer zones between residential rings by houses near the end of some of the mega-site occupations disrupted these flows and may have been one of the reasons for the megasite's demise.[93]

For centuries, mega-sites organized communities numbering in the tens of thousands.[94] There is no evidence for elites, writing, a standing centralized government, or many of the other features that we have come to expect with state government.[95] Instead, we have a society predicated on tradition and an expandable metaphor of house and community. Cucuteni-Trypillian families pioneered Alphonse Karr's aphorism, "*Plus ça change, plus c'est la même chose*" to the extreme—there would be no changes as people moved into mega-sites. People would continue to live in the same way as they had for centuries and make group decisions in assembly houses. Governance, of course, shifted as one moved up the chain of assembly houses or came together at a mega-site's main plaza, but the site's organization gives the impression of a power-from-below system designed to both ensure equal political representation across households and encourage consensus by emphasizing shared experiences and beliefs. Of our three case studies, Cucuteni-Trypillia may have come closest to realizing a political organization of the people, by the people, and for the people.

Power From Below

Can you lead from behind? In our own society, power is often associated with dominance, the ability to impose one's will upon others. There's a decision-making pyramid with the alphas on top—the buck stops here!—and subordinates below. Dominance alone, however, is often anathema to sustained collective action.[96] Emphasizing power-over can lead to violence and tyranny,[97] and there is rich tradition in the West and elsewhere of curbing the power of leaders and inserting more voices into the decision-making process. The *Magna Carta Libertatum*, or Great Charter of Freedoms, is one well-known example, a failed peace treaty between the King of England and a group of rebel barons that sought to protect the latter from arbitrary acts of imprisonment and taxation. The Magna Carta was power from below, and so was British Parliament. "Leading from behind" may sound like an oxymoron, but it is a time-honored dimension of good governance.

Cross-culturally, the governments that acknowledge and successfully respond to its citizens' needs tend to be those that are dependent on broad public participation through tax payments, labor service, and other mechanisms.[98] In theory, more dependency on citizens enables more power from below. More power from below fosters the development of political organizations that are more in the service of their citizens. A virtuous circle ensues that favors power-with leadership strategies that better addresses collective goals.[99] Yet like James Madison, we fear the chaos of unfettered democracy and often break this cycle, returning again and again to the narrow set of Western-derived government models that limit power from below. This fear of chaos seems particularly strong for international governance.

Powering From Below 105

A long tradition of thinking in terms of competing autonomous states has encouraged a winner-take-all, power-over conceptualization of world politics that has stymied our efforts to tackle collective action challenges like climate change. Our case studies suggest possible avenues of reform.

The Zulu homesteads, Tlaxcallan noble houses, and Cucuteni-Trypillia lineages *were* competing autonomous actors and they remained so after incorporation into a broader polity. Each of the leaders in our case studies nonetheless found success through a system that aligned interests without quashing this autonomy. Mpande, the later Zulu king, used his capital as a central hub through which relationships could be channeled. His conversations with different chiefs were personal, often collaborative, and focused on finding common goals. The leaders of Tlaxcallan noble houses came together in a dis-embedded capital that was divorced from the everyday. External affairs were the focus of deliberation, with the houses expected to support each other against foreign aggression. The broader Cucuteni-Trypillia collective was the most temporary, premised on a cyclical process of aggregation and disaggregation. Leaders came together at an assembly house to discuss issues of joint concern, knowing that they would soon return to working within their own household once an action was concluded.

Power-with governance strategies, at least in the case of the Zulu and Tlaxcallan, were necessitated by external existential threats. Buy-in was required to fight off foreign armies, and so leaders made sure that they addressed the needs of their citizens. A similar threat of violence may have loomed over the Cucuteni-Trypillia when mega-sites began to form. Yet in all three case studies, one is struck by the efforts put forth to instill a broader collective identity. Young Zulu men and women gave extended service to the state, eating, sleeping, and fighting alongside compatriots who came from different homesteads. Though not as intense and extenuated as their leaders, every Tlaxcallan participated in extensive initiation ceremonies that were focused on their responsibilities to the state rather than their noble house.[100] The Cucuteni-Trypillia built the ditches, assembly houses, and other features of their mega-sites, working together to create a great circular settlement that defined a broader community.

The Cucuteni-Trypillia mega-sites replicated the houses-circling-plaza organization of smaller villages, and their assembly houses looked likely scaled-up versions of typical homes. Zulu royal residence organization was, and remains, reminiscent of how the private, public, and workspaces of homesteads were spatially organized. Tizatlan, the meeting place for Tlaxcallan, turned the Mesoamerican palace turned inside out, transforming a well-known symbol of hierarchical rule into a place of public deliberation. At least informally, most people were expected to participate in, and influence, political decision-making at the local level in our case studies. Power-with, rather than power-over, was the norm. In making the familiar—and often the familial—writ large in political capitals, thousands of Zulu, Tlaxcallan, and Cucuteni-Trypillian builders architecturally enshrined a power-over ethos at the highest echelon of their polity. Some leaders like Shaka may have wanted to dominate, but the virtuous circle favored those who listened widely, distributed responsibility, and worked for collective interests.

106 *Powering From Below*

The Europeans who encountered the Zulu and Tlaxcallan polities saw weak, ineffective governments. The power of the homesteads and noble houses were something that had to be broken for a properly working government to emerge, and one can only imagine what a Henry Flynn or Hernán Cortés would have thought of the even more acephalous political organization of Cucuteni-Trypillian mega-sites. Power-from-below governance, however, depends on the strength and autonomy of a polity's constituent parts to function. The sustained involvement of so many people in politics, often working at cross-purposes, can seem like a recipe for chaos to Western eyes, but is integral to making a government that is flexible, responsive, and accountable to its citizen needs. In the next chapter, we will face head-on Western fears of chaos by exploring the paradoxical ways in which anarchy allows people to prosper without rulers to guide them.

Notes

1 See Ryan Lizza (2011) The Consequentialist: How the Arab Spring Remade Obama's Foreign Policy. *The New Yorker*, May 2 issue, www.newyorker.com/magazine/2011/05/02/the-consequentialist, accessed on June 23, 2022.
2 See Charles Krauthammer (2011) The Obama Doctrine: Leading from Behind. *The Washington Post*, April 28 edition. www.washingtonpost.com/opinions/the-obama-doctrine-leading-from-behind/2011/04/28/AFBCy18E_story.html, accessed on June 23, 2022.
3 See Joshua Rogin (2011) Who really said Obama was "leading from behind"? *Foreign Policy*, October 27, 2011, https://foreignpolicy.com/2011/10/27/who-really-said-obama-was-leading-from-behind/, accessed on June 23, 2022.
4 See David Unger (2016) The Foreign Policy Legacy of Barack Obama. *The International Spectator* 51(4):1–16; and Eliot A. Cohen, Eric S. Edelman, and Meghen O'Sullivan (2012) Obama's Failed Foreign Policy. *Boston Globe*, November 1, 2012.
5 See Khaleda Rahman (2022) Support for Black Lives Matter Plummets Among African Americans: Poll, *Newsweek*, May 19, 2022. www.newsweek.com/support-black-lives-matter-plummets-among-african-americans-poll-1708122, accessed on June 23, 2022.
6 See Ashitha Nagesh (2020) The Police-Free Protest Zone Was Dismantled—But Was It the End? *BBC News*, July 12, 2020. www.bbc.com/news/world-us-canada-53218448, accessed on June 23, 2022.
7 See Frances Fox Piven (2008) Can Power from Below Change the World? *American Sociological Review* 73(1): 1–14.
8 See Robert A. Dahl (1957) The Concept of Power. *Behavioral Science* 2 (3): 201–215.
9 See Pameal Pansardi and Marianna Bindi (2021) The New Concepts of Power? Power-over, Power-to and Power-With. *Journal of Political Power* 14(1): 51–71.
10 The idea of the social contract was a core tenant of the Enlightenment professed by Thomas Hobbes, John Locke and Jean-Jacques Rousseau and others. Social contract debates tended to be about the just rule of kings. See Ross Harrison (2003) *Hobbes, Locke, and Confusion's Masterpiece: An Examination of Seventeenth Century Political Philosophy* (New York: Cambridge University Press).
11 See Benjamin R. Barber (2003) *Strong Democracy: Participatory Politics for a New Age,* second edition (Berkeley: University of California Press).
12 See Hanna Fenichel Pitkin (1972) *The Concept of Representation* (Berkeley: University of California Press).
13 See Federalist Paper #10 in James Madison (1977) *The Papers of James Madison*, vol. 10, *27 May 1787–3 March 1788*, edited by Robert A. Rutland, Charles F. Hobson,

William M. E. Rachal, and Frederika J. Teute, p. 268 (Chicago: The University of Chicago Press, 1977).

14 Although Hamilton did not use the terms "aristocrats," others portrayed the Senate as such because of their extended terms, and the higher age and residency requirements. For example, see John De Witt III (1787), Editorial, Boston *American Herald*, November 5th edition, In *The Documentary History of the Ratification of the Constitution Digital Edition,* edited by John P. Kaminski, Gaspare J. Saladino, Richard Leffler, Charles H. Schoenleber and Margaret A. Hogan (Charlottesville: University of Virginia Press, 2009). Original source: Ratification by the States, Volume IV: Massachusetts, No. 1, https://csac.history.wisc.edu/document-collections/constitutional-debates/senate/, accessed September 22, 2022. In 1913, the seventeenth amendment of the constitution led to direct elections for United States senators. Originally, state legislators appointed senators with the idea that the Senate would represent state interests and the House would represent popular interests.

15 See Henry Francis Flynn, James Stuart, and D. McK Malcolm (1969) *The Diary of Henry Francis Fynn* (Pietermaritzburg: Shuter and Shooter, 1969).

16 See John Parkington and Mike Cronin (1979) The Size and Layout of Mgungundlovu 1829–1838 *South African Archaeological Society.* Goodwin Series, No. 3, Iron Age Studies in Southern Africa, pp. 133–148.

17 See Flynn et al. (1969), p. 71.

18 See Dan Wylie (1995) "Proprietor of Natal:" Henry Francis Fynn and the Mythography of Shaka. *History in Africa* 22: 409–437.

19 See Johannes W. Raum (1989) Historical Concepts and the Evolutionary Interpretation of the Emergence of States: The Case of the Zulu Reconsidered yet Again. *Zeitschrift Für Ethnologie* 114(1): 125–138.

20 See Donald R. Morris (1965) *The Washing of the Spears: A History of the Rise of the Zulu Nation Under Shaka and Its Fall in the Zulu War of 1879* (New York: Simon and Schuster); James O. Gump (1990) *The Formation of the Zulu Kingdom in South Africa, 1750–1840* (San Francisco: EM Text); and Stephen Taylor (1994) *Shaka's Children: A History of the Zulu People* (London: HarperCollins).

21 See John Wright (2018) 'Izwe La Li Nge Namteto': Reading Discourses on Authority Over Land in the James Stuart Archive. *Journal of Natal and Zulu History* 32(1): 24–37.

22 See Carolyn Hamilton, ed. (1995) *The Mfecane Aftermath: Reconstructive Debates in Southern African History* (Johannesburg: Witwatersrand University Press and University of Natal Press).

23 See Elizabeth A. Eldredge (2014) *The Creation of the Zulu Kingdom, 1815–1828: War, Shaka, and the Consolidation of Power* (New York: Cambridge University Press).

24 Information is far more limited about society in the KwaZulu-Natal region of southern Africa prior to the nineteenth century. Archaeological evidence nonetheless suggests at the very least that smaller chiefdoms rose and fall with the persistence of homesteads organized in a very similar manner for centuries. See Norman Etherington (2004) Were There Large States in the Coastal Regions of Southeast Africa Before the Rise of the Zulu Kingdom? *History in Africa* 31: 157–183; and Gavin Whitelaw (2008) A Brief Archaeology of Precolonial Farming in KwaZulul-Natal. In *Zulu Identities: Being Zulu, Past and Present*, edited by Benedict Carton, Johan Laband, and Jabulant Sithole, pp. 47–61 (Scottsville: University of KwaZutal-Natal Press).

25 See J.F. Holleman (1986) The Structure of the Zulu Ward. *African Studies* 45: 109–133; Adam Kuper (1980) Symbolic Dimensions of the Southern Bantu Homestead. *Africa* 58(1): 8–23; and Martin Hall (1981) *Settlement Patterns in the Iron Age of Zululand*. BAR International Series 119 (Oxford: British Archaeological Reports).

26 See W. D. Hammond-Tooke (2008) Cattle Symbolism in Zulu Culture. In *Zulu Identities: Being Zulu, Past and Present*, edited by Benedict Carton, Johan Laband, and Jabulant Sithole, pp. 62–68 (Scottsville: University of KwaZutal-Natal Press), p. 63.

108 *Powering From Below*

27 For information on Zulu homestead organization, see Eileen Jensen Krige (1950) *The Social System of the Zulus*, second Edition (Pietermaritzburgh: Shuter & Shooter).
28 See Max Gluckman (1964) The Kingdom of the Zulu in South Africa. In *African Political Systems*, edited by Meyer Fortes and E. E. Evans-Pritchard, pp. 25–56 (London: Oxford University Press), p. 41.
29 See Martin Hall (1984) The Myth of the Zulu Homestead: Archaeology and Ethnography. *Africa* 54 (1): 102–179.
30 See Gluckman (1964), p. 37.
31 For example, see Adam Kuper (1993). The "House" and Zulu Political Structure in the Nineteenth Century. *The Journal of African History* 34(3): 469–487; and Paul K. Bjerk. (2006) They Poured Themselves into the Milk: Zulu Political Philosophy under Shaka. *The Journal of African History* 47(1): 1–19.
32 See Sean Hanretta (1998) Women, Marginality, and the Zulu State: Women's Institutions and Power in the Early Nineteenth Century. *Journal of African History* 39(3): 389–415; and Jennifer Weir (2000) 'I Shall Need to Use Her to Rule': The Power of 'Royal' Zulu Women in Pre-Colonial Zululand. *South African Historical Journal* 43(1): 3–23.
33 See Renier H. van der Merwe and Innocent Pikirayi (2019) The Organisation and Layout of Zulu Military Homesteads (Amakhanda). *Azania* 54(1): 75–93; and Elizabeth H. Timbs (2019) The Regiments: Cultural Histories of Zulu Masculinities and Gender Formation in South Africa, 1816–2018. Unpublished Ph.D. dissertation, Michigan State University, Lansing.
34 Debate remains about the degree of penetration of state policy into Zulu-era homesteads. See J.J. Guy (1981) The Political Structure of the Zulu Kingdom during the Reign of Cetshwayo kaMpande. In *Before and After Shaka: Papers in Nguni History*, edited by J.B. Peires, pp. 49–73 (Gramhamstown: Rhodes University); and P.L. Bonner (1981) The Dynamics of Late Eighteenth Century, Early Nineteenth Century Northern Nguni Society, Some Hypothesis. In *Before and After Shaka: Papers in Nguni History*, edited by J.B. Peires, pp. 74–81 (Gramhamstown: Rhodes University) for a discussion of some of the changes, albeit from a king-centered perspective.
35 For a more homestead-orientated vista of the Zulu, see Max Gluckman (1960) The Rise of the Zulu Empire. *Scientific American* 202(4): 157–169; Max Gluckman (1964); and Max Gluckman (1974) The Individual in a Social Framework: The Rise of King Shaka of Zululand. *Journal of African Studies* 1(2): 113–144.
36 See Michael R. Mahoney (2012) *The Other Zulus: The Spread of Zulu Ethnicity in Colonial South Africa* (Durham: Duke University Press).
37 See Kent D. Fowler, Panseok Yang, and Norman M. Halden (2020) The Provisioning of Nineteenth Century Zulu Capitals, South Africa: Insights from Strontium Isotope Analysis of Cattle Remains. *Journal of Archaeological Science: Reports* 31: 102306.
38 See Jeff Guy (1982) *The Destruction of the Zulu Kingdom: The Civil War in Zululand, 1879–1884* (Johannesburg: Ravan Press).
39 Tales of Shaka's madness and depravity were inflated by Europeans to destabilize the Zulu Kingdom. Nonetheless, there is ample evidence to suggest that he used violence as a means to consolidate power. See Carolyn Hamilton (1998) *Terrific Majesty: The Power of Shaka Zulu and the Limits of Historical Invention* (Cambridge: Harvard University Press).
40 See Phillip A. Kennedy (1981) Mpande and the Zulu Kingship. *Journal of Natal and Zulu History* 4(1): 21–38; and James O. Gump (1994) *The Dust Rose Like Smoke: The Subjugation of the Zulu and the Sioux* (Lincoln: University of Nebraska Press).
41 See R. L. Cope (1985) Political Power Within the Zulu Kingdom and the 'Coronation Laws' of 1873. *Journal of Natal and Zulu History* 8(1): 11–31; Charles Ballard (1980) John Dunn and Cetshwayo: The Material Foundations of Political Power in the Zulu Kingdom, 1857–1878. *Journal of African History* 21(1):75–91; and, for a sense of how military service unfolded in the late nineteenth century, see Julian Cobbing (1974) The Evolution of Ndebele Amabutho. *Journal of African History* 15(4): 47–631.
42 See Kennedy (1981), p. 37.

43 For example, see Ian Knight (2010) *Zulu Rising: The Epic Story of isandlwana and Rorke's Drift* (London: Macmillan) and Michael Leśniewski, Michał (2021) *The Zulu-Boer War 1837–1840* (Leiden: Brill).

44 Cortés (1986), p. 66.

45 See Charles Gibson (1952) *Tlaxcala in the Sixteenth Century* (New Haven: Yale University Press); and James Lockhart (1992) *The Nahuas After the Conquest: A Social and Cultural History of the Indians of Central Mexico, Sixteenth Through Eighteenth Centuries* (Stanford, CA: Stanford University Press).

46 See John K. Chance (2000) The Noble House in Colonial Puebla, Mexico: Descent, Inheritance, and the Nahua Tradition. *American Anthropologist* 102(3): 485–502; Delia Annunziata Cosentino (2002) Landscapes of Lineage: Nahua Pictorial Genealogies of Early Colonial Tlaxcala, Mexico. Unpublished Ph.D. dissertation, University of California, Los Angeles; John M. D. Pohl (2003) Royal Marriage and Confederacy Building Among the Eastern Nahuas, Mixtecs, and Zapotecs. In *The Post-classic Mesoamerican World,* edited by Michael E. Smith and Frances Berdan, pp. 243–248 (Salt Lake City: University of Utah Press); Jovita R. Baber (2005) The Construction of Empire: Politics, Law and Community in Tlaxcala, New Spain, 1521–1640. Unpublished Ph.D. dissertation, University of Chicago, Chicago; and Frederic Hicks (2009) Land and Succession in the Indigenous Noble Houses of Sixteenth-Century Tlaxcala. *Ethnohistory* 56(4): 569–588.

47 For a discussion of the Post-Classic political landscape in the region, see Lane F. Fargher, Verenice Y. Heredia Espinoza, and Richard E. Blanton (2011) Alternative Pathways to Power in Late Postclassic Highland Mesoamerica. *Journal of Anthropological Archaeology* 30(3): 306–326.

48 See Lane F. Fargher, Richard E. Blanton, and Verenice Y. Heredia Espinoza (2010) Egalitarian Ideology and Political Power in Prehispanic Central Mexico: The Case of Tlaxcallan. *Latin American Antiquity* 21(3): 227–251.

49 For a discussion of Tlaxcallan deliberations, see Francisco Cervantes de Salazar (1991 [1575]) Cronica de la Nueva Espana. In *Tlaxcala: Textos de su Historia, Tomo 6: Siglo XVI*, edited by Carlos Sempat Assadourian and Andrea Martinez Baracs, pp. 30–113 (Consejo Nacional para la Cultura y las Artes y Gobierno del Estado de Tlaxcala, Tlaxcala).

50 See Verenice Heredia Espinoza, Lane F. Fargher, and Richard E. Blanton (2017) The Independent Republic of Tlaxcallan. In *The Oxford Handbook of the Aztecs*, edited by Deborah L. Nichols and Enrique Rodríguez-Alegría, pp. 535–541 (New York: Oxford University Press).

51 See p. 14 of Lane F. Fargher, Ricardo R. Antorcha-Pedemonte, Verenice Y. Heredia Espinoza, Richard E. Blanton, Aurelio López Corral, Robert A. Cook, John K. Millhauser, Marc D. Marino, Iziar Martínez Rojo, Ivonne Pérez Alcántara, and Angelica Costa (2020) Wealth Inequality, Social Stratification, and the Built Environment in Late Prehispanic Highland Mexico: A Comparative Analysis with Special Emphasis on Tlaxcallan. *Journal of Anthropological Archaeology* 58: 101176.

52 See Fargher et al. (2020).

53 Descriptions of feasts can be found in Toribio Motolinía (1950 [1568]) *History of the Indians of New Spain.* (Berkeley: Cortés Society). For archaeological evidence of feast, see Fargher et al. (2010).

54 See Marc D. Marino, Lane F. Fargher, Nathan J. Meissner, Lucas R. Martindale Johnson, Richard E. Blanton, and Verenice Y. Heredia Espinoza (2020) Exchange Systems in Late Postclassic Mesoamerica: Comparing Open and Restricted Markets at Tlaxcallan, Mexico, and Santa Rita Corozal, Belize. *Latin American Antiquity* 31(4): 780–799.

55 See Buenaventura Zapata y Mendoza, Buenaventura (1995[1689]) *Historia cronológica de la noble ciudad de Tlaxcala*. Transcripción Paleográfica, Traducción, Presentación y notas por Luis Reyes García y Andrea Martínez Baracs (Tlaxcala: Universidad Autónoma de Tlaxcala).

56 See Farger et al. (2020).

110 Powering From Below

57 Perhaps the best summary of these sources remains Lockhard (1992). These documents, of course, reflect life after the Spanish Conquest but the earliest documents show what appears to be a deeply embedded system of autonomous noble houses. For some of the earliest document written by Indigenous authors in Tlaxcala, see Justyna Olko and Agnieszka Brylak (2018) Defending Local Autonomy and Facing Cultural Trauma: A Nahua Order Against Idolatry, Tlaxcala, 1543. *The Hispanic American Historical Review* 98(4): 573–604.

58 See p. 349 of Aurelio López Corral, Ivonne Velasco Almanza, Thania E. Ibarra Narváez, and Ramón Santacruz Cano (2019) Iconografía y Gobierno Colectivo Durante El Posclásico Tardío En Tepeticpac y Tlaxcallan, México. *Latin American Antiquity* 30(2): 333–353, author's translation.

59 See Fargher et al. (2010).

60 See Alfonso Caso (1929) Las ruinas de Tizatlán, Tlaxcala. *Revista Mexicana de Estudios Antropológicos* 1(4): 139–172.

61 See Fargher, Lane F., Richard E. Blanton, Verenice Y. Heredia Espinoza, John Millhauser, Nezahualcoyotl Xiuhtecutli, and Lisa Overholtzer (2011) Tlaxcallan: The Archaeology of an Ancient Republic in the New World. *Antiquity* 85(327): 172–186.

62 See Bernal Diaz del Castillo (1956[1568]) *The True History of the Conquest of New Spain*. Edited by Genaro Garcia. Translated by Alfred P. Maudslay (New York: Farrar, Straus, and Cudahy); and Cervantes de Salazar (1991 [1575]).

63 This view is perhaps best exemplified in Farger et al. (2017).

64 See Chance (2000) and Pohl (2003) for this position.

65 See Fargher et al. (2010).

66 See Laura E. Heath-Stout (2019) Pottery on the Periphery: Contact-Period Ceramics and Regional Integration at La Laguna, Tlaxcala, Mexico. *Journal of Anthropological Archaeology* 56: 101088.

67 See p. 540 of Fargher at al. (2017).

68 See page VI of Linda Ellis (1984) *The Cucuteni-Tripolye Culture: A Study in Technology and the Origins of Complex Society* (Oxford: British Archaeological Reports).

69 For a more recent history of mega-site research in English, see Mykhailo Videiko and Knut Rassmann (2016) Rearch of Different Scales: 120 years Trypillian Large Sites Research. In *Trypillia Mega-Sites and European Prehistory, 4100–3400 BCE*, edited by Johannes Müller, Knut Rassmann, and Mykhailo Videiko, pp. 17–27 (Abingdon: Routledge).

70 See Figures 70–72 in Ellis (1984). The Figures Are Derived From V.P. Dudkin (1978) Geofizicheskaya Razvedka Krupnih Tripol'skih Poselenii. In *Ispol'zovanie Metodov Estestvennih Nauk v Arheologii*, edited by V. F. Genning, pp. 35–45 (Kiev: Naukova Dumka).

71 For example, see Johannes Müller, Knut Rassmann, And Mykhailo Videiko, eds. (2016) *Trypillia Mega-Sites and European Prehistory, 4100–3400 BCE* (Abingdon: Routledge); Bisserka Gaydarska, ed. (2020) *Early Urbanism in Europe: The Trypillia Megasites of the Ukrainian Forest-Steppe* (Warsaw: De Gruyter Open Poland); and Francesco Menotti and Aleksey O. Korvin-Piotrovskiy, eds. (2012) *The Tripolye Culture Giant-Settlements in Ukraine: Formation, Development and Decline* (Oxford: Oxbow Books).

72 See Knut Rassmann, Knut, René Ohlrau, Robert Hofmann, Carsten Mischka, Nataliia Burdo, Michail Yu. Videjko, and Johannes Müller (2014) High Precision Tripolye Settlement Plans, Demographic Estimations and Settlement Organization. *Journal of Neolithic Archaeology* 16: 96–134. Note that "assembly hall" is Chapman's term for these kinds of buildings based on their excavations of a similar structure at the nearby site of Nebelivka, see John Chapman, Bisserka Gaydarska and Duncan Hall (2016) Nebelivka: Assembly Houses, Ditches, and Social Structure. In *Trypillia Mega-Sites and European Prehistory, 4100–3400 BCE*, edited by Johannes Müller, Knut Rassmann, and Mykhailo Videiko, pp. 117–133 (Abingdon: Routledge). Rassmann and colleagues use the term "special building" for Chapman et al.'s "assembly hall".

Powering From Below 111

73 For mega-sites as cities, see Aleksandr Diachenko and Francesco Menotti (2017) Proto-Cities or Non-Proto-Cities? On the Nature of Cucuteni-Trypillia Mega-Sites. *Journal of World Prehistory* 30(3): 207–219; Marco Nebbia (2017*)* Early Cities or Large Villages? Settlement Dynamics in the Trypillia group. Unpublished Ph.D. thesis, Durham University, Durham; and Bisserka Gaydarska, Marco Nebbia, and John Chapman (2020) Trypillia Megasites in Context: Independent Urban Development in Chalcolithic Eastern Europe. *Cambridge Archaeological Journal* 30(1): 97–121.

74 See Thomas K. Harper, Aleksandr Diachenko, Yuri Ya Rassamakin, and Douglas J. Kennett. (2019) Ecological Dimensions of Population Dynamics and Subsistence in Neo-Eneolithic Eastern Europe. *Journal of Anthropological Archaeology* 53: 92–101; Bruce Albert, Jim Innes, Konstantin Krementskiy, Andrew R. Millard, Bisserka Gaydarska, Marco Nebbia, and John Chapman (2019) What Was the Ecological Impact of a Trypillia Megasite Occupation? Multi-Proxy Palaeo-Environmental Investigations at Nebelivka, Ukraine. *Vegetation History and Archaeobotany* 29(1): 15–34; and Wiebke Kirleis and Marta Dal Corso (2016) Trypillian Subsistence Economy: Animal and Plant Exploitation. In *Trypillia Mega-Sites and European Prehistory, 4100–3400 BCE*, edited by Johannes Müller, Knut Rassmann, and Mykhailo Videiko, pp. 195–206 (Abingdon: Routledge).

75 For estimations on requirements for large populations at mega-sites, see Aleksandr Diachenko (2016) Demography Reloaded. In *Trypillia Mega-Sites and European Prehistory, 4100–3400 BCE*, edited by Johannes Müller, Knut Rassmann, and Mykhailo Videiko, pp. 181–194 (Abingdon: Routledge). For a discussion of contemporaneity of megasites, see Müller et al. (2016).

76 Radiocarbon dates do not provide a fine-grained enough understanding of dating to definitively distinguish generational changes in house occupations. For an explanation of evidence pointing to sequential occupation, see Bisserka Gaydarska and John Chapman (2020) Discussion. In *Early Urbanism in Europe: The Trypillia Megasites of the Ukrainian Forest-Steppe*, edited by Bisserka Gaydarska, pp. 415–506 (Warsaw: De Gruyter Open Poland). This scenario fits with data elsewhere in Eastern Europe, such as Aleksandr Diachenko, Mateusz Stróżyk, Marzena Szmyt, and Danuta Żurkiewicz (2021) Why Do We Need to Weigh Burned Daub? Destruction of Wattle-and-Daub Houses and the Internal Chronology of Neolithic Sites. *Journal of Archaeological Science: Reports* 38: 103052. For a contrary view that argues for more contemporality of occupation, see Johannes Müller, Robert Hofmann, Lennart Brandtstätter, René Ohlrau, and Mykhailo Videiko (2016) Chronology and Demography: How Many People Lived in a Mega-site? In *Trypillia Mega-Sites and European Prehistory, 4100–3400 BCE*, edited by Johannes Müller, Knut Rassmann, and Mykhailo Videiko, pp. 133–169 (Abingdon: Routledge).

77 See Gaydarska et al. (2020).

78 This idea is most fully developed in the contributions to Gaydarska (2020).

79 See Chapman et al. (2016); and Robert Hofmann, Johannes Müller, Liudmyia Shatilo, Mykhalio Videiko, René Ohlrau, Vitali Rud, Natalia Burdo, Marta dal Corso, Stefan Dreibrodt, and Wiebke Kirieis (2019) Governing Tripolye: Integrative architecture in Tripolye settlements. *PLoS One* 14(9): e0222243. For a popular account of the assembly houses, see Laura Spinney (2021) The First Urbanites. *New Scientist* 249(3323): 44–47.

80 See Myhailo Videiko and Natalia Burdo (2020) Mega-Structrure from Nebelivka—The Largest Temple in Trypillia Culture. In *Eternitatea Arheologiei: Studii în Onoarea Profesorului Dumitru Boghian la a 65-A Aniversare*, edited by Aurel Melniciuc, Bogdan Petru Niculică, Sorin Ignătescu, and Sergiu-Constantin Enea, pp. 263–286 (Clug-Napoca: Editura Maga).

81 See p. 128 of Chapman et al. (2016).

82 See Marco Nebbia, Bisserka Gaydarska, Andrew Millard, and John Chapman (2018) The Making of Chalcolithic Assembly Places: Trypillia Megasites as Materialized Consensus Among Equal Strangers? *World Archaeology* 50(1): 41–61.

112 *Powering From Below*

83 See Chapman et al. (2016); and Thomas Saile, Martin Posselt, Maciej Dębiec, Mariia Lobanova, and Aleksander Peresunchak (2021) Kozachyi Yar 1: An Enclosed Trypillian Settlement on the Southern Bug River in Kozavchyn (Ukraine). *Praehistorische Zeitschrift* 96(2): 401–412.

84 See Bisserka Gaydarska (2019) If We Want Things to Stay the Same, Things Will Have to Change: The Case of Trypillia. In *Habitus? The Social Dimensions of Technology and Transformation*, edited by Sławomir Kadrow and Johannes Müller, pp. 47–70 (Leiden: Sidestone Press).

85 For the standard interpretations of the era's art, see Dan Monah (2016) *Anthropomorphic Representations in the Cucuteni-Tripolye Culture* (Oxford: Archaeopress). Although figurines (and pottery) change over time, there is remarkable stability across 2,000 years in form and iconography despite the shifts in settlement organization.

86 See Natalia Burdo, Mikhail Videiko, John Chapman, and Bisserka Gaydarska (2013) Houses in the Archaeology of the Tripillia-Cucuteni Groups. In *Tracking the Neolithic Houses of Europe*, edited by Daniella Hoffmann and Jessica Smyth, pp. 95–115 (New York: Springer).

87 See Natalia Burdo (2015) Sacred Dimensions of Megasites. In *Cucuteni and Ancient Europe*, pp. 44–65 (Kiev: МОВА ТА ІСТОРІЯ).

88 See site plans in Rassmann et al. (2014).

89 See Vladimir Kruts (2012) Giant Settlements of Tripolye Culture. In *The Tripolye Culture Giant-Settlements in Ukraine: Formation, Development and Decline*, edited by Francesco Menotti and Aleksey O. Korvin-Piotrovskiy, pp. 70–78 (Oxford: Oxbow Books).

90 See Gayarsaka and Chapman (2020); and John Chapman, Bisserka Gaydarska, and Nebbia Marco (2019) The Origins of Trypillia Megasites. *Frontiers in Digital Humanities* 6, www.frontiersin.org/articles/10.3389/fdigh.2019.00010.

91 See Nebbia et al. (2018).

92 The pilgrimage model is one of several competing assembly models for how mega-site functioned, but all share the sense of a broader community coming together and coming apart. See Gaydarska et al. (2020).

93 See Nebbia et al. (2018). For other reasons for the abandonment of mega-sites and what came after, see Valdimir Kruts (2012) The Latest Stage of Development in Tripolye Culture. In *The Tripolye Culture Giant-Settlements in Ukraine: Formation, Development and Decline*, edited by Francesco Menotti and Aleksey O. Korvin-Piotrovskiy, pp. 230–253 (Oxford: Oxbow Books).

94 Note here that I am not suggesting that tens of thousands of people lived year-round at the mega-sites. Rather, the mega-sites served a population in the tens of thousands.

95 The traits commonly associated with city and states are enumerated in V. Gordon Childe (1950) The Urban Revolution. *The Town Planning Review* 21(1): 3–17. For a discussion of the enduring associated of these traits with urbanism, see Justin Jennings (2016) *Killing Civilization: A Reassessment of Early Urbanism and Its Consequences* (Albuquerque: University of New Mexico Press).

96 For discussions of leadership and dominance in the animal world writ large, see Mariana Rodriguez-Santiago, Paul Nührenberg, James Derry, Oliver Deussen, Fritz A. Francisco, Linda K. Garrison, Sylvia F. Garza, Hans A. Hofmann, Alex Jordan (2020) Behavioral Traits that Define Social Dominance are the Same that Reduce Social Influence in a Consensus Task. *Proceedings of the National Academy of Sciences* 117(31): 18566–18573; and Rebecaa J. Lewis (2022) Aggression, Rank and Power: Why Hens (and Other Animals) Do Not Always Peck According to Their Strength. *Philosophical Transactions of the Royal Society of Biology* 377: 20200434.

97 For a discussion of the pitfalls of power-over governance, see Eric Wolf (1999) *Envisioning Power: Ideologies of Dominance and Crisis* (Berkeley: University of California Press).

98 See Bo Rothstein (2011) *The Quality of Government: Corruption, Social Trust, and Inequality in International Perspective* (Chicago: University of Chicago Press); Bo Rothstein (2014) Good Governance. In *The Oxford Handbook of Governance*, edited by David Levi-Faur, pp. 143–154 (Oxford: Oxford University Press); and Richard E. Blanton, Lane F. Fargher, Gary M. Feinman, and Stephen A. Kowalewski (2021) The Fiscal Economy of Good Government: Past and Present. *Current Anthropology* 62(1): 77–100.

99 For the virtuous circle argument and its limits, see Jennifer Rubenstein (2018) The "Virtuous Circle" Argument, Political Judgment, and Citizens' Political Resistance. *Journal of Intervention and Statebuilding* 12(4): 584–602. Also see Daron Acemoglu and James A. Robinson (2012) *Why Nations Fail: The Origins of Power, Prosperity and Poverty* (New York: Crown Publishers).

100 Every Tlaxcallan went through initiation ceremonies, with those who inspired to leadership position going through an even longer, more arduous period of initiation. See Fargher et al. (2010).

7 Ordering Anarchy

In 1871, the people took over Paris. An elected council of Communards with no president issued crowd-pleasing proclamations—a rent freeze, the return of pawned goods, and the end of military conscriptions—while a welter of neighborhood- and issue-based clubs, committees, and other organizations debated the contours of their new society.[1] For Marx and Engels, the Paris Commune was the realization of their political project. The "Dictatorship of the Proletariat" was afoot in Paris, paving the way for an enduring communist government that might even emerge during their lifetimes.[2] Feminists also glimpsed the future in the workings of the commune,[3] as did socialists, anarchists, and other groups who aspired for alternatives to centralized, hierarchical government. The Paris Commune, however, never got off the ground. After two months, French troops recaptured the city, executing many of the commune's leaders who had not fled into exile.

The Paris Commune, for many of the participants, was a chance to improve upon the short-lived First Republic of France and its unfulfilled promise of "liberté, égalité, fraternité." Both were reactions to the perceived inequities of Western governments inspired by Western critiques of these governments. A line of popular revolt can be traced from the Communards back to the Plebians of Rome who refused to serve in the Roman army in 494 BC, and forward to the protestors who tried to occupy Wall Street in 2011.[4] These power-from-below movements were often utopian projects with little grounding in real-world examples. Slogans like "From each according to his ability, to each according to his needs" sound great,[5] but the nuts-and-bolts of governance were usually not worked out beforehand. The movements were disrupted early on, shattered because of inner turmoil, or curdled into despotism, leaving many onlookers with little faith in alternative forms of governance.[6] When alternatives to liberal democracies and other Western models of governance emerge as they did in the Arab Spring, there is therefore little external support.[7] The world chooses order over anarchy.

This is a false dichotomy. Anarchy derives from the Greek term, *anarchos*, that means "without ruler." The word is commonly defined as disorder, but anarchists have stressed that societal order is possible through voluntary associations without hierarchies since at least 1840 when Proundhon wrote "as man seeks justice in equality, so society seeks order in anarchy."[8] The anarchist symbol, an A (for

DOI: 10.4324/9781003373322-7

anarchy) within an O (for organization), evokes this idea. Most large-scale societies discussed in this volume, nonetheless, contain hierarchical elements. There are societies with well-recognized rulers such as those of the galactic polities of southeast Asia, for example, as well as more heterarchical systems. Heterarchy, like anarchy, can be defined in different ways.[9] I use the term to describe those societies that either have ranked components in parallel, such as the noble houses of Tlaxcallan, or have the potential to shift rankings between components depending on circumstances, such as the Alur segmentary state. In contrast to hierarchy and heterarchy, a basic premise of anarchy is the freedom from domination.[10] Order comes by opting into a collective.

Since the Enlightenment, Western scholars have tended to organize societies along a progression from hunter-gatherers to states, each associated with certain technologies, modes of subsistence, and form of governance that allow larger and more complex polities to form. Anarchy was usually associated with mobile hunter-gatherer lifeways, and most anarchists today, when they consider other extant societies at all, continue to evoke these groups or small-scale gardeners and herders as models.[11] As everyone knows who has tried to make plans with a big group, decision-making gets harder as more people are involved. This "scalar stress" requires fundamental structural changes to successfully navigate.[12] A seemingly inevitable change is to add hierarchy, and cross-cultural studies confirm that there is a general trend toward more centralized, hierarchical societies as societies scale up.[13]

Anarchists therefore often express a certain pessimism about anarchic governance in communities larger than a few dozen people.[14] Even for the faithful, order through anarchy can be seen as a boutique solution, fit for a commune in the woods but incapable of working at scale.[15] Bigger raises the specter of more rules and less freedom, and those who attempt to create larger anarchic collectives can be met with considerable skepticism. For some, the only true anarchists are those that rage against the state through bombs, assassinations, and vandalism.[16] Anarchy's failure to scale in the West, however, stems from a lack of understanding of many of the political, economic, and social actions required to maintain larger voluntary collectives and mitigate the human proclivity for ranking and dominance. The Cucuteni-Trypillian society from the last chapter that encompassed tens of thousands of people could be considered an example of anarchic governance, as could the Indus Valley Civilization that brought together a population that was an order of magnitude larger. Big collectives have thrived for centuries following anarchist principles, and their organizations can be instructive to those considering new possibilities for global governance.[17]

A world order without domination by others is the aspiration of many people. We *want* global anarchy, though fear that it is impossible. Even for many anarchists, our only viable options for global governance are better versions of the variety of the autocracies, oligarchies, and democracies in operation today.[18] This chapter attempts to expand on these options by showing how societies in the past found non-hierarchical solutions to long-distance exchanges, conflict adjudication, mutual defense, and other enduring challenges of collective action. Often

116 *Ordering Anarchy*

explicitly aligned against the state, the organization and associated ethos of these anarchist societies provide some of the requisite nuts-and-bolts necessary to scale up anarchy, and even raise the possibility of effective global governance in the absence of intergovernmental organizations like the United Nations. We begin our journey among the Pomo of central California. As some groups elsewhere in Native North America embraced emerging hierarchies, the Pomo settled into a governance system that would have made Paris' Communards proud.

Pomo

One of the first anthropology programs in the United States was founded at the University of California, Berkeley in 1901. Alfred Kroeber was among the department's founding members, and he soon initiated the Ethnological and Archaeological Survey of California to systematically reconstruct earlier Indigenous lifeways. The focus was on talking to elders about their youth and the stories they heard of earlier generations.[19] It was a salvage project amidst the catastrophic cultural change and population loss after the California Gold Rush in 1849 had brought a massive influx of white prospectors into the region.[20] One of the groups that Kroeber and his students studied was the Pomo, a linguistically related collection of families living just north of San Francisco. The result of their work, when coupled with earlier observations, provides an unprecedented understanding of Pomo life in early nineteenth century.[21] The anthropologists had expected that the Pomo and other California groups would be organized into tribes like those that they were familiar with from many other parts of the United States. They were not.

Kroeber coined a new term, the "tribelet," to describe what he saw in much of California. Tribelets averaged between 200 and 250 members, and were autonomous, property-holding units that did "not recognize any authority or power superior to itself."[22] Each of the Pomo triblets spoke a version of one of seven closely related languages and was anchored by a long-standing central village. The village was the symbolic heart of the community and boasted an assembly hall and sweat lodge.[23] Houses were spread out and ephemeral—people moved in a seasonal round between hunted, gathered, and tended resources—though a tribelet's small territory meant that at most a family was only a few hours walk from their central village.[24] The assembly hall was used to discuss matters of community interest and served as a location for dances, feasts, and other events that brought together tribelet members (Figure 7.1). The sweat lodge was sometimes visited twice a day by men, each carrying logs to feed the central fire.[25] Internal disputes could lead a small group to form a new subsidiary village that, on rare occasions, would become the anchor of a new tribelet.[26]

Open access to all resource zones within a tribelet's territory meant that a Pomo family could usually meet its own subsistence needs. Families also enjoyed routine access to the land of other Pomo tribelets, creating a food safety net in times of local environmental stress.[27] The good will between Pomo groups was fostered through their wider participation in trade feasts, seasonal celebrations, and other events.[28] A particularly important mechanism for pan-tribelet cohesion was the

Figure 7.1 Shoteah Pomo dancers in 1923 preparing for the Expulsion of Sahte ceremony. The ceremony's goal is to drive malignant spirits (the Sahte) away from the community

Kuksu Cult, a secret society dedicated to increasing the community's health and nature's bounty. Members learned many of the same songs and dances, and ceremonies rotated between tribelets.[29] Pomo relations with neighboring linguistic groups like the Miwok could be more hostile, but shell and stone bead money were routinely used to defray hostilities and pay for salt, obsidian, and other imports.[30]

118 *Ordering Anarchy*

Pomo families manufactured some of the beads used in exchanges—they made their own money—and orchestrated their own extra-territorial relationships.[31]

Pomo tribelets nonetheless had one or more hereditary chiefs, who accumulated more shell money and wives than other men. The chiefs were expected to invest their excess wealth and labor in hospitality and other activities that were beneficial to the community.[32] Early-twentieth-century informants made clear to the ethnologists the limits of chiefly power. Kroeber, for example, writes:

> A successful chief was an ornament to his people, and must conduct himself with considerable dignity when the situation demanded it. He had, however, next to no true authority. His role was supposed to be essentially one of using moral influence on the side of wisdom and coordination, and of preventing dissention and trouble from coming up.[33]

Barret further suggests:

> Not even the head captain [Chief] has absolute authority, nor has any captain [extended household head] important judicial power, or power to inflict punishment. In short, the function of the captain is primarily that of adviser to the group. The special duties of the head captain in olden times were to welcome and entertain visitors from other villages, and to meet in council with the other captains concerning matters of general public welfare, and to arrange for and preside over ceremonies.[34]

Finally, Colson's informants told her:

> [T]he chiefs had authority only over members of their families, but they had the additional privilege of lecturing the people of the village morning and evening on the necessity of living a good life.[35]

A chief's principal roles were thus to serve as an example for others and coordinate a few limited affairs. There was wide consensus on the appropriate behavior in common situations, and the chief, along with many others in the community, was there to remind people of how they should act.[36]

More recent scholars have sometimes pointed to signs of greater inequality that were missed or left unexplored by early-twentieth-century anthropologists.[37] The Kuksu Cult, for example, had different tiers of membership, and shamans were routinely paid for their services.[38] There was also a linguistic distinction in the Pomo languages between ordinary people (the "onlookers") and those who had garnered greater prestige.[39] The low-level resource and status inequality that was achieved, however, was capped by a host of other practices that limited social differences. For example, the Pomo emphasized consensus in community decision-making; frowned upon boasting and ostentatious displays[40]; the same person rarely held more than one position of power[41]; megalomania invited serious illness[42]; and, at death, one's accumulated wealth was thrown on the funerary pyre.[43]

Along with other mechanisms, these actions severely limited the development of power-over in Pomo villages, and the atomization of the linguistic group into autonomous tribelets provided a final stop gap to a leader's broader ambitions.

In *Orderly Anarchy*, Robert Bettinger attempts to explain the origins of the California triblets that so fascinated Kroeber.[44] The archaeological record hints at larger, more hierarchically organized societies in central California a few centuries earlier than contact,[45] and Bettinger suggests that the tribelets formed as a reaction *against* hierarchy and the concomitant loss of household autonomy. New technologies like the bow and arrow made families more self-sufficient, as did the manufacture and circulation of bead money. Shrinking societal units made consensus decision-making easier among groups like the Pomo, and entrenched social practices limited the degree of inequality that could develop. The leaders who arose were coordinators with little power-over, often tasked with maintaining relationships between tribelets and outsiders via Kuksu Cult events and other ceremonies. Some 6,000 Pomo speakers prospered for centuries without a ruler and only the barest wisp of a standing government.[46] Six thousand people is an impressive number when speaking of today's anarchic communes—Christiania in Copenhagen was a "last bastion of hippydom" before its 1,000 inhabitants disbanded in less than 40 years[47]—but pales in comparison to our other examples.

Jenne-Jeno

In the mid-twelfth century AD, a chief built a palace in the center of Jenne-jeno, a densely occupied city of more than 20,000 people in the Inner Niger Delta of northwest Africa.[48] Elsewhere on the continent, the event would have been unremarkable—chiefs were by then common in many regions[49]—but Jenne-jeno was different. For more than a millennium, there were no palaces, administrative buildings, temples, rich burials, or even ostentatious homes. The settlement was instead a "rabbit's warren of weaving alleys between tightly packed compounds linked by walls" (Figure 7.2).[50] People did different things at Jenne-jeno: there were farmers, herders, fisherfolk, metalworkers, and other specialists. Yet there is no evidence for any individual or organization that ran the city's affairs. Before the chief's palace was constructed, archaeologists have found no evidence for centralization and only the most subtle indications of hierarchy in and around Jenne-jeno. It was anarchy.[51]

The Inland Niger Delta is part of a vast 30,000 km² floodplain surrounded by a more arid environment. People began settling in the delta near the beginning of the first millennium AD.[52] Families had previously moved seasonally across the region, exploiting different resources before coming together at aggregation sites for a few weeks to trade, conduct group rituals, and engage in other activities.[53] Jenne-jeno was one of the locations in the delta that boasted a nearby range of rich ecological resources. As more people arrived to exploit these resources, mobility decreased and specialization increased to avoid conflict within a crowded landscape. The land that would become Jenne-Jeno's main settlement mound began

120   *Ordering Anarchy*

as gathering place, populated by potters, metalworkers, and other specialists who served those living in surrounding small enclaves.[54]

By AD 400, there was a clustered community of thousands of people. Most people lived in the peripheral enclaves that dotted a shifting landscape of fields, pasture, marshland, rivulets, and other features. Extended family groups called these enclaves home. Each tended to specialize in an activity like farming and weaving, and distinguished themselves from other enclaves by cuisine, clothing, and body modifications to mark separate identities.[55] The main mound followed the same pattern writ small: abutting enclaves were defined by walls and passages. Each enclave, to a degree, was an island of autonomous decision-making and subsistence self-sufficiency.[56] A founding family may have had more influence within an enclave, but they did not speak for those living elsewhere in Jenne-jeno.[57] Governance was thus aided by compartmentalization. Enclaves would continue to be independent decision-making units as the settlement grew.

By 800 AD, 50,000 people lived on the Jenne-jeno's main mound or on one of the dozens of enclaves within a couple hour's walk.[58] More people in one place created more scalar stress, leading to greater specialization and co-dependency. New ties between individuals based on occupation and other shared characteristics also emerged,[59] creating a dense web of interactions that criss-crossed the settlement's clusters. Compartmentalization alone was insufficient to maintain order between families, and at other clustered settlements in the region we see evidence around this time for social ranking and the development of more centralized, hierarchical governance.[60] Jenne-jeno's residents *could* have chosen hierarchy. They went in a different direction.

Roderick McIntosh suggests that there was a "heterarchical grid of authority" that both coordinated collective action at Jenne-jeno and minimized wealth and power differences.[61] The idea is that even at its height there was little power-over in the settlement. Individuals accrued the authority to influence public affairs in a limited area through their ability to access water spirits, for example, or their prowess in metal working. The overlapping authorities of these individuals formed a grid—perhaps better conceived of as a net—that constrained more ambitious leaders from seeking broader political power.[62] The community also actively identified and suppressed threats to the relative autonomy and equality of the enclaves as exemplified by the breaking up of metalworking activities after 400 AD. Metal workers were thought of as magicians who made stone into metal.[63] The splitting up of smelting and smithing activities, and the movement of these activities to the peripheral enclaves, dissipated a potentially disruptive source of power.[64]

The heterarchical grid of authority that limited ranking and centralization was likely further supported by a shared conceptualization of *nyama*. In the region today, nyama is "a fluid energy, invisible and ambivalent" that circulates within humans and non-humans and connects them to each other.[65] To flow properly, nyama requires selfless cooperation with community members.[66] A belief in nyama is recorded in written and oral accounts that date to around Jenne-jeno's abandonment.[67] Today, those of higher rank are said to possess more of this energy,[68] and hence have a heightened responsibility to work on behalf of their compatriots. Yet

Figure 7.2 Jenne-jeno was abandoned around 1400 AD when its last inhabitants moved to nearby Djenné. This street scene from the later settlement was photographed in 1906

the belief in nyama tends to reinforce the status quo because behavioral transgressions are seen as an existential threat to all. One might imagine attempts by some at Jenne-jeno to manipulate the idea of nyama for personal gain. Putting oneself above others, however, *was* a transgressive behavior: doing right in the settlement was working together without hierarchies.

122   *Ordering Anarchy*

The heterarchical grid of authority that maintained anarchy at Jenne-jeno was under stress long before a chief was proclaimed in the mid-twelfth century. Burgeoning trans-Saharan trade raised the possibility of previously unimaginable wealth by the eighth century AD, and subsequent conversions to Islam weakened shared nyama conceptualizations.[69] Two-thirds of Jenne-jeno's clusters were abandoned by the very beginning of the first millennium AD,[70] and it is likely that those who remained slowly accepted a new vision of what society should be like. Anarchy had nonetheless served Jenne-jeno well for centuries. Bounded self-sufficient units formed the backbone of society, supported by a self-reinforcing net of narrow, subject-based authorities that was just roomy enough to allow for coordination between enclaves while preventing the rise of significant hierarchies. Nyama provided a shared morality of selflessness and service to the community. Order was maintained by putting *everyone* in charge.

Akha

For millennia, there was a massive blank spot in the maps of southeast Asia. The spot was a massif almost the size of Europe that towered over southern China, and northern Myanmar, Thailand, Laos, and Vietnam. Millions of people lived on the massif, broken up into hundreds of ethnicities. For those living in the lowland states anchored by irrigated rice pad agriculture, the area was home to the *Zo-mi*, an uncivilized "hill people" who were frozen in time.[71] Zomia was seen as wild, ungovernable, barbaric—an illegible, inhospitable nightmare for tax collectors and soldiers. What lowlanders often failed to understand was that these people had chosen the hills over the lowlands.[72] Zomia was a "society against the state,"[73] designed to deter both the growth of internal hierarchies and the encroachment of foreign powers. The ordered anarchy that these groups developed to keep the outside world at bay paradoxically holds insights into improving global governance.

One of the groups living in Zomia today is the Akha. Half a million strong, the Akha are migratory slash-and-burn farmers who pay little heed to national boundaries.[74] Their origin stories describe a homeland in the southwestern corner of China, *Jadae Mirkhanq*, which was abandoned in the late thirteenth century in the face of state aggressions.[75] The Akha dispersed and atomized, such that the largest political unit today tends to be a village. Each village is divided into patrilineages that trace their ancestry back across centuries.[76] The patrilines are unranked; families are autonomous in their decision-making; and land is used rather than owned.[77] Groups routinely split off to pioneer a new settlement, and villages often move after a few years because of soil exhaustion, foreign intrusion, or other factors.[78] With each move, Akha society needs to be reconstituted.

Akha villages are organized around a suite of ancestral practices known as zá." If "one does the proper procedures with the proper speech attached in the proper circumstances with the proper participants, etc., one is lining up with zá" and ensures a good life for the individual and the community.[79] Zá" is all embracing and embodied, determining how one farms, enters a house, and views sickness. Following zá" makes a person an Akha, and those who are determined to have strayed from ancestral practices can be expelled from a village.[80] The reason for the severity of this punishment is existential: those who do not follow the zá" threaten to disturb the flow of cosmic energy that sustains the village. Proper order and orientation—of homes, villages, and personal lives—are what keeps malevolent, exterior forces at bay.[81] Despite its importance, there is nonetheless no agreed upon list of zá" practices to which all villagers can refer. Disputes are therefore frequent and can be another reason for a village to splinter.

The two pillars of village governance are the priest and council of elders. The priest is charged with ensuring that ancestral practices are followed. He maintains the village gateway, cemetery, main shrine, and other ritual spaces; leads certain ceremonies; and "stands on his open porch and calls out to the villagers" to assert proper behavior and announce deaths, upcoming ceremonies, and other events (Figure 7.3).[82] The council of elders is typically composed of each household head. They choose the priest and routinely consult with him regarding village matters.[83] Households thus come together to govern, using a set of traditional guidelines in the zá" that are flexible enough to adapt to changing circumstances.

Age and gender hierarchies are well marked within households, but the Akha make considerable efforts to ensure equality between households.[84] Subtle wealth differences exist—one household might have an iron rather than a clay pot, or a broom made from horsehair rather than elephant grass[85]—but wealth tends to be effervescent and does not translate into power over others. Akha governance works by having all households on a common footing, so that each head feels that their voice can be heard in council. Too much wealth also leaves a household

Figure 7.3 The gateway (foreground) to the Akha village of Phate in 1971. The gateway helps to keep evil spirits at bay

124   *Ordering Anarchy*

vulnerable to call for greater support at communal events or, worse, accusations that they have run afoul of the zá."

The Akha are tied together by feasts.[86] Most occur within the household, serving to maintain bonds between extended family members. Feasts marking marriage, death, menopause, or other life-stage event for an important household member often also involve other households in one's lineage. Celebrations honor the ancestry and ongoing vitality of the lineage, and attendees are expected to provide some of the food and labor needed to support the event. Larger feasts, such as those associated with the annual ceremonies to chase wild animals back into the forest and to rebuild the gate, require that every villager prepares for, and celebrates, the event.[87] Households and lineages jockey for prestige at these events by serving more meat or using higher quality serving ware, but the gains are limited since everyone contributes something to the event. The egalitarian ethos embedded in zá" also tempers boasting and ostentatious displays at feasts.[88]

Although this section has been written in the present tense, the Akha way of life is rapidly changing. Capitalism, monotheism, and nation-states have made considerable in-roads into Zomia since the 1950s, altering the political, economic, and social make-up of the Akha.[89] Fewer people now follow the ancestral way, dependency on state agencies has increased, and wealth and status differences are rapidly widening. Many have left their villages and moved into lowland cities. Anarchic governance nonetheless worked for centuries because every Akha household insisted on having its own voice in village affairs, the zá" provided a rulebook for living, and a belief in cosmic forces made acting right a communal responsibility. The Akha, like many of the other groups in Zomia, had retreated into the mountains to avoid the onerous demands of states.[90] They built an atomized society of thousands of autonomous households whose members maintained their cultural identity across centuries and could seamlessly join and leave larger collectives when desired. Anarchy gives order to the Akha village, an order that is now under threat.

Ordering Anarchy

Protests over a despot seeking re-election in Benin, tax reform in Costa Rica, soaring prices in Sri Lanka, and coronavirus restrictions in Canada: over the past few years, discontent has been voiced in many cities around the world that can be linked to some of the destabilizing effects of increasing globalization.[91] Most of the time, people gather for only a few hours, but sometimes they have lingered for days, weeks, and even a couple of months. Protest camps emerge that are sometimes pitched as alternatives to the status quo.[92] No leaders, general assemblies, free stuff—the camps often evoke much of the same anarchic ethos that guided the Communards in 1871 Paris. As counter-narratives to the nation-state, these social experiments are occasionally met with violence.[93] Yet the camps tend to break down on their own in the face of formidable logistical challenges. Anarchy is hard for today's revolutionaries, and each failure to sustain and scale-up a utopian vision reinforces arguments for propping up a global order anchored by ranked states and standing bureaucracies like the United Nations.

Ordering Anarchy 125

Although most protestors can only imagine the possibilities of an anarchic governance, it was the status quo for much of human history. We were all highly mobile hunter-gatherers until the end of the last Ice Age.[94] Leadership was tasked-based, family autonomy was paramount, and wealth and status differences were muted.[95] When life began to change for some people a few thousand years ago, an anarchic ethos continued in some locations even as people settled down in one place, adopted full-time agriculture, and moved into cities. These alternatives to hierarchy, exemplified in our three case studies, are now largely extinct or marginalized. Anarchy is something to overcome in the Enlightenment narrative of a march to civilization,[96] and the United Nations and other international organizations are tasked with *imposing* order on anarchy. We see the UN's soaring general assembly hall and its blue helmets as mechanisms preventing the world from descending into chaos. But what if the world needs more anarchy?

Capitalism is built around free markets and autonomous decision-makers. The economic system's ever-deepening global penetration is fueling global flows of ideas, objects, and people that are proving impossible for even the richest and most powerful individuals, corporations, and nation-states to contain.[97] The "anarchy of capitalist consumption" has no ruler,[98] and I suggest that we might learn something from governance systems that were built around the first principles of household freedom and autonomy. Pomo, Jenne-jeno, and Akha families, of course, were not living in a capitalist society, and wealth differences were slight in all three cases. Indeed, the first lesson from our case studies is that significant differences in wealth and status must be actively suppressed for order to come from anarchy. Order in larger collectives is premised on people feeling that they have a voice in community affairs. No person in power imposed restrictions from above, but in each of our case studies, there was something akin to Jenne-jeno's "heterarchical grid of authority" that both limited what individuals could achieve on their own and channeled excess toward community benefit.

A second lesson from our case studies is that room must nonetheless be made for difference. Heterogeneity scales with population size, meaning that differences will inevitably widen as more people come together in one place.[99] Families specialize, and wealth and status differences will rise. Pomo shell money, Jenne-jeno bangles, and Akha brooms were status markers, and effective anarchic governance must find outlets for prestige competitions rather than seek to eliminate them. A third lesson is that anarchic order requires wide participation. People have to go daily to the sweat lodge, routinely engage with other settlement clusters, and contribute to other people's feasts. Assemblies are effective mechanisms for governance when lives are already intertwined—anarchy only works when people want their community to thrive. Finally, anarchy requires adherence to a set of rules governing daily life. Something like the Akha zá" is also found in our other two case studies, and in each case, adherence to these rules was seen as fundamental to the proper functioning of society. Order was achieved by people knowing what to expect in most situations and what was expected of them.

Achieving order through anarchy may sound odd to many readers because the later term has become so closely associated with the violence and destruction of

126 *Ordering Anarchy*

fringe groups seeking to topple existing governments. Yet anarchic governance effectively addresses many of major barriers to collective action that were discussed in the first chapter. Reciprocal obligations, for example, eliminate much of the free-rider problem and ensure a high degree of equity as the rewards for common tasks are well recognized by participants. A commonly accepted set of practices also builds within-group trust, and the downplaying of hierarchies makes it easier for groups to come together to solve problems without jockeying for status positions. Finally, permanence is not a barrier to collective actions in these societies because a family can readily leave the group, and their communal emphasis dissipates much of the tension regarding property and resource rights. Anarchy is therefore ideally suited for collective action. Its problem in the West has been scaling up beyond a few hundred devotees.

Our case studies provide examples of enduring anarchic collectives that wove together thousands of people. Families opted into these collectives, turning their back on more hierarchical alternatives. Pomo, Jenne-Jeno, and Akha life, like many of the other case studies discussed in this volume, are out of step with commonly accepted ways of organizing countries and continents. This is what gives these alternatives their power. As the "anarchy of capitalist consumption" erodes a world order set in motion by European colonial expansion and Westphalian sovereignty, we need to look beyond the Western canon for ways to improve global governance.

Notes

1 See Robert Tombs (2013) *The Paris Commune, 1871* (London: Routledge).
2 Engels uses this term in his postscript to a pamphlet that Marx wrote on the Paris Commune in 1872. See Karl Marx and Friedrich Engels (1934) *The Civil War in France, Including Two Manifestoes on the Franco-Prussian War and Other Writings of Marx and Engels on the Paris Commune* (Chicago: C. H. Kerr).
3 See Carolyn J. Eichner (2003) 'Vive La Commune!': Feminism, Socialism, and Revolutionary Revival in the Aftermath of the 1871 Paris Commune. *Journal of Women's History* 15(2): 68–98; and James Muldoon, Mirjam Müller, and Bruno Leipold (2022) 'Aux Ouvrières!': Socialist Feminism in the Paris Commune. *Intellectual History Review* ahead-of-print: 1–21.
4 See Martin Breaugh (2013) *The Plebeian Experience: A Discontinuous History of Political Freedom*. Translated by Lazer Lederhendler (New York: Columbia University Press).
5 This quote, from Karl Marx's *Critique of the Gotha Program* (1875 [2008], Cabin John, Maryland: Wildside Press, p. 26), evokes a communist goal that was difficult to put into practice. Mikhail Bakunin, a rival to Marx who was one of the founders of the anarchist movement, had a similar talent for picturing utopian societies, such as in this quote from his *Revolutionary Catechism* written in prison in 1851 (from *Bakunin on Anarchy*, 1971, translated and edited by Sam Dolgoff, New York: Vintage Books):

> [E]very individual, every association, every commune, every region, every nation has the absolute right to self-determination, to associate or not to associate, to ally themselves with whomever they wish and repudiate their alliances without regard to so-called historic rights or the convenience of their neighbors.

6 For a discussion of how attempts at anarchy regress to state governments, see Robert Nozick (1974) *Anarchy, State, Utopia* (New York: Basic Books).

Ordering Anarchy 127

7 See Raphael Israeli (2013) *From Arab Spring to Islamic Winter* (London: Routledge).
8 Pierre-Joseph Proudhon was perhaps the first anarchist to develop the idea of how order can be created through anarchy. See Alan Ritter (1969) *The Political Thought of Pierre-Joseph Proudhon* (Princeton: Princeton University Press).
9 For example, see the difference between Carole L. Crumley (1995) Heterarchy and the Analysis of Complex Societies. *Archeological Papers of the American Anthropological Association* 6(1): 1–5; and Dmitri M. Bondarenko (2005) A Homoarchic Alternative to the Homoarchic State: Benin Kingdom of the 13th–19th Centuries. *Social Evolution & History* 4(2): 18–88.
10 See chapters in Benjamin Franks, Nathan Jun, and Leonard Wilson, eds. (2018) *Anarchism: A Conceptual Approach* (London: Routledge); and Carl Levy and Matthew S. Adams, eds. (2018) *The Palgrave Handbook of Anarchism* (New York: Palgrave MacMillan).
11 For example, see the collected works of John Zerzan that includes (2018) *A People's History of Civilization* (Port Townsend: Feral Books); (2008) *Twilight of the Machines* (Port Townsend: Feral House); and (1994) *Future Primitive* (Brooklyn: Autonomedia); Harold B. Barclay's (1990), *People Without Government: An Anthropology of Anarchy*, Revised edition (London: Kahn & Averill) is another example. Although Barclay talks about anarchy in larger, more urban setting, the examples are communities set apart from the everyday.
12 See Gregory A. Johnson (1982) Organizational Structure and Scalar Stress. In *Theory and Explanation in Archaeology: The Southampton Conference*, edited by Colin Renfrew, Michael J. Rowlands, and Barbara A. Wegraves, pp. 389–421 (New York: Academic Press).
13 See David S. Sanderford (2018) Organizational Complexity and Demographic Scale in Primary States. *Royal Society Open Science* (5): 171137; and Marcus J. Hamilton, Robert S. Walker, Briggs Buchanan, and David S. Sandeford (2020) Scaling Human Sociopolitical Complexity. *PLoS One* 15(7): e0234615.
14 See John P. Clark, John (2013) *The Impossible Community: Realizing Communitarian Anarchism* (London: Bloomsbury); and Peter H. Marshall (2010) *Demanding the Impossible: A History of Anarchism* (Oakland: PM Press).
15 For example, see Randall G. Holcombe (2016) Why Government? In *Ordered Anarchy: Jasay and His Surroundings*, edited by Hartmut Kliemt, pp. 147–166 (Abingdon: Routledge). Holcombe argues that governments are imposed by force by aggressors but, at scale, suggests that some form of government remains necessary.
16 See Marc Sageman (2017) *Turning to Political Violence: The Emergence of Terrorism.* (Philadelphia: University of Pennsylvania Press); and A. K. Thompson (2012) *Black Bloc, White Riot: Anti-Globalization and the Genealogy of Dissent* (Oakland: AK Press).
17 For the development of this argument, see David Graeber (2004) *Fragments of an Anarchist Anthropology* (Chicago: Prickly Paradigm Press).
18 For a rare exception, see Scott Turner (1998) Global Civil Society, Anarchy and Governance: Assessing an Emerging Paradigm. *Journal of Peace Research* 35(1): 25–42.
19 See Chapter 2 of Kent G. Lightfoot (2004) *Indians, Missionaries, and Merchants: The Legacy of Colonial Encounters on the California Frontiers* (Berkeley: University of California Press, 2004); and Williams S. Simmons (1997) Indian Peoples of California. *California History* 76(2/3): 48–77.
20 See Benjamin Madley (2016) *An American Genocide: The United States and the California Indian Catastrophe, 1846–1873* (New Haven: Yale University Press).
21 For a discussion of the enduring impact of Kroeber and his students work on our impression of pre-contact California, see Simmons (1997).
22 See p. 99 of Alfred Kroeber (1958) The Nature of Land-Holding Groups in Aboriginal California. *Reports of the University of California Archaeological Survey* 56: 87–120.
23 See Breck E. Parkman (1994) Community and Wilderness in Pomo Ideology. *Journal of California and Great Basin Anthropology* 16(1): 13–40.

128 *Ordering Anarchy*

24 See E. W. Gifford and A. L. Kroeber (1937) Culture Element Distributions: IV, Pomo. *University of California Publications in American Archaeology and Ethnology* 37(4): 117–254; and Samuel A. Barrett (1952) *Material Aspects of Pomo Culture* (Milwaukee: Bulletin of the Public Museum of the City of Milwaukee).

25 See C. Hart Merriam (1955) *Studies of California Indians* (Berkeley: University of California Press).

26 See discussion of the Pomo in Alfred L. Kroeber (1925). *Handbook of the Indians of California* (Washington, DC: Government Printing Office). Ambilocal residency patterns meant that a family had choices of where to live from both sides of marriage, see P. H. Kunkel (1974) The Pomo Kin Group and the Political Unit in Aboriginal California. *The Journal of California Anthropology* 1(1): 6–18.

27 See Omer C. Stewart (1943) Notes of Pomo Ethnogeography. *University of California Publications in American Archaeology and Ethnology* 40(2): 29–62.

28 See Andrew Peter Vayda (1987) Pomo Trade Feasts. In *Tribal and Peasant Economies*, edited by George Dalton, pp. 494–500 (Garden City: New York).

29 See Abraham M. Halpern (1988) *Southeastern Pomo Ceremonials: The Kuksu Cult and Its Successors* (Berkeley: University of California Press).

30 See Jeffery S. Rosenthal (2011) The Function of Shell Bead Exchange in Central California. In *Perspectives on Prehistoric Trade and Exchange in California and the Great Basin*, edited by Richard E. Hughes, pp. 83–113 (Salt Lake City: University of Utah Press).

31 See Barrett (1952).

32 See Kroeber (1925).

33 See pp. 107–108 of Kroeber (1958).

34 See p. 399 of Samuel A. Barrett (1917) *Ceremonies of the Pomo Indians* (Berkeley: University of California Press).

35 See p. 18 of Elizabeth Colson (1974) *Autobiographies of Three Pomo Women* (Berkeley: Archaeological Research Facility, University of California).

36 See Sally McLendon (1977) *Ethnographic and Historical Sketch of the Eastern Pomo and Their Neighbors, the Southeastern Pomo*. Contributions of the University of California Archaeological Research Facility 37 (Berkeley: Archaeological Research Facility, University of California).

37 For example, see Lynn H. Gamble (2012) A Land of Power: The Materiality of Wealth, Knowledge, Authority, and the Supernatural. In *Contemporary Issues in California Archaeology*, edited by Terry L. Jones and Jennifer E. Perry, pp. 175–196 (New York: Routledge); and Lynne H. Gamble (2008) *The Chumash World at European Contact : Power, Trade, and Feasting Among Complex Hunter-Gatherers* (Berkeley: University of California Press).

38 See Brian Hayden (2018) *The Power of Ritual in Prehistory: Secret Societies and Origins of Social Complexity* (New York: Cambridge University Press). One of Hayden's case studies is the Pomo.

39 See Halpern (1988).

40 See Colson (1974).

41 See Halpern (1978).

42 See B. W. Aginsky (1940) The Socio-Psychological Significance of Death Among the Pomo Indians. *American Imago* 1(3): 1–11.

43 See Edward Winslow Gifford (1967) *Ethnographic Notes on the Southwestern Pomo* (Berkeley: University of California Press).

44 See Robert L. Bettinger (2015) *Orderly Anarchy: Sociopolitical Evolution in Aboriginal California* (Berkeley: University of California Press).

45 For a more accessible account of California before European contact, see Brian Fagan (2003) *Before California: An Archaeologist Looks at Our Earliest Inhabitants* (Lanham: Rowman & Littlefield).

46 Archeological excavation confirms that central villages were long occupied, even as houses and communal structures were continually rebuilt. For example, see Thomas

N. Layton (1990) *Western Pomo Prehistory: Excavations at Albion Head, Nightbirds' Retreat, and Three Chop Village, Mendocino County, California* (Los Angeles: Institute of Archaeology, University of California). The estimates of 6,000 Pomo speakers at contact come from Kroeber (1925). Estimates vary but tend to range between 5,000 and 10,000. Today, the Pomo remain in northern California and carry on many of the traditions discussed in this section. For examples, see the Hopland Pomo's website at www.hoplandtribe.com, accessed on September 10, 2022.

47 See Harriet Riley (2007) A Farewell to Freetown. *The Guardian*, September 18th edition. www.theguardian.com/commentisfree/2007/sep/18/farewelltofreetown, accessed on August 18, 2022.

48 See Roderick J. McIntosh *The Peoples of the Middle Niger: The Islands of Gold* (Malden: Blackwell, Malden).

49 See Paul Mitchell and Paul Lane, eds. (2013) *Oxford Handbook of African Archaeology* (Oxford: Oxford University Press).

50 See p. 632 of Susan Keetch McIntosh and Roderick McIntosh (1993) Cities Without Citadels: Understanding Urban Origins Along the Middle Niger. In T*he Archaeology of Africa: Food, Metals, and Towns*, edited by Thurstan Shaw, Paul Sinclair, Bassey Andah, and Alex Okpoko, pp. 622–641 (New York: Routledge).

51 Although researchers at Jenne-jeno do not use the term "anarchy," they do routinely stress the lack of a chief or other form of formal government.

52 See Roderick J. McIntosh (2000) Social Memory in Mande. In *The Way the Wind Blows: Climate, History, and Human Action*, edited by Roderick J. McIntosh, Joseph A. Tainter, and Susan Keetch McIntosh, pp. 141–180 (New York: Columbia University Press).

53 See Kevin C. MacDonald (1997) Korounkorokalé Revisited: The Pays Mande and the West African Microlithic Technocomplex. *African Archaeological Review* 14(3): 161–200; Kevin C. MacDonald (1999) Invisible Pastoralists: An Inquiry into the Origins of Nomadic Pastoralism in the West African Sahel. In *The Prehistory of Food: Appetites for Change*, edited by Chris Gosden and Jon Hather, pp. 333–349 (London: Routledge); and Kevin C. MacDonald and R. H. MacDonald (2000) The Origins and Development of Domesticated Animals in West Africa. In *The Origins and Development of African Livestock: Archaeology, Genetics, Linguistics, and Ethnography*, edited by Roger Blench and Kevin C. MacDonald, pp. 127–162 (London: University College London Press), and Megan Sweeney and Susan McCouch (2007) The Complex History of the Domestication of Rice. *Annals of Botany* 100: 951–957.

54 See Roderick J. McIntosh (1993) The Pulse Model: Genesis and Accommodation of Specialization in the Middle Niger. *Journal of African History* 34(2): 181–212, for evidence from elsewhere in Africa for this scenario of site genesis see Mary E. Clark (2003) *Archaeological Investigations at the Jenné-jeno Settlement Complex, Inland Niger Delta, Mali, West Africa*. Unpublished PhD thesis, Southern Methodist University, Dallas, Texas; Stephen A. Dueppe (2012) *Egalitarian Revolution in the Savanna: The Origins of a West African Political System* (Bristol: Equinox); Douglas Post Park (2011) Climate Change, Human Response, and the Origins of Urbanism at Timbuktu: Archaeological Investigations into the Prehistoric Urbanism of the Timbuktu Region on the Niger Bend, Mali, West Africa. Unpublished Ph.D. dissertation, Yale University, New Haven, Connecticut; and Tereba Togola (2008) *Archaeological Investigations of Iron Age Sites in the Mema Region, Mali (West Africa)*. BAR International Series 1736. (Oxford: Archaeopress).

55 See S. McIntosh and R. McIntosh (1993); and Roderick J. McIntosh and Susan Keetch McIntosh (2003) Early Urban Configurations on the Middle Niger: Clustered Cities and Landscapes of Power. In *The Social Construction of Cities*, edited by Monica L. Smith, pp. 103–120 (Washington, DC: Smithsonian Books). Note the Clark's 2003 dissertation complicates this picture by demonstrating that some of the variation between enclaves is likely temporal.

130 *Ordering Anarchy*

56 See R. McIntosh (1998); and Abagail Chipps Stone (2018) Finding the Ephemeral: Herding Strategies and Socio-Economic Organization in an Urban West African Context. *Quaternary International* 471: 160–174.

57 See R. McIntosh and S. McIntosh (2003).

58 See R. McIntosh (1998) and R. McIntosh and S. McIntosh (2003).

59 See Stephen A. Dueppen (2019) Bridging House to Neighborhood: The Social Dynamics of Space in Burkina Faso, West Africa. *Archaeological Papers of American Anthropological Association* 30: 71–83.

60 See Park (2011) and Togola (2008).

61 See p. 206 of Roderick McIntosh (2005) *Ancient Middle Niger: Urbanism and the Self-Organizing Landscape* (New York: Cambridge University Press). For a recent summary of the dearth of status differences at Jenne-jeno, see Susan Keetch McIntosh (2020) Long-Distance Exchange and Urban Trajectories in the First Millennium AD: Case Studies from the Middle Niger and Middle Senegal River Valleys. In *Urbanisation and State Formation in the Ancient Sahara and Beyond*, edited by Martin Sterry and David J. Mattingly, pp. 521–563 (New York: Cambridge University Press).

62 See R. McIntosh (2000); and R. McIntosh and S. McIntosh (2003).

63 See Håland, Randi (1980) Man's Role in the Changing Habitat of Mema during the Old Kingdom of Ghana. *Norwegian Archaeological Review* 13(1): 31–46.

64 See Susan Keetch McIntosh, Susan Keech (1995) Metals. In *Excavations at Jenné-Jeno, Hambarketolo, and Kaniana (Inland Niger Delta, Mali), the 1981 Season*, edited by Susan Keech McIntosh, pp. 264–290 (Berkeley: University of California Press).

65 See p. 50 of Éric Jolly (2004) Boire avec Esprit: Bière de Mil et Société Dogon (Nanterre: Société d'Ethnologie). Also see Germaine Dieterlen (1950) Les Correspondances Cosmo-biologiques chez les Soudanais. *Journal de Psychologie Normale et Pathologique* 43(3): 350–366; and Geneviève Calame-Griaule (1965) *Ethnologie et Langage: La Parole chez les Dogon* (Paris: Gallimard NRF).

66 See R. McIntosh (2000).

67 The earliest documents from the region are in Arabic and come from the late twelfth century AD. Writing about the region, however, come two centuries later around the time of Jenne-jeno's abandonment. For more on these documents, see the Timbuktu Manuscripts Project at https://artsandculture.google.com/project/timbuktu-manuscripts. The concept of nyama is discussed in Christopher Wise (2006) Nyama and Keka: African Concepts of the Word. *Comparative Literature Studies* 43(1/2): 19–38.

68 See Christopher Wise (2017) *Sorcery, Totem, and Jihad in African Philosophy* (New York: Bloomsbury Academic).

69 See R. McIntosh (2005).

70 See R. McIntosh (1998).

71 The term for "Zomia" was first used by Willem van Schendel (2002) in Geographies of Knowing, Geographies of Ignorance: Jumping Scale in Southeast Asia. *Environment and Planning D: Society and Space* 20(6): 647–668. Van Schendel emphasizes the shared social characteristics of the region, though extends the boundaries of the massif further to the west than most scholars. The need for a term for the region divorced from state-centered depictions is further argued in Jean Michaud (2010) Zomia and Beyond. *Journal of Global History* 5(2): 187–214.

72 This argument is most fully developed in James C. Scott (2009) *The Art of Not Being Governed: An Anarchist History of Upland Southeast Asia* (New Haven: Yale University Press).

73 See Pierre Clastres (1987) *Society Against the State: Essays in Political Anthropology* (New York: Zone Books).

74 See Leo Alting von Geusau (2000) Akha Internal History: Marginalization and the Ethnic Alliance System. In *Civility and Savagery*, edited by Andrew Turton, pp. 142–178 (New York: Routledge).

75 See Micha F. Morton, Jianhua Wang, and Haiying Li (2016) Decolonizing Methods: Akha Articulations of Indigeneity in the Upper Mekong Region. *Asian Ethnicity* 17(4): 580–595.
76 For discussion of Akha village life, see Deborah E. Tooker (2012) *Space and the Production of Cultural Difference Among the Akha Prior to Globalization: Channeling the Flow of Life* (Amsterdam: Amsterdam University Press); and Paul W. Lewis (1968–1970) *Ethnographic Notes on the Akhas of Burma*, vol. 4 (New Haven: Human Relations Area Files).
77 For general descriptions of the Akha village life, also see Robert W. Kickert (1969) Akha Village Structure. In *Tribesmen and Peasants in North Thailand: Proceedings of the First Symposium of the Tribal Research Centre, Chiang Mai, Thailand, 1967*, pp. 35–40 (Chiang Mai: Tribal Research Centre); Hugo Adolf Bernatzik (1970) *Akha and Miao: Problems of Applied Ethnography in Farther India* (New Haven: Human Relations Area Files); and Leo Alting von Geusau (1983) Dialectics of Akhazan: The Interiorization of a Perennial Minority Group. In *Highlanders of Thailand*, edited by John McKinnon and Wanat Bhruksasri, pp. 241–278 (New York: Oxford University Press).
78 See Gordon Young (1962) *The Hill Tribes of Northern Thailand* (Bangkok: The Siam Society).
79 See p. 51 of Tooker (2012).
80 See Deborah E. Tooker (1992) Identity Systems of Highland Burma: 'Belief', Akha Zan, and a Critique of Interiorized Notions of Ethno-Religious Identity. *Man* 27(4): 799–819; and David A. Feingold (2011) On Knowing Who You Are: Intraethnic Distinctions Among the Akha of Northern Thailand. In *Changing Identities in Modern Southeast Asia*, edited by David J. Banks, pp. 83–94 (New York: De Gruyter Mouton).
81 See Deborah E. Tooker (2019) Rethinking Depth Metaphors with a Cosmocentric Self: The 'Steep' and the 'Level' in Akha Emotional Practices. *Ethos* 47(3): 346–366.
82 See p. 226 of Paul Lewis and Elaine Lewis (1984) *Peoples of the Golden Triangle: Six Tribes in Thailand* (London: Thames and Hudson), also see Cornelia Ann Kammerer (1998) Descent, Alliance, and Political Order Among Akha. *American Ethnologist* 25(4): 659–674; and Cornelia Ann Kammerer (2003) Thigh-Eating Chiefs in an Egalitarian Society: The Case of Akha Highlanders of Northern Thailand. In *Founders' Cults in Southeast Asia: Ancestors, Polity, and Identity*, edited by Nicola Beth Tannenbaum and Cornelia Ann Kammerer, pp. 69–86 (New Haven: Yale University Press).
83 See Lewis (1968–1970).
84 See Deborah E. Tooker (1996) Putting the Mandala in Its Place: A Practice-Based Approach to the Spatialization of Power on the Southeast Asian 'Periphery'—The Case of the Akha. *The Journal of Asian Studies* 55(2): 323–358.
85 See Von Geusah (1983).
86 Feasts occur almost exclusively at the village level or below, but Akha who move into a new village would be familiar with feasting practices since the zá" dictates many of the actions. See Tooker (2012).
87 See Michael Clark (2001) Akha Feasting: An Ethnoarchaeological Perspective. In *Feasts: Archaeological and Ethnographic Perspectives on Food, Politics, and Power*, edited by Michael Dietler and Brian Hayden, pp. 144–167 (Washington, DC: Smithsonian Institution Press); Cornelia Ann Kammerer (2003) Spirit cults among Akha Highlanders of Northern Thailand. In *Founders' Cults in Southeast Asia: Ancestors, Polity, and Identity*, edited by Nicola Beth Tannenbaum and Cornelia Ann Kammerer, pp. 40–68 (New Haven: Yale University Press); and Chapter 3 (The Akha, 'Rife with Feasts.') in Brian Hayden (2017) *Feasting in Southeast Asia* (Honolulu: University of Hawaii Press).
88 See Hayden (2017) on this jockeying. Hayden emphasizes the prestige-seeking, but this is being done in a context where Akha prohibitions on such behaviors are breaking down.

132 *Ordering Anarchy*

89 For example, see Cornelia Ann Kammerer (1990) Customs and Christian Conversion Among Akha Highlanders of Burma and Thailand. *American Ethnologist* 17(2): 277–291; Cornelia Ann Kammerer (1996) Discarding the Basket: The Reinterpretation of Tradition by Akha Christians of Northern Thailand. *Journal of Southeast Asian Studies* 27(2): 320–333; Cholthira Satyawadhana (2001) The Akha Struggle for Natural Resources and Forest Conservation in Thailand. *Gender, Technology and Development* 5(2): 323–329; Deborah E. Tooker (2004) Modular Modern: Shifting Forms of Collective Identity Among the Akha of Northern Thailand. *Anthropological Quarterly* 77(2): 243–288; Janet C. Sturgeon (2005) *Border Landscapes: The Politics of Akha Land Use in China and Thailand* (Seattle: University of Washington Press); and Takamitsu Hayakawa, Kaori Ito, and Andrew Burgess (2018) A Study on the Effects of Urbanization on the Housing of the Hill Tribes in Northern Thailand. *AIJ Journal of Technology and Design* 24(56): 339–344.

90 See Scott (2009).

91 See the Carnegie Endowment for World Peace's Protest Tracker at www.carnegieen dowment.org/, accessed on August 31, 2022.

92 See Anna Feigenbaum, Fabian Frenzel, and Patrick McCurdy (2021) *Protest Camps* (London: Zed Books).

93 See Hannah Arendt (2006) *On Revolution* (New York: Penguin Books).

94 See Matt Pope, John McNabb, and Clive Gamble (2018) *Crossing the Human Threshold: Dynamic Transformation and Persistent Places During the Middle Pleistocene* (Milton: Routledge).

95 Hunter-gatherer lifeways are extraordinarily variable, see Robert L. Kelly (1995) *The Foraging Spectrum: Diversity in Hunter-Gatherer Lifeways* (Washington, DC: Smithsonian Institution Press). Yet much of this variation may be a product of accelerated changes near the end of the last Ice Age, see Jessica C. Thompson, David K. Wright, and Sarah J. Ivory (2021) The Emergence and Intensification of Early Hunter-gatherer Niche Construction. *Evolutionary Anthropology* 30(1): 17–27.

96 See Justin Jennings (2016) *Killing Civilization: A Reassessment of Early Urbanism and Its Consequences* (Albuquerque: University of New Mexico Press).

97 There is considerable debate about the degree to which flows are governable. For now classic contrasting views on the nation-state see Paul Hirst and Grahame Thompson (1995) Globalization and the future of the nation state. *Economy and Society* 24(3): 408–442; versus Akhil Gupta (1992) The Song of the Nonaligned World: Transnational Identities and the Inscription of Space in Late Capitalism. *Cultural Anthropology* 7(1): 63–79. More recently, however, views on controlling flows have turned more pessimistic; see contributions over the last few years to the *Journal of Contemporary Politics* as an example.

98 See Guoguang Wu (2017) *Globalization Against Democracy: The Political Economy of Capitalism After Its Global Triumph* (New York: Cambridge University Press).

99 For an introduction to the scaling literature, see Jose Lobo, Luis MA Bettencourt, Michael E. Smith and Scott Ortman (2020) Settlement Scaling Theory: Bridging the Study of Ancient and Contemporary Urban Systems. *Urban Studies* 57(4): 731–747.

8 Finding Better Futures

If one were to survey the world's national governments, among the weirdest might be Switzerland.[1] Inspired in part by the United States Constitution, the Swiss have a bicameral Federal Assembly, as well as a President that stands as head of state. Yet the President rotates each year between the seven members of the Federal Council—the real executive power of the country—who are chosen from among the political parties that get the most votes. The constitutions also require that citizens routinely vote on proposed legislation and allows them to put forth referendums to challenge a passed law or propose a new one. At least four times a year, Swiss citizens vote on issues at every political level: to fund a local road, adjust a canton's taxes, or join an international treaty. The country is unusual because it comes closest to the idea of direct democracy despite a population of more than eight million. Having so many people potentially voice their opinion so often might seem reckless to some, but Switzerland is renowned for both its political stability and economic prosperity.[2]

One way to improve global governance might be to take lessons from the Swiss.[3] An annual rotation of members on the United Nation's Security Council, for example, might prove useful, and perhaps global popular referendums on critical issues are worth exploring. We could also glean ideas from Japan and Nigeria's government, how Oxfam and the World Health Organization interact with local groups, or Nestle and PetroChina's organizational frameworks. Such excavations into the world's more prominent governance mechanism might yield a few ideas as "weird" as those that guide Switzerland. The problem is that today's international outliers are not far enough from the mean to engender the substantive reform required to address the world's more pressing collective action problems.

Switzerland's government traces its origins to the Federal Charter of 1291 that pledged mutual aid between three communities against foreign powers. Over time, communities became cantons, and the cantons multiplied to form a Swiss Confederacy that was, in turn, folded into a federalist state in 1848.[4] It is a mixed confederation-federation government, a product of debates about Rousseau, Hobbes, Greek assemblies, and the Roman Senate. Switzerland's weird political structure is firmly a product of the Western canon, as are those of most of the world's nation-states, international organization, and corporations.[5]

DOI: 10.4324/9781003373322-8

134   *Finding Better Futures*

Governance is the systems and practices used to resolve collective action problems. Since the dawn of humanity, people have found an amazing variety of ways of working together, culminating in the creation of a wide range of long and durable collectives over the past 7,000 years.[6] This book argues that we can benefit by learning from *all* these collectives. One of the consequences of European colonialism is the narrowing of the world's political imagination. Guided by a philosophy of sociocultural evolution in which societies progressed from savagery to civilization, there were only a few proper forms of state-level government.[7] Colonial administrators "civilized" the world from the sixteenth century through early twentieth century by imposing a political order that dismantled, altered, and marginalized those systems that did not fit their expectations for how governments should work.[8] This work has continued into the present, with governance requirements tied to the release of development funds, opening of markets, or the participation in global organizations.[9]

The great winnowing of alternative political organizations over the last few centuries has resulted in a world of sovereign states organized into a few varieties of democracies, republics, monarchies, and dictatorships. These governments, in turn, shape what we think of as the possible ways of organizing global affairs. A problem with this limited imagination is that late capitalism and ever-accelerating globalization threatens the integrity of sovereign states and jeopardizes the world order build around inter-governmental agencies like the United Nations.[10] Common reactions to our increasing inability to get things done have been to try to either shore up existing global governance by tinkering with what we have in hand—add another NGO, shift a budget over—or somehow wall off one's nation from the world in certain arenas.[11] Neither strategy, however, is well positioned to succeed amidst today's accelerating flows of people, ideas, and objects. Instead, we need far more flexible and nimble organizational structures that can quickly adapt to changing circumstances: global governance that is somehow everywhere *and* nowhere, separate *and* together, independent *and* binding. We require collective action mechanisms much weirder than those of Switzerland. We need political systems reminiscent of those that were cast aside in the world's forced march to civilization.

The case studies in this volume have spanned the world over the past 5,000 years. Some of these were collectives of only a few hundred people, others were diverse, enduring collectives of hundreds of thousands. In previous chapters, I discussed how these collectives divided sovereignty, scaled up and down, built consensus, led from below, and ordered anarchy, and then pointed to the possible relevance of these mechanisms for improving global governance today. Many readers will nonetheless remain skeptical. Can lessons from the Pomo, Alur, Vikings, and other ancient and more contemporary marginalized groups actually help us tackle some of today's biggest collective action problems? I am not sure. Doing something like adapting aspects of New Guinea's tee cycle to ameliorate international warfare may not work. But why would we not want to learn more from an institution that successfully channeled decades of violent aggression into mutually beneficial aggrandizement? Thousands of governance mechanisms have been

Finding Better Futures   135

left unexplored because of an *a priori* judgment that they were not relevant in a civilized world. Some of these ideas should be brought to the table for improving global governance.

In 1744, Canasatego urged the colonial commissioners of Pennsylvania to learn from the Haudenosaunee League. "By your observing the same Methods our wise Forefathers have taken," he argued, "you will acquire fresh Strength and Power."[12] The commissioners nodded and did nothing. As our current geopolitical order erodes, there is an opportunity for substantive reform. We seem, however, to be returning once again to the same narrow set of inspirations.[13] This final chapter briefly discusses three of today's most pressing global collective action problems: climate change, pandemics, and cybersecurity. We will look at the scope of each challenge, what is being currently done to address this challenge, and what could be done using some of the governance mechanisms discussed in this book. My goal is *not* to present fleshed-out counter proposals to the status quo, but only to envision what *might* work better in the hopes of inspiring those working on some of today's toughest collective action problems to take alternative governance models more seriously.

Climate Change

In 1988, the United Nations convened the Intergovernmental Panel on Climate Change (IGCC) to produce comprehensive reports on the state of knowledge on anthropogenic climate change, its current and future impacts, and the options to slow this change and mitigate its effects. Each year, the reports enumerate the impacts of accelerating global warming: a 20-centimeter rise in sea level occurred between 1901 and 2018,[14] a 90% decline in multi-year Artic ice between 1979 and 2018,[15] a predicted 1.5°C rise in global temperatures above pre-industrial levels by as early as 2030.[16] Warming has destabilized the world's weather patterns, and is unleashing a litany of terrifying near-term impacts that range from food insecurity to increased arms conflicts and natural disasters.[17] As the IGCC reports makes clear, we now know that the key drivers of anthropogenic climate change are the burning of fossil fuels, the destruction of forests, and farming livestock. We also know many of the actions required to slow these changes.

The IGCC reports are a testament to the potential of collective action. Scientists from dozens of countries co-write the reports, and thousands of others collect the data used in them from every corner of the world. Political action on IGCC's reports, however, has been underwhelming.[18] The 2015 Paris Climate Accord is the framework currently being used to try to keep global temperature from rising more than 2°C above pre-industrial levels.[19] It is an international treaty, signed by 194 nations, that sets emission targets, reporting guidelines, and opportunities for aid. There are nonetheless few consequences for those countries that fail to meet their targets—the biggest one is a meeting with a committee of neutral researchers[20]—and ample evidence that many nations are already falling behind.[21] Much of the pressure on countries to act, as well as on corporations linked to global

136 *Finding Better Futures*

warming, comes from concerned citizens, as well as those touting the economic benefits of greener technologies.

As discussed in Chapter 1, some of the biggest challenges to successful collective action are free riders, expectations for equity, imposed hierarchy, lack of trust, permanence, and unclear property and use rights. One of the great difficulties is addressing climate change is that many of these collective action challenges are amplified when solutions are framed around state actions. Bangladesh, for example, is a former British colony. It currently emits only 0.56% of the world's emissions that cause global warming but ranks seventh in the list of countries most vulnerable to climate devastation.[22] Two-thirds of the country is within five meters of a sea level that is expected to rise 50 cm by the year 2100, displacing some 50 million people. Salinization will destroy agricultural fields, monsoons will become unstable, and typhoons will become fiercer.[23] In a state-centered approach, the voices of Bangladesh's 165 million citizens are muted relative to those of much smaller nations that have done far more to cause the climate change problems that Bangladesh faces.

What from our case studies could be used to improve collective action on climate change? A better approach might be to share sovereignty among those populations most impacted by the different aspects of climate change. To take another example, areas of Artic ice could be taken from the nation-states who currently lay claim to the region and placed under the control of a nested set of socio-political units composed of the communities that currently populate the area.[24] These units might assemble with other Artic units on a rotating basis to reach consensus on actions that should be taken, allowing for the flexible coordination of efforts to protect ice coverage. Funds for these efforts could be made possible through a global tax on emissions,[25] with funding priorities determined through regular consultations across the units that compose the larger Artic ice group. A similar structure could be put in place for other climate change clusters—for coral reefs, vulnerable coastlines, primary forests—as well as groups organized around mitigating, or eliminating, key drivers of climate change like coal-fired plants and cattle ranching.

Since each of these clusters would be composed of community members most affected by a particular aspect of climate change, they would have a vested interest in the success of their group's actions. Those living in Bangladesh would have a stronger hand in shaping the global actions on vulnerable coastlines, and the Indigenous-majority populations living above the Arctic Circle would take greater control over such ice conservation efforts as introducing more herds to the permafrost and building walls to preserve glaciers.[26] *Every* adult in the world would have an active role to play in one or more of these groups, such that coalitions of individuals across nation-state boundaries would drive climate change action. Over time, participation could draw people together around a set of shared principles and mutual sacrifices—a galactic polity of sorts rotating around a shared vision.

Many questions arise that would need to be answered in this alternative scenario—how would stakeholder group membership be determined? How exactly

Finding Better Futures 137

do we coordinate actions between clusters—but one of the great advantages of a political structure like the one proposed is its mutability and independence. We can overhaul the organization of one cluster, while leaving another cluster unchanged. Clusters can merge if desired, and then come apart in novel ways. New principles, and new orbits, can be pioneered as circumstances change. Taking pages out of the political organizations of our case studies, opens new governance possibilities that fall well beyond those typically offered by United Nation administrators, state leaders, and their critics.[27] Perhaps little merit will be found in this and other alternatives to the status quo. Yet I think the "weird" political organizations of the past are worth exploring for the many insights that they can provide on climate change action.

Pandemics

In March 2020, a coronavirus shut down the world. The COVID-19 virus emerged in December of the previous year in central China, and quickly spread via infected travelers. To date, almost seven million people worldwide have died from the virus,[28] and the global economic costs are estimated at more than 12.5 trillion U.S. dollars.[29] Although the global pandemic was a shock to many, epidemiologists were surprised at how lucky we had been before. Pandemics are now an annual occurrence, with the flu circulated the world. Almost every year, a more deadly disease threatens to go global. SARS-CoV-1, another coronavirus, almost broke containment in 2002, for example, as did the 2015 Zika virus spread from mosquitos. Globalization has tied the world together more closely than ever before. Outbreaks of highly contagious diseases are therefore now very difficult to limit to one region, and the time to act has shrank from months to only a few days.[30]

The World Health Organization (WHO) is the institution primarily responsible for coordinating global pandemic efforts. As a long-time agency of the United Nations, the WHO is committed to "the highest attainable standard of health . . . of every human being."[31] To meet this commitment, the WHO has a bureaucratic structure that parallels the United Nations with a headquarters in Switzerland, six regional offices, 150 field offices, and 800 "collaborating centres."[32] The inadequacies of the response to a 2014 Ebola outbreak in West Africa, however, brought the WHO under intense criticism.[33] In response, WHO added more infrastructure by inaugurating the Health Emergencies Programme, while other non-governmental organizations like Médecins Sans Frontières and the Bill and Melinda Gates foundation stepped into help.[34] Thousands of actors and billions of dollars later, the COVID-19 response was still hindered by rogue state actions and failures of global coordination.[35]

Pandemics are another collective action challenge that is poorly suited to a global order organized around sovereign nation-states and fixed bureaucracies. When a possible pandemic is proclaimed, we might be better served by transferring state medical systems to a global collective with dedicated funding. The basic "rules of the game" for this collective should be understood and well accepted,

138 *Finding Better Futures*

but its structure could be made on-the-fly to adjust to the unique contours of a growing epidemic.[36] Containment might occur across the borders of four states, and factories brought on-line on the other side of the world. The response could be led by those on the ground in the most heavily impacted regions, allowing considerable latitude to adjust to local conditions. Consensus-building would be a cornerstone of the organization's operations, encouraging ongoing conversations to rapidly respond to changes such as a virus's genetic mutation or unforeseen health complications.

This proposed alternative to global pandemic responses would likely require a headquarters and a small permanent administrative staff. Yet the remainder of the organization would be inchoate, waiting to take on a form best suited to the world's latest emerging pandemic. Each year, the organization would thus look fundamentally different. These differences would be not only about the disease—factors such as mutation rates and modes of transmission would shape responses—but also about local histories, cultures, and infrastructures. As with the climate change response, there would be wide public participation, and one of the goals of the global collective would be to ensure that disease response involves many people from outside of the immediately effected region. The world needs to think that the latest regional epidemic is their next possible global pandemic, and an effective way of doing so is for everyone to participate in the ongoing work of pandemic prevention.

Many observers argue that nation-states are not the best institutions to manage global pandemics.[37] Most nonetheless work with what we have by trying to improve state responses. Others advocate for an independent pandemic response that begins down the path of what I have outlined in the two previous paragraphs.[38] The exploration of alternatives, however, has been limited by our reliance on the same narrow set of governance models that guides current responses to other global collective action challenges. Power from below does not feel right, and anarchy is something that we should do everything to avoid. Top-down, state-driven responses have nonetheless proved to be a poor fit for containing the COVID-19 outbreak, and for managing vaccination distribution.[39] The case studies in this book offer different kinds of governance that might be better suited to coordinating global responses to pandemics.

Cybersecurity

JBS is the world's leading meat supplier with more than 150 processing plants around the world.[40] On May 30, 2021, the company uncovered a massive cyberattack on their computer systems. The JBS attack began in stealth: a reconnaissance phase in February, followed by three months of data exfiltration that transferred some five terrabytes of information. When the attack was identified, JBS computers were locked by the perpetrators and the data held for ransom.[41] JBS responded by taking some of its servers off-line, disrupting production world-wide and leading to the shut-down of nine plants in the United States.[42] As the days clicked by, anxiety rose in a food industry still reeling from the supply chain disruptions

Finding Better Futures 139

associated with COVID-19. JBS decided to pay the US$11 million in Bitcoin ransom to the cyberthieves.[43]

The group responsible for the JBS attack was REvil, a Russian-based group that used a network of affiliates to distribute its ransomware. REvil's business model was to doubly extort their victims by both locking them out of their computer systems and threatening to publicly release sensitive data. Members of an earlier ransomware organization, GandCrab, likely came together to form REvil in 2019, with the latter group rising to prominence in 2021 with attacks on Apple, Acer, and other companies. Russian security systems broke up the organization in January 2022, but much of REvil's code, as well as some of its platforms, were being used in attacks six months later.[44] GandCrab and REvil are just one of the many storefronts used by a dynamic criminal network that may be impossible to contain.

There is no equivalent of the Intergovernmental Panel on Climate Change for cybersecurity. The closest may be the Five Eyes, an intelligence alliance between the United States, the United Kingdom, Canada, Australia, and New Zealand that is formalized by a multi-lateral agreement.[45] The Five Eyes is a Cold War organization that was not built to take on cybercrimes, but the intelligence systems of these five nations have taken a leading role in coordinating global actions.[46] National law enforcement organizations are also involved in cybersecurity, and a host of non-governmental agencies like the Anti-Hackers Alliance offer guidelines and support.[47] For profit corporations also offer their services to mitigate threats, and university, hospital, and corporate alliances are forming to share information and provide logistical support.[48] In spite of these efforts, the afflicted usually pay off their attackers. Payments both encourage more attacks and raise the amount of ransom requested, creating a feedback loop that threatens to destabilize the world's economy.[49]

Can our case studies also provide insights into improving cybersecurity? The kinds of acephalous, independent, and horizontal organizations discussed in this book should be less susceptible to cyberattack because cascading failures are less likely from a directed attack. Their flexibility also means that these systems can more quickly and easily work around problems when they do occur. Since many of the political structures discussed in this book routinely change each year, they might also present a moving target to those attempting to disrupt their functioning through a cyberattack. A world composed of more of these kinds of governance structures could also be more effective in bridging between organizations, enhancing cooperation through the prospect of mutual aid. Institutional consortiums could more quickly identify threats and mitigate the effects when a breach occurs.

We could thus foster the growth of a power-from-below cybersecurity structure that is more capable of responding to ransomware and other attacks. It may already feel like we are heading toward anarchy in this sector, with many organizations feeling their own way across a shifting legal and political landscape. Yet anarchy, as the case studies in the last chapter indicated, is about finding an order for these efforts that enables groups to better coordinate efforts to reach shared

140   *Finding Better Futures*

goals. Enacting order from above is unlikely to be effective—equity, trust, permanence, and imposed hierarchy concerns will prove challenging—but it is also a mistake to simply trust that an organic process of development will succeed in reaching our goals. Instead, an intellectual and logistical scaffolding for finding common ground needs to be constructed that is rigid enough to provide support but flexible enough to bend with changing circumstances: a zá" of cybersecurity that guides practices and encourages ongoing consensus-building.

Although the first ransomware attack occurred in 1989, cybercrime has only become a significant threat to computer systems since the mid-2000s.[50] The United Nations and its affiliates have been slow to move against this threat, making it easier to imagine how more effective mechanisms of global governance might come to the fore from other political traditions. In the global south, leapfrog technologies are bypassing costly infrastructural investments in such areas as electrical grids and communication networks.[51] A similar leapfrog effect could be had with cybersecurity and other emerging challenges to global collective action if we act before gridlock ensues from too many actors working in the sector who follow the same Western playbook.

Finding Better Futures

As we make our way into the heart of the twenty-first century, we face enormous collective action challenges. Meeting these challenges surely means better supporting what we already have—a properly funded United Nations could do wonders[52]—but we also must look far beyond the status quo for possible solutions. Thousands of successful mechanisms for collective action have been cast aside *a priori* because they did not fit into Western traditions of how people should be organized. Coming from groups that were often dismissed as "savages" and "primitives" until well into the twentieth century, the political systems of these groups were often seen as too acephalous, compartmentalized, heterarchical, or anarchic to be of use during the age of Western expansion: colonists could not build their kinds of governments on such shaky foundations.[53]

The case studies in this book are examples of these alternative governance systems. Pomo, Aymara, and Tlaxcallan governance *are* poor fits for a world where interregional interactions are dictated by sovereign states alone, but we do not live in this world. Global flows of people, objects, and things are complicating the world order. Problems quickly arise, pop up in another region, and then morph into something new. Individuals juggle shifting relationships that cross-cut national borders; a single object is made from parts from a dozen countries. Sovereign states have never truly been sovereign over the affairs of their citizens, and their grip is now weakening every day. As global affairs become more chaotic, the book's case studies should begin to look more appealing to those seeking reform since a sturdy political foundation can also prove to be a brittle one. Other kinds of architecture are needed to meet the challenges of twenty-first-century global governance.

For a long time, we have failed to see the successes of other kinds of collectives. Many of the mountain valleys of the central Andes, for example, are

Finding Better Futures 141

a cascade of agricultural terraces. Millions of hours of labor have been put into their construction and maintenance, and they are emblematic of order imposed on an unruly landscape.[54] Archaeologists assumed for decades that the terraces were the products of political hierarchies—chiefs and kings telling people what to do. Some terraces were the result of state projects, but most were, and continue to be, made by reciprocal labor agreements between families and larger social groups (the same *ayllus* of our Aymara Kingdoms case study).[55] Scaling and power-from-below created the terraced landscapes of the Andes that fed millions, along with many other structures that were long deemed as too "monumental" and "sophisticated" for non-hierarchal societies to produce.[56] Our failure to see these alternative systems at work is a product of a political imagination impoverished after five centuries of European colonialism.

We should not romanticize alternative governance systems. Many are grounded in traditions that reject outsiders, and others are structured around gender or ethnic divides that are out of step with desires for a world of greater equity and inclusion. Nonetheless, The zá", ayllus, and oppida in our case studies were products of governance mechanisms that thrived within turbulent political landscapes, navigating through collective action challenges in unexpected ways. These alternatives make it easier to think of features like divided sovereignty and anarchy as beneficial attributes in politics and show us how they can be effectively employed in a wide variety of contexts. As we stand at a fork in the road for global governance, the case studies offer viable possibilities for reform that have long been ignored.

Every few years, politicians lament the wasted resources in studying remote tribes and ancient cultures.[57] The results might make an interesting read, they argue, but the projects "are at best marginal or at worst frivolous and wasteful."[58] There have been many rejoinders to these laments.[59] Some have emphasized the moral imperatives of decolonization,[60] the value for tourism and cultural heritage,[61] and the need for cross-cultural and long-term datasets to address a range of academic interests.[62] This book is my response to those who might question the value of studying alternative political structures. Tackling today's most pressing collective action problems requires us to free ourselves from the narrow conventions of Western thought. Academics, politicians, diplomats, CEOs, and the many others seeking to make the world a better place need to explore governance alternatives that better fit with today's changing political, economic, and social landscape. The "weird" is not just worth studying because it is interesting. We need to learn more about how Zulu, Trypillian, Alur, and other often-ignored collectives worked because they might be humanity's best hope for survival.

Notes

1 For comparisons of contemporary state governments, see Alan Draper and Ansil Ramsay (2008) *The Good Society: An Introduction to Comparative Politics* (New York: Pearson Longman); Arend Lijphart (2012) *Patterns of Democracy: Government Forms and Performance in Thirty-Six Countries*, second edition (New Haven: Yale University Press); Alan Siaroff (2013) *Comparing Political Regimes: A Thematic Introduction to Comparative Politics*, third edition (Toronto: University of Toronto Press).

142 *Finding Better Futures*

2 For discussions of the Swiss government see Hanspeter Kriesi and Alexander H. Trechsel (2008) *The Politics of Switzerland: Continuity and Change in a Consensus Democracy* (New York: Cambridge University Press); Andreas Ladner, Nils Soguel, Yves Emery, Sophie Weerts, and Stéphane Nahrath (2018) *Swiss Public Administration: Making the State Work Successfully* (Cham: Springer International Publishing AG); and Adrian Vatter (2018) *Swiss Federalism: The Transformation of a Federal Model* (Milton: Routledge).

3 An argument like this has been made in Wolf Linder and Sean Mueller (2021) *Swiss Democracy: Possible Solutions to Conflict in Multicultural Societies* (Cham: Springer International Publishing AG).

4 See Clive H. Church (2013) *A Concise History of Switzerland* (New York: Cambridge University Press); and Tom Scott (2017) *The Swiss and Their Neighbours, 1460–1560: Between Accommodation and Aggression* (Oxford: Oxford University Press).

5 See Randolph C. Head (1995) *Early Modern Democracy in the Grisons: Social Order and Political Language in a Swiss Mountain Canton, 1470–1620* (New York: Cambridge University Press); and Thomas Maissen (2017) The Helvetians as Ancestors and Brutus as a Model: The Classical Past in the Early Modern Swiss Confederation. In *Ancient Models in the Early Modern Republican Imagination*, edited by Wyger Velema and Arthur Weststeijn, pp. 259–284 (Leiden: Brill).

6 See Richard E. Blanton (2016) *How Humans Cooperate: Confronting the Challenges of Collective Action* (Boulder: University Press of Colorado).

7 For example, see Shaunnagh Dorsett and Ian Hunter (2010) *Law and Politics in British Colonial Thought: Transpositions of Empire* (New York: Palgrave Macmillan).

8 For example, Prashant Kidambi (2007) *The Making of an Indian Metropolis: Colonial Governance and Public Culture in Bombay, 1890–1920* (London: Routledge); and D. A. Low (2009) *Fabrication of Empire: The British and the Uganda Kingdoms, 1890–1902* (Cambridge: Cambridge University Press). In many areas, local systems persisted in some form but were characterized as backwards, for example see Colin Newbury (2003) *Patrons, Clients, and Empire: Chieftaincy and Over-Rule in Asia, Africa, and the Pacific* (Oxford: Oxford University Press).

9 For example, see Vincent A. Gallagher (2006) *The True Cost of Low Prices: The Violence of Globalization* (Maryknoll: Orbis Books); Peter James Hudson (2017) *Bankers and Empire: How Wall Street Colonized the Caribbean* (Chicago: University of Chicago Press); and Robert Gildea (2019) *Empires of the Mind: The Colonial Past and the Politics of the Present* (Cambridge: Cambridge University Press).

10 See John Agnew (2009) *Globalization and Sovereignty* (Lanham: Rowman & Littlefield); and George Pavlich and Charles Barbour (2010) *After Sovereignty: On the Question of Political Beginnings* (Abingdon: Routledge).

11 See Geraldine Fraser-Moleketi (2005) *The World We Could Win: Administering Global Governance* (Amsterdam: IOS Press); Marco Verweij (2011) *Clumsy Solutions for a Wicked World : How to Improve Global Governance* (Houndmills: Palgrave Macmillan); and Richard W. Mansbach and Yale H. Ferguson (2021) *Populism and Globalization: The Return of Nationalism and the Global Liberal Order* (Cham: Springer International).

12 Canasatego's speech is recorded on p. 785 of the *Minutes of the Provincial Council of Pennsylvania,* vol. iv published in 1851 (Philadelphia: Theo Fenn).

13 For example, see Jedidiah Purdy (2022) *Two Cheers for Politics: Why Democracy Is Flawed, Frightening—and Our Best Hope* (New York: Basic Books). Purdy returns to ancient Athens to build a better democracy.

14 See the Summary for Policy Makers of *Climate Change 2021: The Physical Science Basis* (2021) prepared by the Intergovernmental Panel on Climate Change, www.ipcc.ch/report/ar6/wg1/downloads/report/IPCC_AR6_WGI_SPM.pdf, accessed on September 8, 2022.

15 See the Summary for Policy Makers of *IPCC Special Report on the Ocean and Cryosphere in a Changing Climate* (2019), prepared by the Intergovernmental Panel of

Climate Change www.ipcc.ch/site/assets/uploads/sites/3/2022/03/01_SROCC_SPM_FINAL.pdf, accessed on September 8, 2022.

16 See the Summary for Policy Makers of *Global Warming of 1.5°C* (2018), prepared by the Intergovernmental Panel of Climate Change, www.ipcc.ch/site/assets/uploads/sites/2/2022/06/SPM_version_report_LR.pdf, accessed on September 8, 2022.

17 See the Summary for Policy Makers of *Climate Change 2022: Impacts, Adaptation, and Vulnerability* (2022), prepared by the Intergovernmental Panel of Climate Change, www.ipcc.ch/report/ar6/wg2/downloads/report/IPCC_AR6_WGII_SummaryForPolicymakers.pdf, accessed on September 8, 2022.

18 See Sushanta Kumar Mahapatra and Keshab Chandra Ratha (2017) Miles to Go: Paris Climate Accord. *Journal of International Development* 29(1): 147–154; and Jordan Johnson (2018) *From Kyoto to Paris: Global Climate Accords* (New York: Cavendish Square Publishing).

19 For the Paris Agreement of Climate Change that was brokered by the United Nations, see https://unfccc.int/sites/default/files/english_paris_agreement.pdf, accessed on September 8, 2022. A good discussion of its content and challenges is Vesselin Popovski, ed. (2018) *The Implementation of the Paris Agreement on Climate Change* (Boca Raton: Routledge); and Geert van Calster and Leonie Reins (2021) *The Paris Agreement on Climate Change: A Commentary* (Northampton: Edward Elgar Publishing).

20 See Alejandro Caparros (2016) L'Accord de Paris Comme Un Pas En Arrière Pour Un Nouvel Élan : Les Leçons à Tirer de et Pour La Théorie. *Revue D'économie Politique* 3(3): 347–356.

21 For the United Nations Framework Convention on Climate Change's *Nationally Determined Contributions under the Paris Agreement. Revised note by the secretariat* (2021), see https://unfccc.int/sites/default/files/resource/cma2021_08r01_E.pdf, accessed on September 8, 2022.

22 See David Eckstein, Vera Künkzel, and Laua Schäfer (2021) *Global Climate Risk Index 2021*, www.developmentaid.org/api/frontend/cms/file/2021/03/Global-Climate-Risk-Index-2021_1.pdf, accessed on September 9, 2022.

23 See Md. Nazrul Islam and Andre van Amstel (2019) *Bangladesh I: Climate Change Impacts, Mitigation and Adaptation in Developing Countries* (New York: Springer).

24 For a discussion of climate change and its effect on humans living in the region, see Grete K. Hovelsrud and Barry Smit (2010) *Community Adaptation and Vulnerability in Arctic Regions* (Dordrecht: Springer Science); and Neloy Khare, ed. (2021) *Understanding Present and Past Arctic Environments: An Integrated Approach From Climate Change Perspectives* (Amsterdam: Elsevier).

25 There are several models for how such a global tax would be implemented. For example, see Peter C. Cramton, Steven Stoft, Axel Ockenfels, and David J. C. MacKay, eds. (2017) *Global Carbon Pricing: The Path to Climate Cooperation* (Cambridge: The MIT Press).

26 See Christian Beer, Nikita Zimov, Johan Olofsson, Philipp Porada, and Sergey Zimov (2020) Protection of Permafrost Soils from Thawing by Increasing Herbivore Density. *Nature: Scientific Reports* 10(1). DOI: 10.1038/s41598-020-60938-y; and John C. Moore, Rupert Gladstone, Thomas Zwinger, and Michael Wolovick (2018) Geoengineer Polar Glaciers to Slow Sea-Level Rise. *Nature* 555 (7696): 303–305.

27 Although note that scholars have advocated for some of these same, see Elinor Ostrom (2010) Polycentric Systems for Coping with Collective Action and Global Environmental Change. *Global Environmental Change* 20 (4): 550–557; and Elinor Ostrom (2011) A Multi-Scale Approach to Coping with Climate Change and other Collective Action Problems. *Leviathan* 39(3): 447–458.

28 For estimates of global COVID-19 infections and deaths, see the WHO's Coronavirus (COVID-19) Dashboard, https://covid19.who.int, accessed on September 10, 2022.

29 Andrea Shalal (2022) IMF Sees Cost of COVID Pandemic Rising beyond $12.5 Trillion Estimate, *Reuters*, January 22 edition, www.reuters.com/business/imf-sees-cost-covid-pandemic-rising-beyond-125-trillion-estimate-2022-01-20/, accessed on September 9, 2022.

144   *Finding Better Futures*

30 For a critical retrospective on the early COVID-19 response, see Sudhvir Singh, Christine McNab, Rose McKeon Olson, Nellie Bristol, Cody Nolan, Elin Bergstrøm, Michael Bartos, et al. (2021) How an Outbreak Became a Pandemic: A Chronological Analysis of Crucial Junctures and International Obligations in the Early Months of the COVID-19 Pandemic. *The Lancet* 398(10316): 2109–2124.

31 See the Constitution of the World Health Organization (1948), www.who.int/about/governance/constitution, accessed on September 9, 2022.

32 See the WHO's website for its organization, www.who.int, accessed on September 9, 2022.

33 See the WHO's own *Report of the Ebola Interim Assessment Panel* (2015) https://cdn.who.int/media/docs/default-source/documents/evaluation/report-ebola-interim-assessment-panel.pdf?sfvrsn=df4e705d_2&download=true, accessed on September 9, 2022.

34 See Time Hanrieder (2020) Priorities, Partners, Politics: The WHO's Mandate beyond the Crisis. *Global Governance: A Review of Multilateralism and International Organizations* 26(4): 534–543.

35 See Jen Gaskell, Gerry Stoker, Will Jennings, and Daniel Devine (2020) Covid-19 and the Blunders of our Governments: Long-run System Failings Aggravated by Political Choices. *The Political Quarterly* 91: 523–533; Colin Kahl and Thomas J. Wright. 2021. *Aftershocks: Pandemic Politics and the End of the Old International Order* (New York: St. Martin's Press); and Scott Kaplan, Jacob Lefler, and David Zilberman (2022) The Political Economy of COVID-19. *Applied Economic Perspectives and Policy* 44 (1): 477–488.

36 Core institutional principles should be in place, but the structure should be organically developed around these principles to meet current needs. See P.K. Suri and Rajan Yadav, eds. (2020) *Transforming Organizations Through Flexible Systems Management* (Singapore: Springer). My proposal, however, is for less standing infrastructure than in normally advocated.

37 See Lynn Eaton and Gary Humphreys (2020) The Need for a Coordinated International Pandemic Response: The COVID-19 Pandemic Has Drawn Attention to the International Agreement Governing Responses to Public Health Emergencies, with Some Experts Calling for Its Revision. *Bulletin of the World Health Organization* 98(6): 378–379; Sudhvir Singh, Michael Bartos, Salma Abdalla, Helena Legido-Quigley, Anders Nordström, Ellen Johnson Sirleaf, and Helen Clark (2021). Resetting International Systems for Pandemic Preparedness and Response. *British Medical Journal (Online)* 375: e067518–e067518; and Matthias C. Kettemann and Konrad Lachmayer, eds. (2022). *Pandemocracy in Europe: Power, Parliaments, and People in Times of COVID-19* (Oxford: Hart).

38 For example, see Paul B. Spiegel (2021) Will This Pandemic Be the Catalyst to Finally Reform Humanitarian Responses? *Nature Medicine* 27(3): 365; Ronald Labonté, Mary Wiktorowicz, Corinne Packer, Arne Ruckert, Kumanan Wilson, and Sam Halabi (2021) A Pandemic Treaty, Revised International Health Regulations, or Both? *Globalization and Health* 17(1): 1–128; and Mario Coccia (2022) Preparedness of Countries to Face COVID-19 Pandemic Crisis: Strategic Positioning and Factors Supporting Effective Strategies of Prevention of Pandemic Threats. *Environmental Research* 203: 111678–111678.

39 Individual countries fared better than others, and much can be learned by state-level responses to the COVID-19 pandemic. My concern here is that top-down state-level responses were ineffective in coordinating a global response. See Anne-Sophie Jung, Victoria Haldane, Rachel Neill, Shishi Wu, Margaret Jamieson, Monica Verma, Melisa Tan, et al. (2021) National Responses to Covid-19: Drivers, Complexities, and Uncertainties in the First Year of the Pandemic. *British Medical Journal* 375: e068954–e068954.

Finding Better Futures 145

40 For more on JBS and its organization, see https://jbsfoodsgroup.com, accessed on November 12, 2022.

41 For more on the ransomware attack on JBS, see Ryan Sherstobitoff (2021), JBS Ransomware Attack Started in March and Much Larger in Scope than Previously Identified. *Security Scorecard Blog*, June 8th edition, https://securityscorecard.com/blog/jbs-ransomware-attack-started-in-march, accessed on November 12, 2022.

42 See Julie Creswell, Nicole Perloth, and Noam Scheiber (2021) Ransomware Disrupts Meat Plants in Latest Attack on Critical U.S. Business. *New York Times*, June 1st edition, www.nytimes.com/2021/06/01/business/meat-plant-cyberattack-jbs.html, accessed on November 12, 2022.

43 See Jacob Bunge (2021) JBS Paid $11 Million to Resolve Ransomware Attack. *Wall Street Journal*, June 9th edition, www.wsj.com/articles/jbs-paid-11-million-to-resolve-ransomware-attack-11623280781, accessed on November 12, 2022.

44 See Fawad Ali (2022) It's Back: REvil Ransomware Makes a Return, Here's What to Do. *Make Use of Us*, June 25th edition, www.makeuseof.com/revil-ransomware-attacks-return-what-to-do/, accessed on November 12, 2022.

45 See Dennis Molinaro, ed. (2021) *The Bridge in the Parks: The Five Eyes and Cold War Counter-Intelligence* (Toronto: University of Toronto Press).

46 See Karen Renaud, Craig Orgeron, Merrill Warkentin, and P. Edward French (2020) Cyber Security Responsibilization: An Evaluation of the Intervention Approaches Adopted by the Five Eyes Countries and China. *Public Administration Review* 80(4): 577–589.

47 See the Anti-Hacker Alliance, website at https://anti-hacker-alliance.com, accessed on September 16, 2022.

48 See Nicola Dalla Guarda (2015) Governing the Ungovernable: International Relations, Transnational Cybercrime Law, and the Post-Westphalian Regulatory State. *Transnational Legal Theory* 6(1): 211–249.

49 See Megan Wade (2021) Digital Hostages: Leveraging Ransomware Attacks in Cyberspace. *Business Horizons* 64(6): 787–797; and Judith Branham and Cheri Carr (2022) The Ransomware Epidemic: Criminals Taking Advantage of Those Working from Home—Including Lawyers and Media Companies. *Communications Lawyer: Publication of the Forum Committee on Communications Law, American Bar Association* 37(1): 37–43.

50 See Philip O'Kane, Sakir Sezer, and Domhnall Carlin (2018) Evolution of Ransomware. *IET Networks* 7(5): 321–327.

51 For example, see Manuel Castells, Mireia Fernández-Ardèvol, Jack Linchuan Qiu, and Araba Sey (2009) *Mobile Communication and Society: A Global Perspective* (Cambridge: MIT Press). Leapfrogging, of course, is easier said than done, but there are nonetheless increased opportunities for innovation when people are not managing the sunk costs of previous investments.

52 See Andy Sumner, Nilima Gulrajani, Myles Wickstead, and Jonathan Glennie (2020) A Proposal for a New Universal Development Commitment. *Global Policy* 11(4): 478–485.

53 See Phillip Dwyer and Amanda Nettelbeck, eds. (2018) *Violence, Colonialism and Empire in the Modern World*, edited by Philip. Dwyer and Amanda (Cham: Springer International Publishing); and Jerry Bannister, Elizabeth Mancke, Denis B. McKim, and Scott W. See, eds. (2019) *Violence, Order, and Unrest: A History of British North America, 1749–1876* (Toronto: University of Toronto Press).

54 See William M. Denevan (2001) *Cultivated Landscapes of Native Amazonia and the Andes* (Oxford: Oxford University Press).

55 See Ann Kendall and Abelardo. Rodríguez (2009) *Desarrollo y Perspectivas de los Sistemas de Andenería en los Andes Centrales del Perú* (Cuzco: Centro de Estudios Regionales Andinos Bartolomé de Las Casas). For a discussion of Andean agricultural

146 *Finding Better Futures*

systems and their contrast with those imposed by the Spanish, see Paul B. Trawick (2003) *The Struggle for Water in Peru: Comedy and Tragedy in the Andean Commons* (Palo Alto: Stanford University Press).

56 For example, see Richard L. Burger and Robert M. Rosenswig, eds. (2012) *Early New World Monumentality* (Gainesville: University Press of Florida).

57 At times, specific projects are targeted as wasteful, such as in Lamar Smith's 2017 op-ed in *USA Today* titled, Fund Science for a New Millennium in America (February 22 edition). The subtitle says it all: "But spending $920,000 to study textile-making in Iceland during the Viking era is not how to do it.", www.usatoday.com/story/opinion/2017/02/22/science-foundation-research-taxpayer-funding-lamar-smith-column/98012732/, accessed on September 16, 2022. At other times, the complaint is part of a more general call for reforming education and funding agencies. See the Browne Report, or *Securing a Sustainable Future for Higher Education: An Independent Review of Higher Education Funding and Student Finance* (2010) British Government, https://assets.publishing.service.gov.uk/government/uploads/system/uploads/attachment_data/file/422565/bis-10-1208-securing-sustainable-higher-education-browne-report.pdf, accessed on September 16, 2022.

58 This quote come from the Smith (2017), op-ed.

59 See Keith W. Kintigh, Jeffrey H. Altschul, Mary C. Beaudry, Robert D. Drennan, Ann P. Kinzig, Timothy A. Kohler, W. Frederick Limp, Herbert D. G. Maschner, William K. Michener, Timothy R. Pauketat, Peter Peregirne, Jeremy A. Sabloff, Tony J. Wilkinson, Henry T. Wright, and Melinda A. Zeder (2014) Grand Challenges for Archaeology. *American Antiquity* 79(1): 5–24.

60 See Joseph Drexler-Dreis and Kristien Justaert, eds. (2020) *Beyond the Doctrine of Man: Decolonial Visions of the Human*, edited by Joseph Drexler-Dreis (New York: Fordham University Press).

61 See Dallen J. Timothy and Gyan P. Nyaupane, eds. (2009) *Cultural Heritage and Tourism in the Developing World: A Regional Perspective* (London: Routledge).

62 See Peter Turchin, Harvey Whitehouse, Jennifer Larson, Daniel Hoyer, Selin E. Nugent, R. Alan Covey, John Baines, Mark Altaweel, Eugene Anderson, Peter K. Bol, Eva Brandl, David Carballo, Gary Feinman, Andrey Korotayev, Nikolay Kradin, Jill Levine, Selin Nugent, Peter Peregrine, Andrea Squitieri, Vesna Wallace, Pieter Francois (2023) Explaining the Rise of Moralizing Religions: A Test of Competing Hypotheses Using the Seshat Databank. *Religion Brain, & Behaviour 13*: 1–28.

Index

Note: Page numbers in *italics* indicate a figure and page numbers followed by an "n" indicate a note on the corresponding page.

Adams, John 1, 5–6
Africa 22, 25–27; Jenne-jeno 119–122; Zulu and 96–98, 107n24
age 123
Akha 122–124, *123,* 125–126
Albany Plan 5; *see also* Franklin, Benjamin
Alur 58–62, *61,* 68
anarchy 114–116, 124–126, 126n5, 129n151; Akha and 122–124; Jenne-jeno and 119–122; Pomo and 116–119
Annan, Koffi 21, 31
Anundshög 90n59
Arab Spring 94, 114
Artic 136
Articles of Confederation 2
authoritarianism 75
ayllu 71n27, 71n28
ayllus 62–64
Aymara Kingdom 62–64, 68, 71n27, 140
Aztecs 98–100

Bakunin, Mikhail 126n5
Baldaeus, Philip 65
Banana Republics 36n77
Bangladesh 136
Bettinger, Robert 119
Big Men 82–83, 92n82, 93n94
Bjarkøy 81
Black Lives Matter 94
Blackstone, William 1
Buddha 67
Buganda *61*

Caesar, Julius 45–46, *48*
California 116–119
Canasatego 7, 8–9, 40, 135
capitalism 3, 57, 124, 125, 134
centralization 72n39
Cetshwayo *96*
chiefs 58–59, 118
China 38, 45
civitas 46–47
climate change 135–137
Colla *64*
collective action 11, 24n15, 31–32; consensus and 85–87; problems of 3–5
Collingwood, William Gersham *80*
colonialism 30, 134
consensus 75–76, 118; collective action and 85–87; New Guinea and 82–85; Uruk and 77–79; Vikings and 79–82; *see also* democracy
constitutions 48
cooperation 3–4, 32
Cortés, Hernán 98, *99,* 106
COVID-19 68, 137–138
Cucuteni-Trypillia 101–104, *102,* 105, 111n76, 115
cultural relativism 27
cybersecurity 138–140

Darwin, Charles 3
Declaration of Independence 5
Deganawida 9–10
democracy: Uruk and 77; *see also* consensus
democratization 75

148 *Index*

democracies 94–96, 104–106; Cucuteni-Trypillia and 101–104; Tlaxcallan and 98–101; Zulu and 96–98
deterritorialization 28
du Simitere, Pierre Eugene 1, *2*
Durant 57

East India Company 18
elders 123
Ellis, Linda 101
Engels, Frederich 114, 126n2
Enlightenment 18, 20; sovereignty and 38
evolution 22–23
exchange chains 82–85

family: Akha and 122, 125–126; Jenne-jeno and 119–120; Pomo and 116–118, 128n26; Uruk Mesopotamia and 77–78
feasts 66, 78, 82, 92n89, 100, 116, 124
feudalism 18
Five Eyes 139
Flynn, Henry 96, 106
Franklin, Benjamin 1, 5, 6; *see also* Albany Plan
free-riders 4, 13, 87
French and Indian War 5
Fukuyama, Francis 75, 87
funding 136, 146n57
futures 133–141

galactic polities 66–67
GandCrab 139
Gauls 45–48, 49
gender 123
Germany 23
global governance 3, 18–21; future of 31–32; globalization and 28–31; League of Nations and 21–23; sovereignty and 39; United Nations and 23–28
globalization 13, 28–29, 75; global governance and 18–21
governance systems 70n2
Great Law of Peace 9–11
Great Seal 1–2, *2, 8, 8, 12,* 14n2
gridlock 30–32, 58
Grotius, Hugo 39
Group of Seven (G7) 29
Group of Twenty (G20) 29

Haudenosaunee Confederacy 9–12, 40, 135
heterarchy 115
heterogenization 29

Hobbes, Thomas 18, 26
Hollar, Wenceslaus *19*
Holocaust 23
homogenization 29
Hopkinson, Francis 8
Huluft, Gerard *65*
human rights 26–27

Iceland 91n61
imperialism 27
individualism 26
Indus Valley Civilization 43–45, *44,* 49, 115
inequality 46, 95, 100, 118, 119
Intergovernmental Panel on Climate Change (IGCC) 135
international government organizations (IGOs) 29–30, 57
International Red Cross 23
Iroquois 9, 16n51, *40,* 49; consensus and 76; sovereignty and 40–42; *see also* Native Americans
Israel 28

Jacobsen, Thorkild 77
Japan 23
JBS 138–139
Jefferson, Thomas 1, 14n1
Jenne-jeno 119–122, *121,* 125–126, 130n67

Kandy *65,* 65–67, 68
Kant, Immanuel 20
Kepele 84
kinship: Aymara and 62; Indus Valley Civilization and 43; states and 69
Kroeber, Alfred 116, 118
Kuksu Cult 117–119
KwaZulu-Natal 107n24

Lafitau, Joseph François 41
Lake Titicaca 62–64
League of Nations 21–23, 31; *see also* World War I
liberal democracies 93n102
Lizza, Ryan 94
Louis XIV 38, 50n1
Lupaqa 62

Madison, James 10, 95
Magna Carta 104
Maidanetske 102, *102; see also* Cucuteni-Trypillia
mandala 65

Index 149

Marx, Karl 114, 126n2
matriarchs 40–42, 49
McDonalds 29
mega-sites 102–104
Mexico 98–101
Mills, John Stuart 21
minority rights 26
moka 83–84, *84,* 86
monarchy 38
Morgan, Lewis Henry 8
Motte, Henri-Paul 48
Mpande 98

Native Americans 6–7; *see also* Iroquois;
  Onondaga
Nazism 26
neighborhoods 45; Cucuteni-Trypillia and
  103; Tlaxcallan and 100
New Guinea 82–85, 86, 91n76, 92n82
nobles 99–101, 105
nongovernmental organizations (NGOs)
  30, 57
nyama 120

oath rings 79, 86; *see also* Vikings
Obama, Barack 94
Occupy Wall Street 94, 114
Ongka 85, 93n94
Onondaga 7; *see also* Native Americans
oppida 45–48
Oxfam 30

Palestine 28
pandemics 137–138
Paris Climate Accord 135
Paris Commune 114, 124
Peace of Westphalia *19,* 20, 31
Pomo 116–119, *117,* 125–126, 128n46,
  129n151, 140
Portillo, Sejas 63
power triangles 60–62
progress 22–23
protest movements 94–95
Protestant Reformation 18

Red Cross 57–58, 68
refugees 85–86
resource rights 4–5
REvil 139
Roosevelt, Eleanor 27
Rousseau, Jean Jacques 18

Sa Ga Yeath Qua Pieth Tow *40*
Saudi Arabia 27

Second Continental Congress 1–3
Security Council 25, 133
segmentary lineage systems 59
segmentary states 58, 69–70
self-reinforcing interdependence 30–31
Shaka 96–98, 108n39
Smuts, Jan 21, 22–23, 25–27
social media 31–32
Southall, Aidan 60–62
Southeast Asia 73n46
sovereignty 1; absolute 38–40, 50n6, 69;
  dividing 48–50; Indus merchants and
  43–45; Iroquois and 40–42; oppida and
  45–48
Special Economic Zones 45
Spencer, Herbert 21
Sri Lanka 66
stability 95
Stamp Act 5
standardization 29
state 68–69; definition of 74n66;
  sovereignty 25
status 125–126
Switzerland 133–134

tee 83–84, 86, 134
Tee Yee Neen Ho Ga Row *40,* 42
*The Articles of Confederation and
  Perpetual Union* 5
things 75, 79–81, *80,* 91n61
Thomson, Charles *12*
time–space compression 28
Tizatlan 100–101
Tlaxcallan 98–101, *99,* 105, 110n57,
  113n100, 140
transnational corporations (TSNs) 30–31,
  36n77, 57
trust 4, 87, 126

Uganda 58–62
Ukraine 101–104
United Kingdom 98; United Nations and
  23–25
United Nations 3, 13, 20–21, 23–28,
  24, 31, 124–125, 134; consensus and
  85; *see also* Intergovernmental Panel on
  Climate Change (IGCC); World War II
United States 5–8, 10–12, 21, 23–28
Universal Declaration of Human Rights 27
Uruk 77–79

Vercingetorix 47, *48*
Vikings 79–82, *80,* 86
violence 83

150 *Index*

Wilson, Woodrow 21–23
women: Iroquois 40–42, 76; Zulu 97,
  105
World Health Organization (WHO)
  137
World Vision 30
World War I 21, 57

World War II 20, 23, 28; *see also* United
  Nations
writing 78, *79*

zá" 123–124, 141
Zomia 122, 130n71
Zulu *96,* 96–98, 105, 108n39